MW00342716

Building a
Career Outside
Academia

Building a Career Outside Academia

A Guide for Doctoral Students in the Behavioral and Social Sciences

EDITED BY
JENNIFER BROWN URBAN and **MIRIAM R. LINVER**

AMERICAN PSYCHOLOGICAL ASSOCIATION
Washington, DC

Copyright © 2019 by the American Psychological Association. All rights reserved. Except as permitted under the United States Copyright Act of 1976, no part of this publication may be reproduced or distributed in any form or by any means, including, but not limited to, the process of scanning and digitization, or stored in a database or retrieval system, without the prior written permission of the publisher.

Chapter 4 was coauthored by employees of the United States government as part of official duty and is considered to be in the public domain.

The opinions and statements published are the responsibility of the authors, and such opinions and statements do not necessarily represent the policies of the American Psychological Association.

Published by
American Psychological Association
750 First Street, NE
Washington, DC 20002
www.apa.org

APA Order Department
P.O. Box 92984
Washington, DC 20090-2984
Phone: (800) 374-2721; Direct: (202) 336-5510
Fax: (202) 336-5502; TDD/TTY: (202) 336-6123
Online: http://www.apa.org/pubs/books
E-mail: order@apa.org

In the U.K., Europe, Africa, and the Middle East, copies may be ordered from
Eurospan Group
c/o Turpin Distribution
Pegasus Drive
Stratton Business Park
Biggleswade, Bedfordshire
SG18 8TQ United Kingdom
Phone: +44 (0) 1767 604972
Fax: +44 (0) 1767 601640
Online: https://www.eurospanbookstore.com/apa
E-mail: eurospan@turpin-distribution.com

Typeset in Meridien by Circle Graphics, Inc., Columbia, MD

Printer: Sheridan Books, Chelsea, MI
Cover Designer: Naylor Design, Washington, DC

Library of Congress Cataloging-in-Publication Data
Names: Urban, Jennifer Brown, editor. | Linver, Miriam R., editor.
Title: Building a career outside academia : a guide for doctoral students in
  the behavioral and social sciences / edited by Jennifer Brown Urban and Miriam R. Linver.
Description: First edition. | Washington, DC : American Psychological
  Association, [2019] | Includes bibliographical references and index.
Identifiers: LCCN 2018007028| ISBN 9781433829529 (alk. paper) |
  ISBN 1433829525 (alk. paper)
Subjects: LCSH: Psychology—Vocational guidance. | Social sciences—
  Vocational guidance. | Doctoral students.
Classification: LCC BF76 .B85 2019 | DDC 150.23—dc23 LC record available at
https://lccn.loc.gov/2018007028

British Library Cataloguing-in-Publication Data
A CIP record is available from the British Library.

Printed in the United States of America
First Edition

http://dx.doi.org/10.1037/0000110-000

10 9 8 7 6 5 4 3 2 1

Contents

CONTRIBUTORS *vii*

INTRODUCTION *3*
Jennifer Brown Urban and Miriam R. Linver

I

How to Decide on Your Optimal Career Path 9

1. Academia or Not? What Moderates a Doctoral Student's Career Decisions *11*
   Jennifer Brown Urban and Miriam R. Linver

2. Leaving and Returning to Academia: Can You Ever Go Home Again? *21*
   Lisa Lieberman

II

Career Paths for Behavioral and Social Science Doctorates 31

3. Postdoc: The Next Logical Step? *33*
   J. Zoe Klemfuss

4. Government: Using Your Skills for the Public Good *45*
   Layla E. Esposito and Valerie Maholmes

5. Private Foundations: The Other Side of the Research Coin *57*
   Sarah Clement

6. Consulting: Applying Your Skills in New Arenas *67*
   Scott R. Rosas

7. Think Tanks: Applying Your Academic Skill Set to Policy Research *79*
   Lisa A. Gennetian

8. For-Profit Corporations: Finding Your Way in the World of Business *89*
   Debra Mazloff

9. Nonprofits: Bridging the Research–Practice Divide *99*
   Jonathan F. Zaff

10. Non-Tenure-Track Academic Jobs: The Side of Academia You Didn't Know Existed *109*
    Jane L. Powers and Lisa A. McCabe

III

Preparing Yourself for the Nonacademic Job Market 121

11. How to Get the Most From Your Mentoring Experience *123*
    Patricia L. Mabry

12. Preparing for and Conducting Job Searches Outside Academia *135*
    Kerin McQuaid Borland, Terri LaMarco, and Amy Hoag Longhi

13. Networking: How to Market Yourself and Your PhD *151*
    Alan Pickman and Lisa Chauveron

14. Interviewing: What to Expect and How to Prepare *161*
    Dana M. Foney and Olivia Silber Ashley

APPENDIX *171*

INDEX *181*

ABOUT THE EDITORS *189*

Contributors

Olivia Silber Ashley, DrPH, RTI International, Research Triangle Park, NC

Kerin McQuaid Borland, MA, University of Michigan, University Career Center, Ann Arbor

Lisa Chauveron, MEd, Impact Development & Assessment, Brooklyn, NY

Sarah Clement, PhD, John Templeton Foundation, West Conshohocken, PA

Layla E. Esposito, PhD, *Eunice Kennedy Shriver* National Institute of Child Health and Human Development, Bethesda, MD

Dana M. Foney, PhD, The National Council for Behavioral Health, Washington, DC

Lisa A. Gennetian, PhD, National Bureau of Economic Research, New York, NY

J. Zoe Klemfuss, PhD, University of California, Irvine

Terri LaMarco, MA, University of Michigan, University Career Center, Ann Arbor

Lisa Lieberman, PhD, Montclair State University, Montclair, NJ

Miriam R. Linver, PhD, Montclair State University, Montclair, NJ

Amy Hoag Longhi, MEd, University of Michigan, University Career Center, Ann Arbor

Patricia L. Mabry, PhD, Indiana University Network Science Institute and School of Public Health, Bloomington, IN

Valerie Maholmes, PhD, *Eunice Kennedy Shriver* National Institute of Child Health and Human Development, Bethesda, MD

Debra Mazloff, PhD, Invesco, New York, NY

Lisa A. McCabe, PhD, Cornell University, Bronfenbrenner Center for Translational Research, Ithaca, NY

Alan Pickman, PhD, Lee Hecht Harrison, New York, NY

Jane L. Powers, PhD, Cornell University, Bronfenbrenner Center for Translational Research, Ithaca, NY

Scott R. Rosas, PhD, Concept Systems, Inc., Ithaca, NY

Jennifer Brown Urban, PhD, Montclair State University, Montclair, NJ

Jonathan F. Zaff, PhD, America's Promise Alliance, Washington, DC; Boston University School of Education, Boston, MA

Building a
Career Outside
Academia

Jennifer Brown Urban and Miriam R. Linver

Introduction

The number of new psychology and social science doctorates has been steadily increasing, with roughly 9,095 doctoral degrees granted in psychology and the social sciences in 2013 (up from 6,027 in 1985; National Center for Science and Engineering Statistics [NCSES], 2017). Alongside this increase, however, there has been a concurrent decline in the number of available tenure-track academic positions (Ginder, Kelly-Reid, & Mann, 2017; McKenna, 2016). In 2015, 59.6% of psychology and social science doctoral degree recipients obtained traditional academic positions (NCSES, 2017).

Increasingly, recent psychology doctoral program graduates are seeking alternative positions in government (11.6%), industry or business (16.2%), nonprofit organizations (9.1%), and other or unknown fields (3.4%; NCSES, 2017). The approach to doctoral education used by academic institutions in this country has not kept pace with these shifting employment trends. In fact, students who are interested in nonacademic or more applied careers are often marginalized in their graduate programs. This is exacerbated by a lack of resources available to help navigate a nonacademic career path.

Most professional development courses for doctoral students in the behavioral and social sciences focus on preparation for careers in academia. However,

http://dx.doi.org/10.1037/0000110-001
Building a Career Outside Academia: A Guide for Doctoral Students in the Behavioral and Social Sciences,
J. B. Urban and M. R. Linver (Editors)
Copyright © 2019 by the American Psychological Association. All rights reserved.

nearly half the students in these classes are unlikely to obtain or even want to pursue academic careers. Doctoral students may choose to pursue a career outside of academia for many reasons: compensation is often higher in nonacademic jobs, there may be more geographic flexibility, applied work is valued, and one has the opportunity to make a meaningful difference in people's lives.

Given the need for professional development for those pursuing nonacademic careers, why has the academy been so slow to respond? One reason may be that professors feel most comfortable teaching what they know, and that is the world of academia. However, it is a disservice to many students not to prepare them for the nonacademic job market. Given most professors' inexperience with careers outside of academia, there is a great need for books that can help guide students pursuing such careers. A scan of available books revealed a dearth of such resources. Therefore, we decided to create such a book ourselves. This book was built out of our own experiences as graduate students considering potential career paths and in our work teaching and mentoring doctoral students with ambitions beyond academia.

As a graduate student at Cornell University, Jennifer was intent on pursuing a nonacademic career and was frustrated that her professional development class focused entirely on preparing for tenure-track academic positions. To better prepare herself for the nonacademic job market, she helped start a student organization, Policy and Advocacy in the Social Sciences, whose mission was to provide a support network and professional development opportunities for doctoral students interested in pursuing nonacademic careers. After graduation, she served as a Society for Research in Child Development Executive Branch Policy Fellow and was placed in the Office of Behavioral and Social Sciences at the National Institutes of Health. She ultimately decided to pursue a career as a tenure-track professor, and in that capacity, she has been charged with developing and teaching the program's doctoral professional development course. One of the primary readings for this course is *The Compleat Academic* (Darley, Zanna, & Roediger, 2004), which serves as an excellent resource for students and emerging scholars pursuing academic careers. The hope is that this book can serve as a counterpoint for those pursuing nonacademic careers.

Miriam also followed an indirect path to her current tenured position. Commencing her PhD program immediately after her bachelor's degree, she was unsure of the direction her career would take. Her program did not offer a formal professional development course; all professional development was imparted informally via mentor–student interactions. While still a PhD candidate at the University of Arizona's Family Studies & Human Development program, she moved across the country to New York. Still unsure of exactly which direction her career should take, she interviewed for research positions at think tanks and nonprofits and in the end took a position as a part-time research associate in a lab setting at Columbia University's Teachers College. After completing her doctorate, she continued in the lab as a postdoctoral researcher and then as a research scientist. When the opportunity arose, and the timing was right, she transitioned into her current tenure-track position.

Intended Audience

This book was written primarily for doctoral students in the behavioral and social sciences, including those earning a PhD, EdD, or PsyD in such disciplines as psychology, education, sociology, human development, family science, anthropology, demography, economics, and political science, to name a few. Although those who have earned or are in the process of earning a doctorate are the primary focus of this book, those who have or are working toward a master's degree in the behavioral and social sciences may also find the tips and strategies provided herein applicable to their job search. A secondary audience for this book are the mentors and advisors who support graduate students. Those who teach professional development courses for doctoral students may also find this book to be a helpful resource for their classes.

What makes this book unique among career guides for doctoral students is that it provides real-life stories from the trenches. When students approach us wondering what career path is right for them, we often tell them to conduct informational interviews with people who work in sectors of interest to them. This book brings a full spectrum of informational interviews to you. In a single, concise, accessible book, you will be exposed to a diverse array of potential careers. Across a range of sectors, the authors of each of the chapters in Part II of this book address questions such as, How did you get to where you are today? What types of jobs are available? What skill set should students work on building to be competitive? How can a doctoral-level skill set be applied? and What is a typical day like? Part III of the book provides the tools and resources you need to prepare yourself for the nonacademic job market, including advice on how to find a supportive mentor, how to prepare for and conduct nonacademic job searches, and how to effectively network and interview.

It is important to note that this book is not meant to be a comprehensive review of all possible career opportunities outside academia. For example, we do not offer guidance for building a career as a clinician. Nor do we cover careers in school, environmental, or forensic psychology. For resources on careers in clinical psychology, we encourage you to see books by Walfish (2010) and Pope and Vasquez (2005). The American Psychological Association website also features stories from psychologists in a variety of nonacademic careers.[1]

Integrating Themes

We have organized the book into four parts: (a) how to decide on your optimal career path, (b) career paths for behavioral and social science doctorates, (c) preparing yourself for the nonacademic job market, and (d) an appendix listing organizations that

---

[1]For example, see http://www.apa.org/science/resources/careers/index.aspx, http://www.apa.org/careers/resources/profiles/index.aspx, and http://www.apa.org/action/careers/index.aspx for more information.

hire PhDs in the behavioral and social sciences. Part I outlines the pros and cons of pursuing an academic or nonacademic career path, including topics such as work–family balance, flexibility (work schedule, geographic location), moving in and out of the tenure-track academic path, and financial compensation. This section is intended to help you think through whether a nonacademic career path may be appropriate for you.

Part II provides firsthand descriptions from behavioral and social science PhDs who have pursued nonacademic career paths. This section is intended to give you a sense of both how the authors got to where they are today and what it is like to work in various nonacademic sectors. Each of the chapters in Part II begins with the authors answering the question "How did you get to where you are today?" These are presented as short vignettes that provide an introduction to the chapter. As you read the vignettes, consider whether any of the authors' experiences resonate with you. This may help you identify whether a nonacademic career is for you and, if yes, which sector is the right fit. The remainder of the chapters includes a discussion of the different types of jobs available in that sector, what skill set you should work on building to be competitive in that sector (e.g., taking more statistics classes, writing for academic audience publications vs. practice-oriented publications, honing critical thinking skills by volunteering to serve as a peer reviewer, working well in a team setting), how a PhD-level skill set can be applied in that sector, what a typical day is like for the authors, what they enjoy and don't enjoy about working in that sector, and specific advice for students who may be interested in pursuing a career in that sector.

Part III provides specific and detailed information on how best to prepare for the nonacademic job market. These chapters include advice on how to find supportive mentors who will help guide you on a nonacademic career path, the best way to prepare for a nonacademic job search, how to effectively network, and how to successfully interview for nonacademic jobs. The book concludes with an appendix that lists organizations that typically hire behavioral and social science doctoral graduates.

Practical Tips for Using This Book Effectively

There are several ways you can approach reading this book. For graduate students who are just starting to consider a career outside of academia, we suggest reading the book in a linear fashion from start to finish. Graduate students who are more secure in their decision to pursue a nonacademic career may want to first go to Part II and read about various career options before turning to Part III's practical advice for pursuing a nonacademic job.

Mentors and instructors of professional development courses may want to use the book the way we do. When a student expresses an interest in a particular non-academic career path, we share the appropriate chapter with them. In professional development classes, you may choose to cover a subset of potential careers outside of academia and have students read the chapter that corresponds with that day's topic. You could also have students read chapters from Part III as a prelude to completing an assignment such as a draft resume or mock interview. However you choose to use this book, we hope you find it to be a practical and useful resource.

Concluding Thoughts

Our hope is that this book will put anxious minds at ease. If you thought you were alone in wanting to pursue a nonacademic career, you're not. If you've felt as though you needed to keep your nonacademic dreams a secret, you don't. If you haven't been sure where to turn for advice and guidance, you now have a place to start. A nonacademic career is not second rate, and pursuing one does not mean that you couldn't cut it in academia. There are many reasons you may have decided to expand your career vision beyond academia, and we support you in those efforts.

As you'll hear over and over from the chapter authors, networking is the key to success. So once you've finished reading this book, start networking! Better yet, don't wait until you've finished the book—start now. Informational interviewing is a great way to learn more about potential career paths. Talk with people who have the job you think you'd like to hold one day. Ask them to describe their experience. Ask them the questions that serve as headings in Part II of this book. Learn as much as you can, and ask them to refer you to at least two additional people.

Setting yourself up for success in a nonacademic job is not that different from what you would do to prepare for an academic job. You should still focus on publishing in academic outlets. For many nonacademic jobs, publishing is one of the factors that can make you a competitive candidate. Take as many statistics and methodology courses as you can. Rarely in your career will you have the opportunity to devote yourself to learning a broad array of methods and statistical techniques. Take full advantage of this opportunity in graduate school. You will be glad you did, whether you later find yourself in an academic or nonacademic career.

You are highly educated and have an enviable skill set. Now, go put it to use.

References

Darley, J. M., Zanna, M. P., & Roediger, H. L., III. (2004). *The compleat academic: A career guide* (2nd ed.). Washington, DC: American Psychological Association.

Ginder, S. A., Kelly-Reid, J. E., & Mann, F. B. (2017). *Enrollment and employees in post-secondary institutions, fall 2015; and financial statistics and academic libraries, fiscal year 2015: First look (provisional data)* (Report No. NCES 2017-024). Washington, DC: U.S. Department of Education, National Center for Education Statistics.

McKenna, L. (2016, April 21). The ever-tightening job market for Ph.D.s: Why do so many people continue to pursue doctorates? *The Atlantic.* Retrieved from https://www.theatlantic.com/education/archive/2016/04/bad-job-market-phds/479205/

National Center for Science and Engineering Statistics. (2017). *2015 doctorate recipients from U.S. universities* (Report No. NSF 17-306). Arlington, VA: National Science Foundation. Retrieved from https://www.nsf.gov/statistics/2017/nsf17306/static/report/nsf17306.pdf

Pope, K. S., & Vasquez, M. J. T. (2005). *How to survive and thrive as a therapist: Information, ideas, and resources for psychologists in practice*. Washington, DC: American Psychological Association.

Walfish, S. (2010). *Earning a living outside of managed mental health care: 50 ways to expand your practice*. Washington, DC: American Psychological Association.

HOW TO DECIDE ON YOUR OPTIMAL CAREER PATH

Jennifer Brown Urban and Miriam R. Linver

Academia or Not?
What Moderates a Doctoral Student's Career Decisions

1

octoral students often struggle with the decision of whether or not to pursue an academic career. For example, you may find you love doing research but do not like working in the academy. Or you may be limited by geography and don't want to widen your job search. There are many reasons why a nonacademic job may be more appealing to you. Perhaps you are struggling with whether to pursue an academic or nonacademic career and need some help thinking through your decision.

This chapter presents the pros and cons of nonacademic and academic (i.e., tenure-track) career paths and will help you think through whether a nonacademic career path is right for you. As you are deciding on your next career move, it pays to be armed with knowledge of recent statistics about behavioral and social science PhD graduates. What do recent graduates look like, in terms of demographic characteristics? How have PhD graduates changed over the past decade? What implications do these shifts have for your job search?

http://dx.doi.org/10.1037/0000110-002
Building a Career Outside Academia: A Guide for Doctoral Students in the Behavioral and Social Sciences,
J. B. Urban and M. R. Linver (Editors)
Copyright © 2019 by the American Psychological Association. All rights reserved.

Getting Your Career Off The Ground, or "Has My Life Actually Started Yet?"

Do you ever get the feeling that you're not really a true adult quite yet? While your friends from college may have gotten married, been in good-paying jobs for 10 years, started a family, and bought a house, you're still slaving away at your dissertation. To make matters even worse, if you want an academic career, you'll probably need to spend an additional 2 to 3 years in a low-paying postdoctoral position, after which you'll likely have to relocate yet again. If you do eventually land that tenure-track job, there's no guarantee you'll get tenure, and if you don't, you'll be looking to relocate for perhaps the second or third time since finishing graduate school. If you're itching to "start your life," chances are that pursuing a nonacademic career is for you.

Compensation

Conventional wisdom is that your earning power is higher if you work in a nonacademic setting. However, some argue that in the long run, you can make just as much as an academic as you can working in a nonacademic sector (Koprowski, 2015). This is no small concern, especially when you factor in any debt you may have. In fact, the mean education-related debt of a social science PhD recipient is $34,999, and 22% have more than $70,000 in debt (Jaschik, 2016; McKenna, 2016). If it is important to you to command a high salary immediately after completing your doctorate, academia is probably not for you.

More than ever before, PhDs in psychology and social sciences are taking postdoctoral positions before entering a tenure-track position (National Center for Science and Engineering Statistics [NCSES], 2017). The average postdoc salary ranges from $42,000 to $50,000. It's only slightly better once you land that elusive tenure-track position, in which the median annual salary for newly minted PhDs in psychology and the social sciences is $60,000. Compare that with sectors such as industry and business ($90,000), government ($85,000), nonprofits ($70,000), and other sectors ($75,500), in which the starting salaries are significantly higher (NCSES, 2017).

Geography: Opportunities to Choose Where You Live or Relocate

Having a career in academia means less freedom to select where you live and fewer opportunities to relocate. There are only so many universities with open positions in your field at your rank at any given moment in time. Although it is possible to narrow your job search on the basis of geography, this can limit the number of available opportunities and may mean you will have to make other compromises (e.g., taking a position at a less prestigious university or outside your immediate area of expertise) to prioritize location.

Finding a position close to family is often important to job candidates. Academics often have to forgo being close to family and friends, at least when considering their first academic appointment. We've noticed that many people spend their careers trying to get closer to where they grew up. Jennifer was fortunate in that her first academic position was at a university located in her hometown, less than 5 minutes from her parents' house. Not everyone is that lucky.

Geographic flexibility is further hampered if you have a partner who is also pursuing a tenure-track position or another geographically inflexible career (e.g., military, medicine). This is known as the *two-body problem*. Now, not only do you need to find that rare tenure-track position in your field in a place you are willing to live, but your partner also has to find a tenure-track position at the same or a nearby university. The two-body problem has put a strain on many relationships. It's not all that unusual for partners to live in different states and even raise children while living separately.

Nonacademic positions provide much greater freedom to select where you live. You don't have to wait for that one perfect position in the perfect location to materialize. There are many jobs in many locations you are qualified to do. When searching for nonacademic jobs, geography is often the first selection criterion. Try asking yourself which is more important, living in a certain location or obtaining a specific job? If you picked location, then a nonacademic job could be for you. This isn't to say that you can't also have your dream job—it just might not be in the academy.

Travel

Are you someone who likes to travel, or do you need to stay close to home? You have options in both academic and nonacademic settings. If you want to travel as an academic, you have many opportunities to do so through conference attendance and collaborative research projects. If, however, you prefer to stay closer to home, you can pick and choose which conferences you attend and limit your collaborative work to local colleagues and web-based meetings. If you are considering a nonacademic setting and have strong feelings about travel, be careful in selecting your nonacademic sector. If you enjoy traveling, working as a consultant or in industry or business could be a good fit for you. If, however, you prefer not to travel, consider working for a local nonprofit or foundation, which is likely to have fewer travel requirements.

Job Security

Academia is known for providing good job security if you are able to get tenure. At some institutions, it's difficult to know where you stand leading up to tenure. You know you're expected to publish and bring in grants, but how many publications are enough, and how much money and what types of grants actually count? Figuring out and fulfilling tenure requirements can be a challenging and grueling process, but once you do make it to tenure, you have job security unlike anything you see in most other sectors.

If having job security is high on your priority list but you also want to pursue a nonacademic career, consider a job in government. Many federal government positions offer a high degree of job security and can be found all over the country, not just in Washington, DC.

Intellectual Freedom

One of the greatest advantages of academic positions is having the freedom to pursue your own ideas. You get to set your research agenda and can follow your own interests. You can also shift your research agenda over time as you see fit. If you need to fund your research program, you will need to be attuned to the funding climate and pursue avenues of inquiry of interest to funders. With tenure comes even greater latitude in exploring your research interests, which could allow you to study underexplored or potentially even controversial topics.

You do not have the same freedom to pursue your own ideas and interests in nonacademic settings. Typically, your work is guided by client needs and/or the priorities of your organization. This may mean that in a nonacademic job, you jump from project to project, and at times some of your work tasks may not be in your wheelhouse.

You also do not have the same amount of time for contemplation and reflection as you do in academic positions. Although the pressure to publish in academia can be exhausting, it does afford you the opportunity to think about your work and how it relates to the broader scientific literature. In nonacademic jobs, having time to publish is often a luxury, and publishing often needs to be done on your own time. Although publishing in scientific journals is rewarded in academia, it is not particularly valued in most nonacademic settings. However, publications for a lay audience are typically valued in nonacademic settings, whereas they are undervalued in academia. Think about the kind of audience you enjoy writing for. Do you prefer translating science for a lay audience (nonacademic), or do you prefer doing the original research and writing for a scientific audience (academic)?

A Typical Day

As you will see in Part II of this book, which focuses on various nonacademic sectors, nonacademic jobs offer opportunities to engage in a variety of activities. For some of the chapter authors, their tasks vary tremendously from day to day, and sometimes even within the same day. They could be meeting with clients, managing staff, writing proposals, and tracking budgets all in one day. Almost all the authors describe being responsible for administrative tasks. These are typically the least enjoyable aspects of a nonacademic job, but don't think you can avoid administrative tasks by working in academia.

One of the best kept secrets about academia is that many academics don't actually spend all that much time teaching, and once you're established, you often don't spend much time analyzing data, either. So, what are you doing? You're pursuing grant opportunities; performing (often frustrating and time-consuming) administrative duties such as serving on committees, mentoring students, and managing people; and writing, writing, writing. If you run a research lab or center, you'll probably feel more like a small-business entrepreneur than an academic, and most likely, you never received any business training. In some cases, you'll be lucky enough to find an amazing collaborator at your institution (as we have). In other cases, you'll be on your own and could even find yourself in a department that is more competitive than collegial.

Although you might not be excited about having to perform administrative duties, chances are you're going to spend time on these in both academic and nonacademic positions, and you probably weren't trained to handle them as part of your doctoral work, either. Regardless of what sector you decide to pursue, try and take at least one business administration class. You'll be glad you did.

Flexibility in Managing Your Time

Academic jobs are known for allowing you to have flexible work hours. You prefer working late at night? No problem. You need to take your child to the doctor? No need to worry about clocking personal leave time. This degree of flexibility does have its downsides, though. To be a successful academic, you need to be intrinsically motivated and able to set your own goals and hold yourself to account. If you are someone who prefers to have more structure, academia may not be for you.

Although flexibility is typically considered the hallmark of academic positions, many nonacademic positions provide a similar level of flexibility. As several authors of chapters in Part II note, their organizations provide work-from-home options and credit them for work completed outside of standard business hours. If you thrive on flexibility and know you want to pursue a nonacademic career, make sure you ask questions about this before accepting a position. Different organizations and even different supervisors have vastly different opinions on the matter.

Opportunities to Mentor

As a graduate student, you may have had opportunities to mentor junior students, undergraduates, or research assistants. This can be one of the most gratifying aspects of an academic position. Knowing that you are playing a role in a pivotal moment of someone else's life is a wonderful feeling. By mentoring students, you impact not only their life but also the future direction of your field. Mentoring also is rewarding for mentors in that their mentees can help keep them abreast of parallel research areas and new statistical techniques.

Opportunities for mentoring in nonacademic jobs are not always as apparent as they are in academia. However, depending on your job sector and role, you may have opportunities to mentor junior colleagues. If mentoring is important to you and you are pursuing a nonacademic position, try and learn more about the organizational structure of your potential employer. Do people work in teams in which one person serves as the project lead? Is people management part of the role responsibilities? Will you be expected to mentor junior colleagues?

In addition to learning about opportunities to serve as a mentor, you may also want to consider asking about opportunities to be mentored (regardless of whether you are pursuing an academic or nonacademic career). For more about how to find a supportive mentor, see Chapter 11 of this book.

Teaching

If you are passionate about teaching, you can pursue your passion as both an academic and a nonacademic. As a tenure-track faculty member, you will be expected to teach a certain course load each semester. The amount of time you spend teaching varies tremendously depending on the type of academic institution. At research-intensive universities, this could mean a minimal teaching load. At a liberal arts college or community college, this could mean a teaching load of four or more classes per semester. Your teaching load may include classes on topics you care deeply about, but you may also have to teach classes on topics you know little about or would prefer not to teach. As a member of a department, you will be expected to do your part and make sure all of the courses your department offers are covered.

If you pursue a nonacademic career and decide to teach on the side, you will most likely be working as an adjunct professor. Chances are you will be teaching a subject matter you care about deeply. You have the flexibility to take a semester or two off from teaching, and you have the freedom to turn down any courses you would rather not teach. That being said, adjuncts and part-time university instructors typically make very little money. This may not be an issue if you are working in a sector that pays well and are teaching more for personal gratification.

Applied Research, or Making a Difference in the World

One of the most common reasons we have heard for wanting to pursue a nonacademic career is the desire for one's work to be meaningful and have real-world consequences. This was a big reason Jennifer was so intent on a nonacademic career while in graduate school. It's true that most universities undervalue applied research. There are some exceptions (including Montclair State University, where we work). For example, land-grant universities have a mission to bring research from the university into the community and tend to be more open to applied research programs. By and large, however, if your focus is on doing applied research and/or integrating research and practice, you will find more opportunities outside of academia than within it. Doing research that has real-world consequences often means working at a much faster pace than you are accustomed to. This can be incredibly invigorating and gratifying as you will be able to see the results of your work on a faster timeline than is typically found in academia.

Job Market Landscape for Behavioral and Social Science PhD Graduates

In addition to considering the factors outlined above, it is helpful to know who you are up against on the job market. The following sections provide demographic statistics forming a landscape analysis of behavioral and social science doctorates. Having this information will give you a sense of where you fit in, how many others on the market are like you, and what demographic trends might mean for your own career goals.

Earning a doctorate is a big commitment; aside from the financial burden of paying back debt accumulated during your program, on average behavioral and social science graduates invest 7 to 9 years of their lives from beginning their graduate work until earning a PhD (NCSES, 2017). Many in the academic world have suggested this time frame needs to be shortened (Berger, 2007), yet it has remained unchanged in recent years. As we stated in the introduction to this volume, the sheer number of PhD graduates in the behavioral and social sciences is on the rise, and as tenure-track position openings are becoming less plentiful, many graduates are seeking positions outside of the academy.

In 2015, there were 9,095 psychology and social science doctoral recipients (NCSES, 2017). About 42% of these received degrees in psychology, including the subfields of clinical psychology (13%), counseling psychology (5%), developmental and child psychology (2%), cognitive psychology and psycholinguistics (2%), industrial and organizational psychology (2%), social psychology (2%), experimental psychology (2%), human development and family studies (1%), neuropsychology (1%), and school psychology (1%). The remaining 58% of degrees were in the social sciences, which include anthropology (5%); economics (14%); political science and government (9%); sociology (8%); and other related fields (22%), such as gender and women's studies and criminology (NCSES, 2017).

The post-PhD time can be extremely stressful if you're a woman because the years spent earning your PhD can collide with the height of your childbearing years. This combination is exacerbated by the finding that having a child has the most significant effect on wage loss for women who are highly educated (Sonfield, Hasstedt, Kavanaugh, & Anderson, 2013; see Chapter 2, this volume, for a more detailed discussion of this topic).

An analysis of the Survey of Doctorate Recipients found that in the social sciences, gender disparities exist in hiring, promotion, and salaries, even at the full professor rank (Ginther, 2005). For example, in the social sciences, women are 8% less likely to get tenure than men and the salary gap between men and women full professors is also 8%, differences partially explained by familial factors. Women with children are often paid less than women without children (Waldfogel, 1998). And in the academic world, the "baby penalty" is felt by women but not men: Women are penalized (less likely to be hired, more likely to receive lower salaries, and less likely to get tenure) when they have children, whereas men are rewarded (Mason, 2013). Ironically, women who are unmarried and childless actually earn more than single men (and nearly as much as married men; Mason, 2013).

Ginther (2005) suggested that the discrepancies between men and women in social science academic jobs may be attributable to a cumulative advantage model in which men are rewarded for having more years of experience overall and thus are more likely to be promoted and to be more highly compensated. This model has merit, as more men than women pursue an academic career immediately following their doctorate, as we discuss later in this chapter. Chapter 2 probes in more depth how gender and age can interact in making career decisions.

How Have PhD Graduates Changed?

The percentage of PhD graduates who have a job commitment at the time they earn their degree is declining; in 2004, 72% of graduates had job commitments, but by 2014 that number had slipped to below 69% (Jaschik, 2016). At the same time, the percentage of women earning PhDs in the behavioral and social sciences increased, from 55% in 2005 to 59% in 2015 (NCSES, 2017).

As the number of behavioral and social science doctoral degrees awarded has increased, racial and ethnic diversity has steadily increased as well. For U.S. citizens and permanent residents,[1] the number of degrees granted in the behavioral and social sciences increased from 5,431 in 2005 to 6,698 in 2015 (a 23% increase). The percentage of degrees going to non-White graduates (U.S. citizens and permanent residents) increased from 22% in 2005 to 28% in 2015 (NCSES, 2017).

Where Do I Go From Here? Trends in Postgraduation Career Paths for Behavioral and Social Science Doctorates

When making decisions about the next step in your career, it can be helpful to know the path others have taken after earning their PhD, in terms of both their career track and their geographic location. Postdoctoral study is fairly common among recently minted psychology and social sciences PhDs (38%), followed by academic employment (37%), industry employment (10%), and employment in other sectors, includ-

---

[1]The National Center for Science and Engineering Statistics (2017) reported racial and ethnic breakdowns for U.S. citizens and permanent residents only; racial and ethnic data on temporary visa holders are not available.

ing government, nonprofit, and elementary or secondary schools (15%). There is variation in post-PhD plans by subfield. Academic positions are most common for recent PhDs in anthropology (46%), economics (46%), political science and government (58%), and sociology (58%). Postdoctoral positions are most common for recent PhDs in psychology (58%). Nonacademic positions are common across all subfields, especially economics (41%) and psychology (23%; NCSES, 2017).

There are also gender differences in post-PhD career plans, with more women (43%) than men (31%) pursuing postdoctoral studies and more men (42%) than women (33%) going directly into an academic position. Men are also slightly more likely to pursue nonacademic careers than women (27% and 24%, respectively). When examining the same data by discipline within the behavioral and social sciences, similar patterns emerge across each field. In psychology, a higher percentage of women (60%) than men (54%) pursue postdoctoral study, although that is the most common choice for both genders. More men than women turn to employment in academia (22% for men vs. 18% for women) and industry (13% for men vs. 10% for women).

For all other fields in social science, an academic track is the most common post-PhD career track. Men follow the academic path at a slightly higher rate than women for all fields, including anthropology (48% of men, 45% of women), economics (46% of men, 45% of women), political science and government (59% of men, 57% of women), and sociology (61% of men, 56% of women). Postdoctoral positions are the second most common career choice in the fields of anthropology (33% of men, 40% of women), political science and government (22% of men, 28% of women), and sociology (24% of men, 26% of women). Postdoctoral positions are the least common option for those with economics PhDs (15% of men, 12% of women); graduates in economics select industry at a higher rate than any other field (17% of men, 25% of women) or pursue "other" fields (23% of men, 18% of women). New sociology doctorates enter industry at a low rate (5% for both genders) and pursue other career paths (10% of men and 14% of women; NCSES, 2017).

Where geographically are PhD graduates headed? The overwhelming majority (91%) reported planning to remain in the United States after graduation, specifically in the regions of New England (10%), Middle Atlantic (14%), East North Central (12%), West North Central (6%), South Atlantic (19%), East South Central (3%), West South Central (7%), and Pacific (15%; NCSES, 2017). Nine percent planned to relocate outside of the United States. The distribution was slightly different across social science subfields; for example, more of those with psychology degrees planned to remain in the United States (97%), and more of those with economics degrees planned to relocate to outside of the United States (29%).

Conclusion

Deciding whether to pursue a nonacademic or academic career is a deeply personal decision. Whatever decision you make, you will have opportunities to apply what you've learned in graduate school. As someone with a PhD in the behavioral and social sciences, you have a very marketable skill set. Transitioning to a nonacademic career will likely be much smoother for you than for someone with a doctorate in, say, physics. There are many sectors in which expertise in researching human beings is highly valued. Your job is to figure out which of those sectors is most appealing to you. No matter where you are headed after your degree is in your hand, your destiny is under your control. We hope you use the knowledge gained by reading this book to find the best career match for your skill set, interests, familial situation, and life goals.

References

Berger, J. (2007, October 3). Exploring ways to shorten the ascent to a Ph.D. *The New York Times*, p. B9. Retrieved from http://www.nytimes.com/2007/10/03/education/03education.html?_r=0

Ginther, D. K. (2005, December). *The economics of gender differences in employment outcomes in academia.* Paper presented at the National Academies Convention on Maximizing the Success of Women in Science and Engineering: Biological, Social, and Organizational Components of Success, Washington, DC. Retrieved from https://www.ncbi.nlm.nih.gov/books/NBK23781/

Jaschik, S. (2016, April 4). The shrinking Ph.D. job market. *Inside Higher Ed*. Retrieved from https://www.insidehighered.com/news/2016/04/04/new-data-show-tightening-phd-job-market-across-disciplines

Koprowski, E. (2015, November 16). Pros and cons of continuing into an academic career. *PhDstudies.com*. Retrieved from https://www.phdstudies.com/article/Pros-and-Cons-of-Continuing-into-an-Academic-Career/

Mason, M. A. (2013, June 17). In the Ivory Tower, men only. *Slate*. Retrieved from http://www.slate.com/articles/double_x/doublex/2013/06/female_academics_pay_a_heavy_baby_penalty.html

McKenna, L. (2016, April 21). The ever-tightening job market for Ph.D.s: Why do so many people continue to pursue doctorates? *The Atlantic*. Retrieved from https://www.theatlantic.com/education/archive/2016/04/bad-job-market-phds/479205/

National Center for Science and Engineering Statistics. (2017). *2015 doctorate recipients from U.S. universities* (Report No. NSF 17-306). Arlington, VA: National Science Foundation. Retrieved from https://www.nsf.gov/statistics/2017/nsf17306/static/report/nsf17306.pdf

Sonfield, A., Hasstedt, K., Kavanaugh, M. L., & Anderson, R. (2013). *The social and economic benefits of women's ability to determine whether and when to have children.* New York, NY: Guttmacher Institute.

Waldfogel, J. (1998). The family gap for young women in the United States and Britain: Can maternity leave make a difference? *Journal of Labor and Economics, 16*, 505–545. http://dx.doi.org/10.1086/209897

Lisa Lieberman

Leaving and Returning to Academia

Can You Ever Go Home Again?

2

For many PhDs, the familiarity and comfort of their academic homes result in their going directly to the academy and remaining there for their entire career. As noted in Chapter 1, however, fewer than half (37%) of behavioral and social science PhDs go directly to academia (National Center for Science and Engineering Statistics, 2017). Those who do not go directly to academia may find that the first step on a nonacademic career path can lead to many places.

The question I explore in this chapter is, Once off the academic track, can you ever go home again? I discuss reasons that may drive a new PhD graduate to delay a career in academia and identify important preparations for a potential later-in-life return. In discussing the potential twists and turns of a nonacademic career path, I seek to explore and alleviate the stress of a decision not to immediately seek a tenure-track faculty position. Making this decision initially or at any point in a career does not mean that a tenure-track position is no longer an option. I'll begin with my own story.

http://dx.doi.org/10.1037/0000110-003
Building a Career Outside Academia: A Guide for Doctoral Students in the Behavioral and Social Sciences,
J. B. Urban and M. R. Linver (Editors)
Copyright © 2019 by the American Psychological Association. All rights reserved.

How I Went Home Again

I defended my dissertation for a PhD in public health on the day before my 30th birthday. Because of family and financial obligations, I had been working full-time at a research institute, using data from a project there for my dissertation. It was an exciting and satisfying work environment, filled with supportive colleagues, in a beautiful midtown Manhattan building. There was a strong academic influence and approach to the work of the organization. My colleagues were publishing, and many moved from this organization into strong academic careers. After completing my PhD, I remained there for another 2 years, during which time my first child was born. When he was 8 months old, my dream faculty job opened at a prestigious university, a 1-hour drive from my home. I was fortunate to be hired for a full-time, tenure-track position.

At this university, I worked with accomplished colleagues and taught inspiring students in classes I loved to teach, with an afternoon and evening teaching schedule that allowed me to spend time with my son in the mornings. I had secured a federal grant to do work about which I was passionate. I balanced and managed those evening courses, daytime meetings and committees, my research, and student advising as most of us do—with a combination of juggling balls, spinning plates, and masterful calendar management. Unlike many others, I also had the advantage of a wonderful, willing, and capable partner who helped manage the challenges at home.

Three years into my faculty position, when I was 36, my daughter was born. I took a leave for the spring and summer semesters while continuing to supervise staff on my research grant. My biological clock had stopped ticking; however, the tenure clock had not. I returned that fall, sleep deprived, anxious, and depressed. Papers that needed to go through the lengthy publication process were looming, and the commute, along with my children's sleep schedules, had me pulling off the highway to a gas station at 10 p.m. some nights to close my eyes. By the end of that academic year, I realized that fulfilling my responsibilities at school were at the expense of both my family's and my own health. I believed I could "have it all," as my progressive mother had trained me, but recognized, then, that "all" didn't have to be entirely at one time. I made the decision to honor my own needs and those of my family, and I resigned from my tenure-track position. Friends and colleagues wondered how I could walk away from a top-notch university halfway to tenure, with such a bright career ahead of me, but I knew that this was what I needed to do. I was fortunate to be able to negotiate moving my grant to the research institute at which I had previously worked so that I could manage it from there while working part-time. I knew in my heart I would return to academia someday.

The professional connections I made through the grant and my career led to opportunities to provide consulting work for various nonprofit agencies and the local health department where I lived. Over time, the part-time work that had helped me balance my family's needs grew into a full-time independent consulting practice. For the next 17 years, I provided program evaluation research and services to health departments, nonprofit agencies, schools, and government agencies. I had the flexibility to plan my work around school hours (often returning to the computer late at night) and to get involved in local causes that added to my own sense of accomplishment and satisfaction. In fact, I spent 9 of those years as an elected local school board member, applying my professional skills in that volunteer arena and contributing to the community in which I lived. In addition, I taught a graduate course about once per year as an adjunct instructor in a public health program that was closer to home. Ultimately, the downturn of the economy in 2008 resulted in more challenging prospects for new consulting work. I started dreaming again about that academic career that seemed only a few turns back. My time had come.

As if the universe knew, I ran into a professional colleague who told me that an exciting new master's program at his university was seeking a full-time faculty member. The school was 30 minutes from my home, and the job description appeared to have been written specifically for me. I enthusiastically returned to academia in a tenure-track position at the age of 54. In the hiring process, I had a few advantages over others at the beginning of their careers: a lifetime of field-based experiences that I could bring to the classroom, some publications, and teaching experience.

I also had a few disadvantages, however. The nature of consulting was such that either much of the work was not publishable or I had not had the time or luxury to publish when a project ended. Thus, I had fewer publications than would be expected for someone at this point in a career. Further, the institution for which I had been teaching as an adjunct did not require ongoing course evaluations or assessments, and the chair of the department in which I worked had never observed me, so I had no evidence of my teaching ability or success. As a direct result of these challenges, I was offered my position at the rank of assistant professor. In addition, the landscape of college campuses had changed with respect to online course management systems and changing student expectations, and the learning curve was steep. Although it was never explicitly mentioned, my advanced age was unusual for this entry-level rank, creating some degree of stress for me based on the pressure to prove I was up to the task.

Role of Gender in Driving Decisions About Academia

My personal story is replete with examples of how gender played a role in my decisions. Much has been written about the gender gap in tenure (Wolfinger, Mason, & Goulden, 2008), including the lesser likelihood that women will be awarded tenure and the "leaky pipeline" (van Anders, 2004) whereby women are more likely than men to drop out of the academy before reaching higher ranks. Gender has been well established as a factor in the likelihood of getting hired in a tenure-track position in the first place. Among doctoral-level scientists in tenure-track positions at 4-year colleges and universities, fewer than a third are women (Perna, 2001). Married mothers of preschool-age children are 35% less likely to get tenure-track jobs than married fathers of preschool children. Thus, early academic careers appear to be influenced by gender and childbearing and create discrepancy further along the career track. For example, only one in four women are full professors (Wolfinger, 2013) and publish fewer scholarly papers than men (Schucan Bird, 2011). These differences have been attributed to motherhood, specifically, and gender bias, more generally. Although a full discussion of gender bias is outside the scope of this chapter, there has been limited attention paid to the simple fact that the crucial timing of the tenure process, itself, is on a collision course with fertility (Armenti, 2004).

The average age of conferral of the PhD for women is 33 (Mason, 2009). As discussed in Chapter 1, the majority of newly minted PhDs move directly to either academia or a postdoctoral position. This places women who enter academia squarely in the midst of their most fertile years. Stated more directly,

> the average age of a [female] PhD recipient is now nearly thirty-three, compared to thirty-one two decades ago. If this pattern holds or intensifies, the problematic nature of the timing of faculty careers and family formation may greatly affect future generations of doctoral students. (Mason, Goulden, & Frasch, 2009, p. 16)

Thus, if the most typical or expected path from a PhD is directly to an academic appointment, then the tenure period, ranging from 5 to 7 years, coincides with the period during which professional women are most likely to begin their families. The childbearing opportunity is "do or die"; you either bear children when you are fertile, or you don't. Notably, the tenure process is also "do or die"; you either meet the criteria within that 5- to 7-year window to warrant tenure, or you don't.

University policies and structures that might address this, such as part-time tenure-track options, delayed or relaxed tenure clocks, flexible scheduling, and on-site child care, have been the subject of other publications (O'Meara & Campbell, 2011). One example is a reversible part-time option for tenure-track faculty. More than half of American corporations allow part-time options for parents, yet fewer than one in 10 colleges and universities do so (O'Meara & Campbell, 2011). Such solutions have the potential to dramatically improve opportunities for women in the academy. Here I make the perhaps controversial case that delaying entrance to a tenure-track academic position is another scenario that can address these challenges. Most important, this scenario is by no means an endpoint that precludes returning to academia.

Gender and childbearing may not be the only factors delaying entrance to academia or resulting in leaving academia to return at a later date. Academics are sometimes faced with the two-body problem when their partner is also an academic. Wolf-Wendel, Twombly, and Rice (2000) reported that 80% of full-time academic faculty had spouses or partners who were also working professionals, often other academics: 35% of male faculty and 40% of female faculty were partnered with other academics. Universities are often not able to offer both parties a position; thus, one person accepting his or her dream job may mean a separation from academia for the other partner. Unless the position is in a large urban area, the potential of another college or university in close proximity at which a partner can be employed is also limited. As a result, one partner may find himself or herself seeking employment outside of academia. Alternatively, for those with clinical degrees, a professional practice may grow or be more attractive than an academic career for financial or personal reasons.

And finally, there simply may be opportunities outside of academia that are just too attractive to turn down. As noted throughout this volume, doctoral training is applicable to positions in many settings, including research, development, government, foundations, and business. These may be attractive in terms of salary, benefits, lifestyle, and opportunities at some point in one's career.

"Retiring" to Academia

Many people who want an academic position late in their career are not necessarily looking for a tenure-track position. "Retiring" to academia is a way to teach what you have spent a career learning and doing, without the requirements of doing research, publishing, having committee responsibilities, and advising students. This path may be more common among business or hard science PhDs than among behavioral and social science PhDs, in part because of the greater potential for higher paying jobs and opportunities that may draw newly minted doctorates to work outside of academia.

"Later" may be a potentially satisfying way to experience academia for those in the behavioral and social sciences who have served in research roles at foundations, nonprofit organizations, and public schools. Opportunities to teach as an adjunct or in a clinical position may not necessarily require a full-time tenure-track commitment to academic research, service, and teaching. For those who do seek an academic career, however, there are ways to do so.

What If I Want an Academic Career Later?

The short answer is that you *can* go home again. It is likely that the opportunity you find may be somewhat different than what you envisioned while writing your dissertation. It may require some concessions; for example, you might be more constrained by geography. You may also consider an institution that you would not have considered earlier in your career, as you have a better perspective on what is now most important to you. Ultimately, if you love academia but it doesn't meet your needs immediately or shortly after finishing your doctorate or postdoc, you *can* go home again! The key, however, is to prepare *now* for that eventuality.

If I'm Thinking of an Academic Position Later in My Career, What Do I Need to Do Now?

If you want to keep your options open, there are several things you can do now that will help you maintain your competitiveness on the academic job market later. These include publishing, teaching, staying involved in professional organizations, and documenting all of your work. These activities are explored in more detail below. Keep them in mind as you continue on your nonacademic career path.

PUBLISH, PUBLISH, PUBLISH

There may be many opportunities to write about the work you are doing outside of academia, if only you think about them in academic terms. If you are in a research position, do everything you can to ensure that your name appears on scholarly publications. If you are in a think tank, foundation, nonprofit, or government position, look for ways to work on projects that can be published, and be the catalyst to getting the work published.

Unless you are in a research institution, publishing may be outside the scope of your responsibilities or the expertise of your colleagues. There is, however, no more important attribute than a list of publications to make you attractive when you want to return to academia. One of my largest consulting projects was with a local health department evaluating the county's tobacco control initiative. The public health staff were overextended, underpaid, and struggling with shrinking public budgets. They did not have the time or energy to publish, and their job evaluations did not depend on peer-reviewed publications. But our work was groundbreaking, and I knew it needed a larger audience. I became the instigator behind publishing our work together, struggling at times to get their input and material in a timely way, but finding it well worth the effort when that work got published in a top public health journal, marking the county as having one of the lowest smoking rates in the nation (Lieberman et al., 2013). Seeing their work highlighted in print brought the staff great pride. In addition, they were able to share it with local legislators, who ultimately decided to maintain critical funding for their programs.

Opportunities to publish may vary depending on the type of setting in which you are employed. In government jobs (Chapter 4), you may be limited by vetting requirements (Green, 2016). As a result, publishing may simply take longer. Foundations (Chapter 5) are typically focused on funding projects rather than conducting them, but there are still opportunities to publish discussion papers and reflections on the direction of your field. Consulting (Chapter 6), which was my primary role, provides myriad possibilities for publication, but it can be challenging because of the need to move rapidly from project to project. When a project or assignment ends, the consultant moves on and must set aside significant time and attention to publish on a previous project. Working in think tanks (Chapter 7) will likely provide opportunities to generate documents not typically published in peer-reviewed journals. Look for opportunities to translate these documents into perspectives, opinions, or other pieces that may be of interest to academic journals. Publishing within an industry or business setting (Chapter 8) may perhaps be more challenging because of proprietary issues. In nonprofits (Chapter 9), look for opportunities to conduct and publish evaluation studies or to contribute to other researchers' work. Ultimately, seeking opportunities to share your work in professional journals is critical to landing an academic job down the road.

A related, and potentially great, way to stay connected to research in your field is to serve as a reviewer for scholarly journals and to seek editorial positions on journal boards and advisories. The peer review process relies on careful and reliable peer reviewers who put time and effort into their reviews, send them back on time, and provide specific and substantive feedback on manuscripts. Such reviews are highly valued by journal editors and can be a great way for you to stay connected to publications in your field, keep up with the literature, and identify opportunities to publish your current work. You can start this process during your doctoral studies by asking mentors and professors if you can work with them on mentored reviews to learn the process. At least one journal, *Health Education & Behavior* (n.d.), recently started a doctoral reviewer mentoring program to train the next generation of peer reviewers and expand its own peer review network. For doctoral candidates who may not be seeking an academic career immediately after graduation, this kind of opportunity can be invaluable in staying connected to the literature and the publishing process.

TEACH, TEACH, TEACH

Depending on the position to which you eventually apply, you will likely be expected to teach at the graduate or undergraduate level. Those who interview you may be impressed with the real-world credibility of a candidate from outside academia, but they may have concerns about your potential to "profess." Thus, whatever work you are doing, if you want to one day return to academia, having teaching experience at local colleges, community colleges, or online may be critical in your academic application.

Importantly, collect evidence of effective teaching along the way. This evidence may include letters from supervisors or chairs of departments in which you teach, formal or informal observations of your teaching, and formal and informal student evaluations. Not all universities offer or require adjunct faculty to be evaluated by students, but individual instructors can seek their own student feedback using anonymous written or online surveys. Whatever or wherever you teach, be sure to document and collect the evidence that you are an effective teacher.

STAY INVOLVED IN PROFESSIONAL ORGANIZATIONS

Although requirements for a nonacademic position may not include attending, belonging to, or holding leadership positions in professional societies, these remain critical connections to the academy, should you choose to return there. The parameters of your existing job will likely drive which organizations you join or meetings you attend. You'll want to stay connected, however, to large national organizations in your field, even if these are not the primary focus of your nonacademic position. These organizations are a great source of knowledge about open academic positions, as well as connections to academics who can recommend you or give you inside information. There are likely to be advantages of your attendance at such national meetings for your nonacademic employer, but unless you are in an academic or research setting, it will be up to you to seek out those opportunities and advocate for the time and financial support of your employer to attend.

KEEP YOUR EYES OPEN FOR LOCAL OPPORTUNITIES

In addition to large national organizations, staying involved with professional organizations in your state or region will keep you connected to and aware of the local universities offering programs in your field. The local and regional connection is critical because if you return to academia well into your career, it is less likely that you would be moving across the country as you might for a position right out of graduate school. Thus, it is important to stay abreast of schools in your region that have programs in your field, get to know their faculty, and be aware of research taking place there. Find ways to connect with those people or places, and consider collaborating on projects, attending their workshops or professional development events, and becoming the person they might seek out if a full-time or adjunct position opens.

Conclusion

PhDs often start their career in the academy during or immediately after earning their degree. Some are well suited to a lifetime in the academy; a range of financial, family, and other considerations, however, make it less than optimal for others. The main point is that, ultimately, you *can* go home again to academia. With planning and attention to the factors that drive the academic world (i.e., publications, leadership, and teaching), a successful career in academia is possible, even after diverging from the academic track.

References

Armenti, C. (2004). Women faculty seeking tenure and parenthood: Lessons from previous generations. *Cambridge Journal of Education*, 34, 65–83. http://dx.doi.org/10.1080/0305764042000183133

Green, L. W. (2016). Reflections on government service rotations by an academic health education professional. *Health Education & Behavior*, 43, 11–16. http://dx.doi.org/10.1177/1090198115621868

Health Education & Behavior. (n.d.). *Student peer-reviewer application process*. Retrieved from http://journals.sagepub.com/pb-assets/cmscontent/HEB/Expectations_of_Student_Reviewers.pdf

Lieberman, L., Diffley, U., King, S., Chanler, S., Ferrara, M., Alleyne, O., & Facelle, J. (2013). Local tobacco control: Application of the essential public health services model in a county health department's efforts to Put It Out Rockland. *American Journal of Public Health, 103*, 1942–1948. http://dx.doi.org/10.2105/AJPH.2013.301284

Mason, M. A. (2009, October 21). *Why so few doctoral-student parents?* Retrieved from http://www.chronicle.com/article/Why-So-Few-Doctoral-Student/48872/

Mason, M. A., Goulden, M., & Frasch, K. (2009). Why graduate students reject the fast track. *Academe, 95*(1), 11–16.

National Center for Science and Engineering Statistics. (2017). *2015 doctorate recipients from U.S. universities*. (Report No. NSF 17-306). Arlington, VA: National Science Foundation. Retrieved from https://www.nsf.gov/statistics/2017/nsf17306/static/report/nsf17306.pdf

O'Meara, K., & Campbell, C. M. (2011). Faculty sense of agency in decisions about work and family. *The Review of Higher Education, 34*, 447–476. http://dx.doi.org/10.1353/rhe.2011.0000

Perna, L. W. (2001). Sex and race differences in faculty tenure and promotion. *Research in Higher Education, 42*, 541–567. http://dx.doi.org/10.1023/A:1011050226672

Schucan Bird, K. (2011). Do women publish fewer journal articles than men? Sex differences in publication productivity in the social sciences. *British Journal of Sociology of Education, 32*, 921–937. http://dx.doi.org/10.1080/01425692.2011.596387

van Anders, S. M. (2004). Why the academic pipeline leaks: Fewer men than women perceive barriers to becoming professors. *Sex Roles, 51*(9–10), 511–521. http://dx.doi.org/10.1007/s11199-004-5461-9

Wolfinger, N. H. (2013, July 29). For female scientists, there's no good time to have children. *The Atlantic*. Retrieved from https://www.theatlantic.com/sexes/archive/2013/07/for-female-scientists-theres-no-good-time-to-have-children/278165/

Wolfinger, N. H., Mason, M. A., & Goulden, M. (2008). Problems in the pipeline: Gender, marriage, and fertility in the ivory tower. *The Journal of Higher Education, 79*, 388–405. http://dx.doi.org/10.1080/00221546.2008.11772108

Wolf-Wendel, L., Twombly, S., & Rice, S. (2000). Dual-career couples: Keeping them together. *The Journal of Higher Education, 71*, 291–321.

CAREER PATHS FOR BEHAVIORAL AND SOCIAL SCIENCE DOCTORATES

II

J. Zoe Klemfuss

Postdoc
The Next Logical Step?

3

I decided in the fifth grade that I wanted to become a psychologist. This may sound precocious, but really, I had the same narrow sense of what it means to be a psychologist as most of the lay public. The psychologist I am today has little to do with the psychologist fifth-grade me envisioned: someone who listened to people's problems in an attempt to help them feel better.

As an undergraduate at the University of California (UC), Berkeley, the psychologist I am today began to take shape. I enrolled in a breadth of courses, including those from across disciplines within psychology (e.g., social and personality, cognitive, developmental, biological) and became especially drawn to developmental psychology because I found it fascinating to think of basic psychological concepts in the ever-changing landscape of development. This interest was solidified through my part-time job as a substitute preschool teacher and my experience volunteering as a research assistant in a developmental psychology lab on campus.

As graduation approached, however, I felt the pressure that is common among soon-to-be college graduates—I wasn't sure what to do next. I had a vague feeling I wanted to pursue a doctorate in developmental psychology,

http://dx.doi.org/10.1037/0000110-004
Building a Career Outside Academia: A Guide for Doctoral Students in the Behavioral and Social Sciences,
J. B. Urban and M. R. Linver (Editors)
Copyright © 2019 by the American Psychological Association. All rights reserved.

but I didn't know in what specific area, nor was it clear to me what I would do with a doctorate. Instead of attempting graduate school applications right away, I chose to take a year to think. I worked odd jobs and volunteered in a new research lab to broaden my research experience. For me, this time was most useful for focusing on reading and thinking carefully about what research topics interested me enough to motivate years of hard work getting a PhD. Luckily, I was successful in finding my motivation and in finding a graduate program that would foster my interests. I went on to get my MA and PhD in developmental psychology from the Department of Human Development at Cornell University.

This time, as I approached graduation, I faced another common set of challenges. First was the decision about what to do with my PhD. I was fairly confident I wanted to pursue a faculty position at a research university, but I wasn't sure how to achieve this goal. I earned my PhD in 2011, and at the time it was becoming increasingly common—in fact, often expected—that a psychologist would complete a postdoctoral position before being offered a faculty position at a research institution. This is even more true now. There were many exceptions, of course, but these exceptions were typically for applicants who came out of their PhDs with several high-impact empirical publications, at least some of which were first authored, and a clear sense of their independent research area. I felt I still had some growing to do as an academic before I would be competitive on the job market, which made pursuit of a postdoctoral position the perfect decision for me.

After graduation, I completed a 2-year postdoctoral position in the Department of Psychology and Social Behavior at UC Irvine, during which I broadened my research knowledge and experience, honed my independent research program, and bulked up my curriculum vitae (CV), making me more competitive on the academic job market. Out of my postdoc, I worked as a tenure-track faculty member in the Psychology Department at Florida International University for 3 years, and I have now returned to UC Irvine as a tenure-track faculty member.

My hope is that my brief autobiography highlights a few basic points for you. First, although this book focuses on alternatives to traditional academic paths, my perspective is necessarily one of an academic because that's what I am. However, I make a concerted effort to present potential alternatives. Second, the position under discussion, the postdoc, is not a career in itself but a path to a career. This second point is important given that the decision whether to take a postdoctoral position and the decision about what type of postdoctoral position to take can direct your career path, so it's important to be strategic and forward thinking. Third, making career decisions can be hard, even though we often pretend it's not. Seek information from as many sources and experiences as possible, use that information to help guide you through your planning (reading this book is a good start!), and think deeply about what you find professionally exciting and motivating. In the following sections, I provide a brief overview of what a postdoc is and what a postdoctoral position might entail, offer tips for deciding whether a postdoctoral position is right for you and suggestions for achieving a postdoctoral position, and discuss potential career trajectories following completion of a successful postdoc.

What Is a Postdoctoral Position?

A postdoctoral position is a training opportunity for recent PhD graduates. Most often, postdoctoral positions require you move to a new lab at a new university and work directly with a faculty mentor. Postdoctoral positions in the behavioral and social sciences typically last 2 to 3 years, but the range can vary quite a bit. Some postdoctoral positions are only a year long, though they can also extend longer than 3 years, and some people choose to complete more than one postdoctoral position consecutively. Keep in mind that if you accept a 1-year postdoctoral position and plan to go on the academic job market, you have to start applying for your next job within a couple of months of starting the postdoc. This buys time for manuscripts already in your queue to be published, which might be all you need, but it's unlikely you'll be able to add any manuscripts from your postdoctoral position to your hiring CV.

What Do You Do During a Postdoctoral Position?

What you do during a postdoctoral position inevitably varies depending on the nature of the postdoc (and the characteristics of the person in the position). The nature of the postdoctoral position lies on a continuum with endpoints that can be described as *independent* and *project specific*. Independent postdoctoral positions can offer almost complete intellectual freedom. This category of postdoc is typically not tied to funding for a specific project or projects. It also requires a lab model and a primary investigator (PI) that foster independence.

A typical week in a postdoctoral position of this type is similar to that of a faculty member who has no teaching or service responsibilities. The majority of the week is spent writing manuscripts and perhaps grant proposals, and a manuscript or proposal draft or two would change hands with the postdoc mentor. A significant portion of time is dedicated to active data collection and data processing activities, including meeting with and training students and staff assisting on research projects. Other important activities include designing and launching new independent research (e.g., submitting institutional review board applications). A couple of hours each week are also likely spent meeting with the postdoc mentor or attending a meeting of the entire research group.

Similar to an independent postdoctoral position, a project-specific postdoctoral position is likely to contain many of the same activities. However, you would spend less, or even no, time during the regular workweek working on independent projects. Instead, you might be asked to focus on carrying out the PI's projects, supervising students and staff assigned to these projects, and contributing to manuscripts and grant proposal preparation as a junior author, data analyst, or editor. There are a range of variants in the continuum of postdoc types from nearly complete independence to project-specific positions. These variants exist largely because postdoctoral mentors, like doctoral mentors, vary in their supervision styles and how they (micro) manage, regardless of the source of the funding for the position.

Some postdoctoral positions include teaching requirements or teaching opportunities in the course of the position. Teaching, especially teaching well, is an important but time-consuming activity. Thus, there necessarily are trade-offs among teaching, research, and other professional activities. Before accepting a postdoctoral position that requires teaching, or before accepting teaching opportunities offered during a postdoctoral position, it's important to decide whether the trade-offs make sense for your professional ambitions. It is probably worth asking your graduate mentor and others in your intended profession for advice about whether additional teaching experience would strengthen your CV for the job you want given the likely dip in research productivity.

Although most postdocs are considered academic positions intended to further prepare PhDs for faculty positions at research universities, there are notable exceptions. Some postdoctoral positions are designed for practitioners, policymakers, or those who will be conducting research within institutions other than universities (e.g., national laboratory, federal institution). Typical activities within these types of postdocs are likely to be more geared toward real-world application of research. For example, a clinical psychologist interested in gaining expertise in a novel intervention might take a postdoc within a psychiatric hospital specializing in this technique. A legal psychologist interested in crime detection and prevention might complete a postdoc within the Federal Bureau of Investigation (FBI). A developmental psychologist interested in government policies affecting child well-being might pursue a postdoc with the *Eunice Kennedy Shriver* National Institute of Child Health and Human Development.

When applying to postdoctoral positions, it is important to think carefully about what type of postdoc can best help you achieve your professional goals. This includes considering your preferred mentorship style and level of structure within the postdoc. In order to find a postdoctoral position that is the best fit for you and your aspirations, gather as much information as possible about each potential PI's mentorship style and lab structure, and determine the nature of the postdoctoral positions of interest. It is best to do this before applying, and certainly before accepting, a postdoctoral position. If applicable, find out where previous postdocs from this lab ended up working after their postdoctoral position.

How Will I Use the Skills I Learned During Graduate School in My Postdoc?

As a postdoc, you will likely use the knowledge and skills you learned in graduate school every day. Presumably you will have chosen a postdoctoral position that is similar but tangential to your main topic of graduate training, and thus you'll be building on the content you learned through your graduate coursework and working under your graduate advisor. You will also likely engage in research activities almost exclusively if you're completing a postdoctoral position under a PI at a university research lab or to some varying extent if you've taken another type of postdoc. Therefore, all of your experience assisting with and independently conducting research projects will come in handy, as will your methodological and statistical training. It's also likely you'll spend a significant portion of your time writing, and thus you will make use of your graduate experience writing manuscripts, chapters, class papers, grant proposals, and so forth.

Another important point to remember is that you will have earned a PhD and thus are an expert in your field of study. This can, and should, make your postdoctoral position a mutually beneficial experience for you and your PI. You are in your postdoctoral position to learn and gain experience, but you will also be able to contribute your specialized knowledge and experience to the lab through collaborative activities such as meetings, research projects, student training, data analysis, and writing.

How Do I Decide Whether to Apply for Postdoctoral Positions?

If you are a doctoral student who is interested in pursuing a tenure-track faculty position at a research institution, you should probably apply for postdoctoral positions. This does not preclude you from also applying for tenure-track positions, but it allows for more potential career options in the future. And given that it is becoming increasingly expected that behavioral and social scientists will complete a postdoctoral position prior to becoming faculty, you may need one to achieve the tenure-track faculty position you want. The good news is that the faculty job market is typically a bit earlier in the season than the market for postdoctoral positions. For typical late summer or early fall start dates, most faculty positions are posted a year before, between the preceding August and November, whereas postdoctoral positions are usually posted in the spring. This means you will likely hear from faculty positions to which you've applied before you have to decide whether to accept a postdoctoral position.

There are a number of reasons why a postdoctoral position can help prepare you and make you marketable for academic positions in research universities. In other words, applying for postdoctoral positions can be a good idea for reasons other than "everyone else is doing it." First, completing a postdoctoral position gives you the opportunity to broaden and deepen your expertise. You might choose to take a postdoctoral position because you're interested in incorporating a new method into your research program or in merging a different subfield with your primary research area, or simply because you think a new perspective could improve the depth of your work. Relatedly, you may wish to complete a postdoctoral position because you feel that your work is overly similar to that of your graduate adviser's. Typically, faculty hiring committees are looking for a candidate with a unique research line that demonstrates independent thinking and creativity. A postdoctoral position that broadens your perspective can help you find your novel area of contribution to the field.

Second, a postdoctoral position is an intermediary step between being a graduate student and being a faculty member. A well-chosen postdoctoral position can help you hone the skills that will be most needed in your future profession. This may mean you get additional experience conducting independent research, working with graduate and undergraduate students in a supervisory role, learning specialized statistical techniques, teaching, getting experience applying what you learned in graduate school to real-world settings (e.g., seeing clients, contributing to policy), and so on.

Third, a postdoctoral position buys you time. If you already have multiple strong publications when you graduate from your doctoral program, you probably don't need this extra time. If, however, you have several manuscripts in the works (e.g., under review, in preparation) or the more daunting prospect of nothing significant yet in your pipeline, a postdoctoral position gives you the opportunity to continue to educate yourself while giving your CV time to mature. Another perk of a postdoctoral position is that it helps you build additional relationships with academics who share your interests. Behavioral and social science fields are no longer composed of individual scientists conducting work in isolation. Learning to network and collaborate with others within and across disciplines is a valuable and necessary skill.

If you are not on an academic track, the decision about whether to take a postdoctoral position is likely more complicated. I mentioned that some postdoctoral positions provide opportunities to gain experience in areas other than research (e.g., teaching, policy applications). However, research is typically a central component of most (but certainly not all) postdoctoral positions.

How Can I Prepare Myself to Be a Competitive Applicant for a Postdoctoral Position?

What it takes to be a successful applicant for a postdoctoral position will vary somewhat depending on the type of postdoctoral position you want. You will need to have completed a PhD (or equivalent degree) before starting the position or perhaps soon after starting. You will want to foster strong, positive relationships with faculty who will be able to write you letters of recommendation or, better yet, who will directly get in touch with colleagues with open postdoctoral positions on your behalf. It's also helpful to put thought into what your intellectual interests, skills, and strengths are so you can market yourself accordingly and convince your desired employer of the mutually beneficial fit. In terms of how you should commit your time and efforts while in graduate school, the best method is to think beyond the postdoctoral position and model your CV after those who have attained the job you eventually want to have. If you are successfully working toward that goal, it's likely your CV will be competitive for the type of postdoctoral position you want.

For example, if your end goal is a faculty position at a research institution, you should invest most of your time and effort in research resulting in peer-reviewed publications. Showing you collaborate with others is also helpful, so having publications on which you're not first author can be beneficial. However, first-authored publications will hold the most weight because they show you are capable of independent thought and of carrying a project successfully through to dissemination. If academia is your goal, you can also round out your CV with practice-oriented publications or chapters and encyclopedia entries; these will not count as much to an academic audience, however, so don't prioritize these over empirical publications. Your publications, especially first-authored publications, say a lot about who you are as a researcher and your specific area of interest. So be strategic and programmatic, especially when you're starting to build your CV, so you can start to establish yourself as an expert in your chosen topic.

You've probably already been advised that coursework is less of a priority in graduate school than it was during your years as an undergraduate. In my experience this is certainly true, as long as you're performing in line with your cohort. Think of your graduate courses as opportunities to add both breadth and depth to your knowledge base and skill set for your desired career. If that career involves research, then take advantage of as many methods and statistics courses as you can, especially if they focus on methods you will likely use in your field of research. Indeed, if you've taken specialized coursework of particular interest to an employer (such as a new statistical methodology), this can make you more marketable. Consider taking courses outside your primary research area, and maybe outside your department if you think it will help you think more creatively about your work. Although your coursework does not always play much of a role in whether you land your ideal postdoctoral position, it could go a long way in helping you develop the knowledge and skills you will make use of during your postdoctoral years and beyond.

How Do I Find Postdoctoral Positions?

There are multiple avenues for finding a postdoctoral position. You can search behavioral and social science job listings as you would for a faculty job. *The Chronicle of Higher Education*, for example, posts jobs across disciplines, and you can set filters for "social & behavioral sciences" and for academic or research positions. You can also search by region, if you so choose, and you can look specifically for postdoctoral positions by including *postdoctoral* or some variant as a search term. Many academic job sites have separate listings for postdoctoral positions. For example, the job search website for the American Psychological Association (APA) allows you to filter job results for fellowships. The Association for Psychological Science (APS) job search site offers a separate listing of postdoctoral positions around the world, called the APS Postdoc Exchange. You can also check listings for specialized organizations or subdivisions for listings within your subfield (e.g., APA Division 7, Developmental Psychology; APA Division 41, American Psychology-Law Society; National Council on Family Relations; Population Association of America; Society for the Scientific Study of Religion).

There are a number of annual fellowship opportunities that can function like applied postdoctoral positions. For example, those interested in postdoctoral positions within a national laboratory or federal research facility might consider looking at opportunities offered through the Oak Ridge Institute for Science and Education.

Developmental psychologists can check out the Society for Research in Child Development for fellowship opportunities that place successful applicants within federal agencies or congressional offices for a year or longer. Several other professional organizations offer similar opportunities within the federal and state governments.

Another method for attaining a postdoctoral position is to seek out informal options. This method works for positions in university research labs (it's the route I took to get my postdoc), but I can't vouch for whether it would work for other types of organizations. Come up with a list of mentors for whom you're interested in working. Actually, try to limit your list to labs in which you'd be excited and overjoyed to work. Make sure these labs could fulfill your goals for the postdoctoral position, including teaching you a new method, subfield, or application of your previous work. Keep in mind that it costs money to hire you (i.e., your salary and benefits), so the mentors on your list should have a history of successful grant funding, strong potential for successful grant funding, or access to institutional funds to hire a postdoc, or you should make these contacts far enough in advance—probably at least a year before your desired start date—so that you can apply for your own funding (see below). Make contact with the mentors on your list as early as you can, and convey professionalism and enthusiasm.

There are a number of different ways you can start to develop contacts that might eventually result in an informal offer of a postdoctoral position. Meeting people at professional conferences can be a great mechanism, particularly if you have someone to facilitate the meeting. For example, if you're interested in someone's work and your faculty advisor knows him or her, ask your advisor if he or she would be willing to introduce you. Similarly, your advisor might be able to facilitate a "meeting" over e-mail if you are not expecting to see your potential mentor in person in the near future. You can also take advantage of formal meet-and-greets like "meet the scientist" lunches. In some cases, you may be able to unearth a postdoctoral position through cold e-mailing—that is, contacting a potential mentor to express interest without having prior contact or anyone to facilitate the introduction.

The specific approach you take with your potential mentor will likely vary by person and context, but some basic etiquette will serve you well:

- *Do your homework.* Read up about your ideal mentors and their contributions so you can have informed interactions with them. Think about how you want to pitch your interests and how they align with what your ideal mentor does.
- *Ask for advice.* Get multiple (valued) opinions about how, specifically, to approach your ideal mentor.
- *Be professional.* Professionalism will convey that you are serious about your career and will work hard in a postdoctoral position.
- *Be enthusiastic.* If you're pursuing a postdoctoral position, you should be enthusiastic about the work you are doing and want to be doing in the future. Conveying this enthusiasm, while staying professional, should indicate to your potential mentor that you have the energy and motivation to perform well in a postdoctoral position.

A third route to finding a postdoctoral position is to create a position for your-self with federal funding. For example, both the National Institutes of Health (NIH) and the National Science Foundation (NSF) offer mechanisms for funding post-docs. The major funding mechanisms to investigate within the NIH are F32 awards and K-awards. The F32 is also called the Postdoctoral Individual National Research Service Award, or NRSA for short. The award funds individual researchers to get postdoctoral research training in health-related fields, broadly construed. NRSAs are offered through multiple programs within the NIH—for example, the *Eunice Kennedy Shriver* National Institute of Child Health and Human Development and the National Institute of Mental Health. Similarly, there are a number of K-awards that can fund postdoctoral training. K-awards are typically for career development at the early career phase (this can include postdocs). Within NSF, you can apply for a Social, Behavioral, and Economic Sciences (SBE) Directorate Postdoctoral Research Fellowship (SPRF). This award supports research and training during a postdoc of up to 2 years.

Of note, there are also award mechanisms specifically designed to support post-doctoral scholars from underrepresented minority groups. If this applies to you, it is a great option to consider. For example, if the faculty member for whom you would like to work has an existing NIH grant, he or she might be eligible to apply for fund-ing for you via a category of administrative supplements called Research Supplements to Promote Diversity in Health-Related Research. This means that they can apply for funding for you that would be added to an existing funded grant. Within NSF's SPRF mechanism, described above, you can apply for Track 2: Broadening Participation in the SBE Sciences (SPRF-BP), described in the general program solicitation (NSF 16-590). This is a branch of the SPRF program that is designed specifically to increase the rep-resentation of underrepresented minorities in the social, behavioral, and economic sciences.

It is important to note, first, that these fellowships are highly competitive and coveted and thus by no means guaranteed. Second, taking this route requires you to plan far in advance. For example, for NIH's F32 mechanism, there are three funding cycles each year—that is, three opportunities to submit a proposal to request funding. Submission deadlines are typically in early April (Cycle I), August (Cycle II), and December (Cycle III). The earliest possible start dates for projects that are successfully funded through this mechanism are September or December (Cycle I), April (Cycle II), and July (Cycle III). You should also expect to submit at least one resubmission to have a chance at being funded; resubmissions follow the same schedule. In other words, if your goal is to have postdoctoral funding available in July of 2020, a reasonable timeline would be to submit your proposal for the first time in August of 2019 and resubmit it in December of 2019. Taking another step back, it means that you will want to actively begin developing your funding proposal and accompanying materials several months in advance of the August 2019 deadline.

Although this option may seem daunting, it comes with a slew of benefits. First, it gives you flexibility in where and with whom you complete your postdoctoral position. Most mentors would be happy to take a qualified postdoctoral fellow, but costs can be prohibitive. If the mentor doesn't have to pay for the postdoctoral position from his or her own funds . . . voila! Happy mentor. Given the limited availability of postdoctoral positions in any given year, independent funding can be a particularly beneficial solution if you have additional restrictions on your job search, such as geographic location or partner or family considerations.

Second, experience applying for federal funding and success in attaining funding are becoming increasingly important in behavioral and social science departments. Thus, if you're interested in achieving a faculty position, demonstrating you have this experience already can go a long way. Many other organizations (e.g., RAND Corporation) are similarly motivated to attain external funding and would likely find an applicant with experience successfully attaining funding desirable. Third, funding can beget more funding, and experience writing grant proposals helps you write better grant proposals. Thus, if you start early (it's even better if you've already gotten practice applying for grants as a graduate student), it can only help.

When you're a student on the job market for a postdoctoral position, or for any position, it usually pays to make your career ambitions known to faculty in your current department and to any connections you have outside of your department and university. If people know you're on the market, or about to be on the market, and they know what types of positions you're looking for, they can send information your way. This can include letting you know about new postings that come up that you might have missed, letting you know about a colleague who just received a large grant and will be looking to fill a postdoctoral position, or sending you information about funding opportunities that could help pay for your postdoctoral position. If they really like you, and if you ask them, they might even contact potential employers they know on your behalf.

What Am I Qualified to Do After Completing a Postdoctoral Position?

In my experience, completing a postdoctoral fellowship in the behavioral and social sciences often leads to academic positions. However, I return to my earlier caveat that as an academic, my experience is mostly with academic career paths. I can think of a number of examples of graduate students who went on to take "applied" postdoctoral positions (for lack of a better term). This category includes fellowships within the NIH, the FBI, hospitals, and psychiatric clinics. Most of these individuals ultimately ended up in faculty positions. However, many of the faculty positions were within departments with a focus on applied or translational research. Examples also come to mind of PhDs who completed traditional research-focused postdoctoral positions and went on to take teaching positions or administrative positions within private research institutions. These examples, however, are the exception and not the rule in my experience.

This is not to say that a postdoctoral position is not for you if your career ambitions are outside of the university setting. For example, if you have hopes of achieving a research position within law enforcement, a postdoctoral position with the FBI can make you highly marketable. Or if you are seeking a position in which you can contribute to policy development within the government, a fellowship with the *Eunice Kennedy Shriver* National Institute of Child Health and Human Development might be right for you (e.g., through a Society for Research in Child Development fellowship).

Because (as this book illustrates) there is a wide range of professions you can pursue with a PhD in the behavioral and social sciences, there is a wide range of potential paths to get there. The best things you can do are to identify where you want to end up, find people who are already there, and figure out what they did to get there. For some, the answer might be a postdoctoral position, but for many others, it might not.

Conclusion

A postdoctoral position is a short-term training opportunity for recent PhDs. Historically, behavioral and social scientists rarely took postdoctoral positions, but today they are becoming standard for future academics. Postdoctoral opportunities have also diversified to include options for placement in private research centers, government agencies, and hospitals. Although postdoctoral positions are not suited for everyone, they can be a great way to use what you learned during graduate school to gain additional experience, knowledge, and skills prior to beginning your more formal career.

There are a number of different ways to find or create a postdoctoral position that fits your individual goals, and some of these options (e.g., applying for funds to self-support) require getting an early start, so it's never too early to start planning. The wide range of types of postdoctoral positions available means there is potential to pursue a wide range of specialized career paths upon completion of a postdoctoral position. There are many types of postdoctoral positions to explore that can make one qualified for positions in a multitude of nonacademic settings.

My hope is that this chapter serves as a springboard for graduate students who are beginning their investigation into potential paths to take after earning their PhD. As you approach the end of your doctoral studies, you have invested so much time and effort in your education that it can be exciting, challenging, and daunting to imagine what to do next, and hard to know where to begin. Asking questions early and often and gathering information from a variety of sources can guide a well-informed decision about the next step in your career path, including whether to pursue a postdoctoral position and, if so, what type of postdoctoral position to pursue.

Additional Resources

American Psychological Association jobs: https://www.psyccareers.com
Association for Psychological Science jobs: https://jobs.psychologicalscience.org
National Institutes of Health Research Training and Career Development Individual
 Fellowships: https://researchtraining.nih.gov/programs/fellowships

National Institutes of Health Research Training and Career Development Research Career Development Awards: https://researchtraining.nih.gov/programs/career-development

National Science Foundation Social, Behavioral, and Economic Sciences Postdoctoral Research Fellowships: https://www.nsf.gov/funding/pgm_summ.jsp?pims_id=504810

Oak Ridge Institute for Science and Education: https://orise.orau.gov/stem/internships-fellowships-research-opportunities/postdocs.html

Powell, K. (2015). The future of the postdoc. *Nature, 520,* 144–147. http://dx.doi.org/10.1038/520144a

RAND Corporation: http://www.rand.org

The Chronicle of Higher Education jobs: https://chroniclevitae.com

Layla E. Esposito and Valerie Maholmes

Government
Using Your Skills for the Public Good

4

V alerie's career path was quite circuitous. She didn't take a straight path to her work in federal service. In fact, she initially wanted to have a career in journalism. She really enjoyed the process of investigation and telling a good story. While preparing for that field, she took what she thought would be a short-term position in an admissions office at a local college. She had been a work-study student in the graduate admissions office while a student, so she thought she could continue working in that area until she found the job she wanted. Unbeknownst to her, this job would be a stepping-stone to her future.

During her tenure as the director of admissions, she traveled to school districts around the New York–New Jersey–Connecticut tristate area and saw firsthand the impact of economic disadvantage on educational performance and attainment. In stark contrast, she saw how adequate resources and support prepared students for higher education and success in later life. She was still very much interested in pursuing a career in journalism; however, now she had a burning question—Why do these disparities exist?—which set her on a journey to try to address this issue. That question led her to pursue doctoral studies in educational psychology.

This chapter was coauthored by employees of the United States government as part of official duty and is considered to be in the public domain. Any views expressed herein do not necessarily represent the views of the United States government, and the authors' participation in the work is not meant to serve as an official endorsement.

http://dx.doi.org/10.1037/0000110-005
Building a Career Outside Academia: A Guide for Doctoral Students in the Behavioral and Social Sciences,
J. B. Urban and M. R. Linver (Editors)

Through her postdoctoral training, she learned about child and adolescent development and the role of social policy in affecting outcomes for children and families. At the end of her training, having completed a technical and quantitative doctoral program and a clinical postdoc, she felt unprepared to study social policy. With the insistence and support of her mentor, she learned to map social policy issues onto her skill set. Ironically, it was the focus on social policy that led her to apply for a fellowship through the Society for Research in Child Development (SRCD) and the American Association for the Advancement of Science (AAAS) with placement at the *Eunice Kennedy Shriver* National Institute of Child Health and Human Development (NICHD). The fellowship experience allowed her to see how she could bring to bear her passion for journalism and her training in science on policies that impact children and families.

It was her good fortune to have the opportunity to work in several offices and divisions at NICHD in areas of science she was not familiar with. This experience took her out of her comfort zone but at the same time reassured her that she had something to offer and that if she really paid attention, she could find a way to add her perspective to our work. She was also tasked with shadowing a program official in the Child Development and Behavior Branch at NICHD. She was familiar with most of this research, and by now she could integrate what she learned from other assignments to enhance her knowledge and understanding of child and adolescent development research. The program official whom she had the privilege to shadow moved on to other things, and she was fortunate to apply for and get hired in that position.

A few years later, the NICHD established a new branch that would bring together research in pediatric critical care medicine, emergency care, injury prevention, and trauma. She did not initially think this would be an area of science to which she would have anything to contribute. However, a colleague reminded her of her earlier experiences as a fellow and how she could foster multidisciplinary collaboration in this new field. She applied and was hired as chief of the Pediatric Trauma and Critical Illness Branch.

What she learned through all of these experiences is that just as with the process of scientific inquiry, in career development one often has to be open to uncertainty and follow where the opportunities lead.

From as far back as the beginning of high school, Layla knew she wanted to work in the field of child psychology. She took every opportunity available to volunteer or intern in a variety of settings to help narrow her interest and focus. These opportunities included research assistantships and clinical experiences in which she worked with both typically and atypically developing populations in schools, hospitals, and residential facilities.

In college, she decided she wanted to pursue her PhD in clinical psychology, although she was still very interested in developmental and social psychology. Her graduate training reflected this diversity; her master's training was a mix of clinical and developmental psychology and her doctoral training a mix of clinical and social psychology. She had entered her doctoral program expecting to end up in academia with maybe some clinical work on the side, but after hundreds of hours working with clients and years of exposure to the life of academics, she decided she didn't want to pursue either path.

Her program, like many clinical psychology programs, did not expose students to other careers that might be available to those with our qualifications. She felt a little lost and started her own exploration in search of a career that would fulfill her love of science and research and her passion for the psychological well-being of children. She was fortunate enough to hear about a science policy fellowship sponsored through SRCD and AAAS. This fellowship allowed her to learn about the intersection of science and policy making in the federal government and placed her at NICHD at the National Institutes of Health (NIH). After 2 years as a fellow, she took a position as a program official and now oversee a portfolio of research on social and emotional development, child and family processes, and childhood obesity. It ended up being a perfect fit, but her path was serendipitous.

Although this chapter discusses careers for behavioral and social scientists in government, we mainly discuss federal jobs at NIH. We describe how to find positions in government, the types of positions common for behavioral and social scientists at NIH, requisite skills for these jobs, typical activities in these positions, and the rewards and challenges of our work. But let's start with a general overview of the federal government and potential job opportunities.

The government is divided into three distinct branches: the legislative branch, which makes laws; the executive branch, which carries out those laws; and the judiciary branch, which interprets the meaning and constitutionality of those laws. Behavioral and social scientists work in numerous capacities within these branches. For example, in the legislative branch, they contribute knowledge of science and scientific evidence to inform policy decision making, and in the judiciary branch, behavioral and social scientists provide insight on the implications of judicial decisions on social conditions. In the executive branch, where we work, behavioral and social scientists contribute to the functioning of the government in a variety of ways, which we describe next.

How Do I Find Positions in the U.S. Government?

There are many benefits to taking a federal job, and as a whole, the U.S. government is the largest employer in the country, so there is a wide variety of positions for scientists in the various agencies within the executive branch. Compared with jobs in academia or industry, federal jobs tend to be more secure. The salary and benefits are competitive, and there are ongoing efforts to promote work–life balance across many of the agencies. There is a lower risk of layoffs compared with industry positions, and unlike a "soft money," or grant-funded, position in academia, you are not under pressure to secure external funding every 3 to 5 years to support your work or to provide your salary. Given the large number of positions in a variety of different organizations (from NIH to the National Oceanic and Atmospheric Administration), there are many opportunities for individuals with backgrounds in all areas of science. Even if an organization's work focuses on a scientific discipline that is outside your area of study, the skills you learn in your doctoral program can be applied to various positions at that organization, which we will discuss in more detail later in this chapter. Job listings are posted on www.usajobs.gov; the website has a lot of useful information, and it is worth spending some time exploring it. There is also a website that ranks the "best places to work in the federal government" (http://bestplacestowork.org/BPTW/index.php) that may help narrow down your choices or bring to light options you had not yet considered. Both of these resources will give you the bigger picture of the types of positions that are available across the federal government.

In addition to these opportunities, there are other routes to getting into the federal government. We came to government through science policy fellowship opportunities sponsored by SRCD and AAAS. These opportunities afforded us the chance to learn about the government as a whole and where our interests and expertise would allow us to contribute. There are other options for gaining experience in government before securing a permanent position through various professional societies (e.g., American Psychological Association) or the Presidential Management Internship, which is a prestigious 2-year training and development program at a U.S. government agency administered by the Office of Personnel Management (https://pmf.gov/opportunity/index.aspx). After successful completion of the fellowship, agencies have the option to noncompetitively appoint fellows to permanent positions. One of the benefits of taking an alternative route to government service through these types of fellowships is that you have the opportunity to try out various roles and responsibilities throughout the government before deciding on the agency or department that provides the career development opportunities best for you.

As a result of our fellowship experiences, both of us chose to stay at NIH. A subcomponent of the Department of Health and Human Services, NIH comprises 27 different Institutes and Centers (ICs) each focusing on a specific area of health, disease, or body system. The ICs are guided by the Office of the Director of NIH but have their own individual missions, strategic plans, and cultures.

What Kinds of Positions Are Available in the U.S. Government?

There are many career opportunities within the federal government in which social and behavioral scientists can make important contributions. In this section, we focus on NIH, where we have spent our government careers, and we describe four types of positions that we think can be filled by behavioral and social scientists or public health professionals.

PROGRAM OFFICIAL

The NIH program official is a liaison among applicants who are seeking grant funding, grantees who are carrying out their federally funded research, and NIH. Program officials are responsible for overseeing a portfolio of research in a specific area of science.

This position includes helping scientists submit applications by shepherding them through the process from submission to peer review to (hopefully) funding. Program officials help solicit applications in emerging or promising areas by writing funding opportunity announcements, providing feedback to applicants when they send their ideas, discussing the critiques they receive from the review process, making funding recommendations, and providing stewardship of the grants that are awarded. Program officials also serve as experts to the IC in their area of research in order to guide strategic planning and communication with the broader scientific community. They work closely with scientific review officers and grants management specialists at different stages of the grant process. In addition, there are institute-, NIH-, and governmentwide committees that program officials may be a part of, often to coordinate efforts around a specific topic or program. Program officials (and scientific review officers [SROs]) are officially called "health scientist administrators," reflecting that the job duties combine science and grant administration.

SCIENTIFIC REVIEW OFFICER

The scientific review officer is responsible for the peer review process that grants undergo when they are submitted to NIH. SROs are also PhDs or MDs and oversee grant reviews in their area of expertise. The job of an SRO is to recruit reviewers to serve on the review panel, assign applications to reviewers with the right expertise, run the review meeting, and prepare summary statements of the reviews for applicants. They work closely with program officials, but there is a deliberate firewall that ensures the review process is not influenced by program staff. Aside from their scientific content expertise, SROs are versed in review policies and review criteria for the various grant mechanisms such as career development (K) and fellowship (F) awards, as well as the various types of research project grant awards (e.g., R01, R21, R03).

SCIENCE POLICY, LEGISLATION, AND PUBLIC POLICY

The interface between science and policy is another place that calls for doctoral-level positions at NIH. There are two types of NIH offices that focus on the arena of science policy and public policy, and although they might seem off the beaten path, you should consider them. Each IC may have a slightly different name for the office of science policy and program analysis, but these offices serve a similar and important function. People working in these offices analyze and report on the programs of the institute and their impact; provide information for requests from other parts of NIH, the Department of Health and Human Services, Congress, the White House, or other federal agencies; and coordinate science planning and policy activities of the institute. A solid understanding of science and analytic skills are essential in these positions.

Another office (which also goes by different names depending on the institute) is the Office of Legislation and Public Policy (OLPP). This office serves an important role in relating to the legislative branch of the federal government. The OLPP advises the IC director and other staff on significant policy issues and is a liaison with Congress and other public policy officers serving across the executive branch. In addition, staff in the OLPP frequently meet with scientific, advocacy, and public interest groups. Those with expertise in the behavioral and social sciences can contribute to the communication of the IC's activities, especially when it comes to creating scientific reports and materials used in hearings, briefings, and meetings.

COMMUNICATIONS

Communicating with the public about the important health-related research findings that come from NIH is an important job of the offices of communications. These offices usually interact with other government agencies, nongovernment agencies, professional societies, the news media, and the public. Each of the 27 ICs has a communications office, and there are positions for those with science backgrounds as well as those with more traditional communications training. Being able to translate complex and nuanced research into plain language is a valuable skill and not one that every scientist possesses. Individuals who work in this space interface with the public via the Internet, social media, television, video and radio, newspapers, and other print media. They coordinate press releases about high-impact scientific discoveries and sometimes interview grantees. They are also involved in community outreach programs, public health campaigns, and other public engagement. For example, the NICHD Communications Office has led the "Safe to Sleep" campaign promoting best practices for infant sleep and a program called "Media-Smart Youth" to help youth understand the role the media plays in physical activity and nutrition.

INTRAMURAL RESEARCHER

Although the majority of the NIH budget is allocated for funding extramural researchers, there is a large intramural research program as well. The intramural program consists of approximately 1,200 principal investigators and more than 4,000 postdoctoral fellows, making it the largest biomedical research institution in the world. The science conducted by NIH intramural scientists includes basic, clinical, and translational work and often involves high-risk, high-reward projects that might otherwise be difficult to conduct in other settings. A few laboratories are focused on the behavioral and social sciences, such as NICHD's Child and Family Research Section (https://science.nichd.nih.gov/confluence/display/cfr/Home) and the Division of Intramural Population Health Research (https://www.nichd.nih.gov/about/org/diphr/Pages/default.aspx). The intramural program also uses the NIH Clinical Center, the largest hospital devoted solely to clinical research.

How Can I Prepare Myself to Be a Competitive Applicant for a Position in the U.S. Government?

In order to be well positioned to apply to NIH for the types of positions described above, you would be best served if you prepared as if you were going for a career in academia. Many program officials and SROs come to NIH from academic positions, so the competition can be stiff. NIH is a research enterprise, so course work in research methods, study design, and advanced statistics is very helpful. Course work in public health can also be useful and appealing, and many of the doctoral-level staff at NIH have a master's degree in public health.

As in applying for an academic job, a track record of publications in peer-reviewed scientific journals and conference presentations is desirable. You should seek out opportunities for hands-on experience with research projects. The more experience with independent research or research program administration, the better. If you are interested in a position in a communications office, course work in communications would be beneficial, as would having experience with communicating research findings to scientific and lay audiences.

NIH's description of the health scientist administrator (HSA; which includes program officials and SROs) notes that characteristics of successful HSAs include

> competence in science—recognizable accomplishment and career progression
> in a research activity related to health or biomedical/behavioral sciences;
> competence in management—ability to communicate effectively, to plan,
> to initiate, to administer, and to evaluate a scientific program successfully;
> familiarity with the dynamics of health-related research—understanding not
> only the internal relationships of the organization with which the research is
> identified and conducted but also the practices and policies affecting national
> health research efforts; and ability to work effectively and cooperatively with
> others. (NIH, 2017, para. 8)

We have each served in the program official role for more than a decade, and by developing these competencies, we have had significant impacts on public health concerns in our respective areas of science.

What Are the Essential Knowledge, Skills, and Attitudes Needed to Be Successful in the Government?

Among the most important skill sets for work in federal service are the abilities to be flexible in your thinking, to manage competing priorities, and to respond quickly, even if the product takes a while to come to fruition. These skills are not explicitly taught in doctoral programs; however, they are an essential part of the doctoral learning experience and vital to earning a terminal degree. During our time as fellows, it quickly became apparent that to do our jobs effectively, we had to rely on more than our technical skills and knowledge in the social and behavioral sciences. We needed first and foremost to draw upon our implicitly learned skills. In government service, it is not unusual to be called upon to contribute to and possibly take a leadership role in areas that may be outside of your specific areas of training and expertise. Many in government service have had very successful and productive careers working in areas outside of their specific field of interest. In most cases, these individuals found ways to map their expertise and experiences onto their new roles and responsibilities to build a stronger set of skills upon which to draw for future projects.

In addition, many scientific initiatives take a good deal of time and effort to launch. This is in part because it is necessary to collaborate with other colleagues and seek input to have the initiative reflect the specific interests of all parties invested in funding or supporting the initiative. It also takes time to identify important research gaps for scientific investigators to address and to forecast the information needed by intended beneficiaries of the research so that the initiative has the best possible chance of success. These types of collaborative efforts require good problem solving, planning, and project management skills. There will often be competing priorities and time-sensitive issues requiring rapid, yet thorough and well-thought-out responses.

Working in federal service requires a commitment to fostering and preserving public interest and public trust. Aside from the technical skills of the particular scientific discipline and area of expertise brought to bear on this work, communication skills are also essential. As a steward of federal funds and resources, you have a responsibility to ensure there is transparency in communicating research, policies, and other information in ways that are accessible and easily understandable to the lay public. In 2010, President Barack Obama signed the Plain Writing Act of 2010 as a way to encourage federal government agencies to write in simple and easy-to-understand language and to not create unnecessary barriers between the government and the people it serves. There are few instances in which this is more important than in communicating information regarding public health and public safety to the public. In response to the Plain Writing Act, NIH followed with a plain-language initiative to ensure that scientific writing and information disseminated to the public are clear, to the point, and free from scientific jargon and that they tell readers what they need to know and how the information is intended to benefit them.

What Is a Typical Day Like for a Program Official?

One of the perks of our jobs at NIH is that there is a lot of variability and flexibility in how our days are structured and how we spend time doing our jobs. It is rarely predictable, mundane, or uneventful. However, there are several main job functions for which all program officials are responsible.

TECHNICAL ASSISTANCE

Generally speaking, NIH receives grant applications three times per year, so many of the activities we do cluster around those receipt dates. There is a flurry of phone calls and e-mails as applicants are preparing to submit their applications. We spend a significant amount of time speaking with applicants on the phone or corresponding via e-mail about ideas for projects and requirements for submission.

We spend several months in "study sections," or meetings in which the scientific and technical merit of the grant applications is reviewed; we often average 100 applications on diverse scientific topics per funding round. Thus, some days are spent listening to hours of grant application reviews and taking notes so we can help provide feedback to applicants about the strengths and weaknesses of their proposed research and ways to improve it if they want to consider a resubmission.

These activities are followed by calls from applicants to discuss the "summary statement," which is the official written critique developed by the scientific review office. In addition to discussion of the scientific merit of the application, we also advise on program relevance, protection of human subjects or animal welfare, budget, and inclusion of diverse populations.

Finally, we prepare for the institute's National Advisory Council meeting, in which the second level of review occurs. The Council is composed of scientists from the extramural research community and public representatives. Members are chosen by the IC and are approved by the Department of Health and Human Services. For certain committees, members are appointed by the president of the United States. At this meeting, the Council discusses the recently reviewed grant applications that program staff recommend for funding and advises the institute leadership on funding decisions and other matters relevant to the institute's mission and priorities.

In addition to the time we spend working with new applicants and making funding recommendations, we are simultaneously reviewing progress reports from our current grantees and counseling them if issues arise while the research is being conducted. This is the customer service aspect of the job, meaning that one of our main priorities is to be responsive to the public. As a result, there is a lot of communication among the program official, researchers, and sponsored program officers in academic institutions or other research settings. Other commitments, meetings, and scholarly activities are sprinkled on top of these priorities, making every day somewhat different than the one before.

LIAISON TO THE EXTRAMURAL COMMUNITY

One of the exciting aspects of our jobs involves opportunities to liaise with the scientific and professional communities outside NIH through activities on professional boards and associations and by giving funding talks and presentations on current or future research directions. We are often asked to consult with scientific societies on such topics as the state of the science and the relevance of research needs identified by these societies to our institute's mission and vision. We provide reports and other information regarding NIH investments in various areas of science. We also provide guidance in the use of public information tools such as the NIH RePorter (https://projectreporter.nih.gov/reporter.cfm), a public, searchable database of funded research projects, so that the extramural community can query the system to help answer their specific funding questions.

The need to promote career development for early-stage investigators is a shared priority, and we are frequently invited to speak about pipeline issues whenever possible. We conduct grand rounds and give talks at universities, hospitals, and scientific conferences and meetings. In many instances, we are invited to have small-group and one-on-one meetings with applicants, current grantees, early-career scholars, and others who want to know more about how the NIH grant-making process works and whether their proposed projects are in line with our program priorities.

PORTFOLIO ANALYSIS AND PROGRAM DEVELOPMENT

Program officials are tasked with reviewing the current research in their field and analyzing their portfolio of grants to identify gaps and promising areas for future study. We also convene workshops and meetings with outside experts to help identify research priorities on certain topics. With this information, we can write funding opportunity announcements (FOAs) to help solicit the right applications to fill these gaps, which can lead to scientific advances that fulfill the mission of the institute. This is a lengthy process, but on any given day we might spend some time working toward the development of requests for applications (RFAs) or program announcements (PAs), which are two different types of FOAs. RFAs identify a more narrowly defined area for which one or more NIH institutes have set aside funds for awarding grants; they usually have a single receipt (i.e., received on or before) date specified in the RFA announcement, and they are usually reviewed by a scientific review group convened by the IC that intends to fund the successful applications. A PA identifies areas of increased priority or emphasis for a specific area of science; it is usually accepted on standard receipt dates on an ongoing basis and often remains active for 3 years from the date of release unless the announcement indicates a specific expiration date. There is usually no set-aside of funds for PAs. The process of writing a FOA can include narrowing down the specific type of research projects we are soliciting, working with other ICs to include their participation on the FOA, determining the right funding mechanism (e.g., R01, R21, R03), considering special review criteria that may be needed, and working with various NIH offices on the process of getting a FOA published.

SUPERVISION AND MENTORING

There is also a major supervisory component to our work. In our institute, the extramural programs are organized into branches that have a specific scientific mission and corresponding priorities. The chief of a scientific branch is responsible for fostering collaboration across the various programs, managing the branch's budget, and ensuring that scientific investments are aligned with the overall mission and goals of the branch and, by extension, the institute. Branch chiefs and program officials also spend considerable time mentoring interns, fellows, and other trainees looking for a career-enhancing experience. Depending on the nature of the fellowship, some of these experiences may be for a summer, a semester, or a year or more.

COLLABORATION

Meetings are certainly a part of the job. There are institute-wide meetings, branch or division meetings, and a large assortment of committee meetings. Many program officials serve on trans-NIH or interagency committees focused on a specific topic (e.g., obesity) to share information, coordinate efforts, and keep abreast of what other activities may be happening in that area. Often, we participate in these meetings as a representative of our institute or agency. In this capacity, we work with our colleagues to ensure that important priorities are included in policy and programmatic decision making. These meetings may result in changes in the way science is conducted and reported or in important guidelines for including and protecting study participants.

Another way we try to keep abreast of the most current and cutting-edge science is to attend workshops, conferences, or other scientific presentations. The main NIH campus is somewhat like a university setting in the sense that there are always lectures, seminars, and webinars open to the NIH community. There is never a shortage of opportunities to expand our knowledge both on and off campus.

Last, program work is heavily administrative. Managing grants and conducting the business of the institute require a commitment to sundry administrative tasks, which are mostly computerized. We spend a lot of time behind a computer screen, which should come as no surprise.

What Are the Rewards and Challenges of Working in the U.S. Government?

As with any career, there are rewards and challenges. One of the challenges we experience is managing the competing priorities discussed in this chapter. For example, we have to make decisions about how much time and effort we will devote to developing a funding opportunity or collaborating with colleagues versus spending time on the customer service aspects of our jobs. Because there is a continuous cycle of reviewing and funding grants, it is very easy to become overwhelmed by the volume of work and the rapid turnaround required when responding to an expansive constituency of administrators, policy makers, researchers, students, and colleagues.

Having said that, we enjoy the breadth and scope of the work we get to do. Most of our responsibilities involve meeting with researchers at all career levels to talk about their work and how they might obtain federal funding for their projects. It is most rewarding to work with applicants from the conceptualization of their ideas, to a fully executable study, all the way to publication of findings. Although in the extramural context we do not have opportunities to participate in the conduct of studies, we do have the privilege of stewardship over public funds to address important public health problems. In that capacity, we have the opportunity to see the big picture and to use our power to convene to bring groups together who work on similar issues but from different disciplinary perspectives. We derive a great deal of pleasure from seeing investigators find new partnerships and collaborations that inform each other's work and take their respective fields of science into new vistas of exploration and discovery.

Conclusion

We believe that the federal government, and especially NIH, has many career opportunities for behavioral and social scientists. The types of positions we've covered may be of interest to those interested in the research enterprise, grant administration, science policy, or communications. The wide variety of activities that our jobs encompass provides for an exciting, challenging, and engaging experience. For those with the right qualifications and an interest in serving the public, federal careers should certainly be a consideration.

Additional Resources

Best Places to Work in the Federal Government: http://bestplacestowork.org/BPTW/index.php

Eunice Kennedy Shriver National Institute of Child Health and Human Development, Child and Family Research Section: https://science.nichd.nih.gov/confluence/display/cfr/Home

Eunice Kennedy Shriver National Institute of Child Health and Human Development, Division of Intramural Population Health Research: https://www.nichd.nih.gov/about/org/diphr/Pages/default.aspx

National Institutes of Health, NIH RePORTER Tool: https://projectreporter.nih.gov/reporter.cfm

USAJOBS: www.usajobs.gov

U.S. Office of Personnel Management: https://pmf.gov/opportunity/index.aspx

References

National Institutes of Health. (2017). *Health scientist administrator.* Retrieved from https://jobs.nih.gov/announcement-links/healthadministrator.htm

Plain Writing Act of 2010, Pub. L. 111–274, 124 Stat. 2861 (2010).

Sarah Clement

Private Foundations
The Other Side of the Research Coin

5

When I was an undergraduate, I would ask every visiting scholar and guest about their career path. What steps did they take? Did they participate in internships throughout college? Did they seek out specific mentors? I thought that if I could identify the essential elements of a successful career trajectory, I could chart a path to my own dream job. Of course, I was consistently frustrated and disappointed when guest after guest described a series of standard experiences (college, internships, increasing responsibility) interspersed with random circumstances: "Well, I was lucky; they created this position for me" or "I guess I kind of fell into this job" or "My friend happened to know the incoming director, and they were looking for someone with my skills." How could I systematically chart my career path if it was dependent upon, at least to some extent, chance? The strategic planning skills that served me well as a student seemed to be failing me as I considered my career trajectory. As a near-term solution, I decided to focus on obtaining the necessary requirements for the types of positions I found interesting. That meant continuing with my undergraduate studies in child development and psychology and pursuing internships during summer breaks to get a better sense of the specific jobs available.

http://dx.doi.org/10.1037/0000110-006
Building a Career Outside Academia: A Guide for Doctoral Students in the Behavioral and Social Sciences,
J. B. Urban and M. R. Linver (Editors)
Copyright © 2019 by the American Psychological Association. All rights reserved.

I greatly enjoyed my internship experiences and the opportunity to work directly with community members. As a result, I decided to enroll in a master's degree program that offered an applied track. Through this program, I was able to participate in an intensive, semester-long internship that culminated in a capstone paper. The idea of continuing to develop my research skills while simultaneously applying them in real-world settings was extremely compelling to me. I didn't realize it at the time, but I had already begun to envision a career outside of academia.

After I earned my master's degree, I took a year off from school and worked as a research coordinator for a study that examined middle school students' exposure to and experiences with violent video games. It was a wonderful experience, and it was clear I still wanted to learn more about how I could lead my own studies. Therefore, during that year, I applied to and then enrolled in a PhD program in developmental psychology at Cornell University. I received excellent training at Cornell and even spent 2 additional years training as a postdoc, but when it came time to apply for a job, I found that I was repeatedly drawn to job postings outside of academia. In truth, some of the academic positions were appealing as well, but becoming an assistant professor wasn't a forgone conclusion for me.

As time went by, I looked at fewer and fewer job postings at universities and instead began to target nonprofit and philanthropic organizations in the Philadelphia area. My family is from Philadelphia, and although I was open to living in several different cities, I thought I might as well begin looking in my top-ranked city. The job search itself was far more haphazard than I would have preferred. At the time, there wasn't a well-established listserv, website, or database for these types of positions. I did hear about at least one website—Versatile PhD (https://versatilephd.com)—that posted nonacademic jobs, but I was worried about logging on to such a site and having my name be associated with a nonacademic search. I would like to think that my fears of being "found out" as someone interested in nonacademic positions were unfounded, but in fact this type of search—at least among certain academic circles—is still discussed in hushed tones. In fact, the Versatile PhD website is member only, and the home page notes, "Versatile PhD understands your situation, respects your privacy and sees your potential." Nonacademic positions are more widely accepted today than they were in the past, but at the time, I was hesitant to broadcast my interest in such positions.

Given the lack of high-profile databases or websites to reference during my search, I simply looked for leading organizations in the Philadelphia area and then checked to see if they had an open position. That is when I stumbled across a job posting for a program officer in the Character Development Department at the John Templeton Foundation (JTF). I was intrigued by the description but quickly dismissed it, thinking, "I don't have a degree in character development." I was used to looking for positions in my field or, even better, in my subfield. I soon realized I needed to recalibrate my expectations for the overlap between the words on my diploma and the words in a job description. After a few weeks, I revisited the foundation's website and reread the description. Although I didn't have a degree in character development (in fact, no such PhD exists), I met most of the qualifications, and I realized my background could be a great fit for the position. I applied that day and the rest, as they say, is history.

Identifying a lucrative nonacademic career path for a newly minted PhD can be a daunting process. The purpose of this chapter is to provide you with a better sense of what it is like to work at a private foundation. The chapter includes discussions of the types of positions available at foundations and the core responsibilities and requisite skills of a foundation officer and provides guidance on how to search for this type of job. The chapter concludes with some advice to future foundation officers on how to maximize your knowledge and skill set to create positive change in the world.

What Kinds of Positions Are Available at Foundations?

For PhD candidates interested in pursuing a career in philanthropy, the most commonly held position is that of program officer. In this role, you will be responsible for the development and maintenance of a portfolio of grants in a particular topical area. Of course, depending upon your experience and the particular foundation, there may be some variation in the title (e.g., senior program officer, director of programs).

In addition to the program officer position, there are other options for PhD candidates, including positions in a policy department or an evaluation or learning department. Policy officers, as you might imagine, focus on the development of new policy initiatives related to a particular topical area. Foundation staff in evaluation and learning departments often find they do some combination of internal (e.g., evaluation of a particular grant strategy) and external (e.g., What was the impact of Grant X?) evaluations. These are exciting and valuable roles, but because most PhD candidates interested in philanthropy apply to be a program officer, this chapter focuses specifically on that position.

What Are the Core Responsibilities of a Program Officer at a Foundation?

Most job postings for a program officer position note that grant making is the core responsibility. At JTF, our program officers are responsible primarily for managing the proposal review process, which includes five steps: (a) review and selection of letters of intent from potential grantees, (b) intake of full proposals, (c) identification of peer reviewers, (d) synthesis of reviewer feedback, and (e) recommendation of proposals to our board of trustees. Throughout this process, the program officer typically has numerous communications with applicants that continue throughout the life of the grant. Program officers monitor grant activities through phone calls with grantees and review of regular reporting requirements. Program officers also typically make site visits for their grants, but the frequency and number of visits vary by foundation.

At JTF, our grant portfolios include both unsolicited proposals and staff-generated proposals. Whereas unsolicited proposals can be submitted by anyone with an idea and an Internet connection, staff-generated proposals—as the name suggests—begin with staff members generating ideas on a particular topic of interest. The relevant staff member then selects an external partner, typically a university scholar, to lead the project. Staff and external partners typically spend anywhere from 6 months to 2 years developing the proposal that will be considered by JTF's board of trustees.

The structure of grants that JTF supports varies, but they are all project-based grants, as opposed to operating grants or unrestricted funds. In essence, this means that applicants must identify specific, time-limited activities and goals and must report on how funds were spent to support these activities and goals. Within the structure of project-based grants, however, there is a lot of flexibility to fund different kinds of activities, including pilot studies, lab-based research, field-based research, development of book manuscripts, conferences, workshops, curriculum development, classroom-based interventions, and many others.

Foundations vary as to whether or not they accept unsolicited proposals, the number and length of review cycles throughout the year, and the size of each department's grant portfolio. In some cases, a program officer may have a portfolio of 10 or 15 grants, and in others, the portfolio can include as many as 70 to 100 grants. Regardless of the size of the portfolio, grant review and grant monitoring will likely constitute the majority of your core responsibilities and daily activities as a program officer.

Beyond grant review and grant monitoring, program officers are expected to remain current in their field of study; this includes reading relevant journal articles and books and traveling to professional conferences and events. These activities are an excellent way to remain involved in academic life while embedded in a nonacademic setting. Of course, there are also conferences and meetings for grant makers, including those that are specific to your topic area or geographic region (e.g., Grantmakers for Education [https://www.edfunders.org/], Philanthropy Roundtable [http://www.philanthropyroundtable.org/], Philanthropy Network Greater Philadelphia [https://philanthropynetwork.org/]).

Even after going to school for over 20 years to become a subject matter specialist, you'll find that these meetings are incredibly valuable opportunities to learn more about grant making from your peers. During these meetings you can learn how other foundations structure their grant agreements and reports, the extent to which they engage with their grantees during the life of the grant, and what the opportunities and challenges may be for certain types of grants (e.g., projects, convenings, networks). Further, by engaging with your peers in philanthropy, you can obtain a better sense of overall grant making in your field. You can find out which foundations are funding which scholars and what ideas are surfacing as important next steps in the field, and you can even potentially collaborate across foundations to achieve greater impact.

Finally, a portion of your responsibilities will involve administrative duties. These responsibilities include executing grant agreements, tracking and reviewing grant reports and financials, organizing and hosting meetings (particularly when investing in a new area), and executing contracts for partnerships with external collaborators.

What Are the Essential Knowledge, Skills, and Attitudes Needed to Be Successful at a Foundation?

A successful program officer at a foundation must be both a subject matter expert and a generalist. First and foremost, you must have a thorough understanding of the literature in your subject area, including the leading theories, scholars, and methodology. Unlike academic positions, you will not be judged—at least not as strictly—on the number of first-authored publications you have in top-tier journals. However, it is always encouraging to see that an applicant for a program officer position is actively engaged in the field through authoring publications and presentations. To that end, publications are certainly desirable and should still be featured in your application, but first authorship and the ability to obtain external funding are not weighed as heavily for program officers as they are for assistant professors.

Despite the lack of focus on first-authored publications in top-tier journals, you will be hired on the basis of your ability to act as a representative of your field or subfield. Whether you will be the only representative of that field at the foundation or one of 50 is dependent upon the size of the specific organization. Because it may be the case that you are the lone representative of your field, you must also be adept at explaining research in your field to colleagues who work outside of your area. Further, you may find that others expect you to have a broad understanding of fields related to your field of study. For example, as a psychologist, I sometimes receive inquiries from my colleagues about social science research more broadly. This requires both the ability to translate complex research ideas to others outside the field and the ability to craft big-picture narratives that convey general trends and findings.

Overall, you will be expected to have a broader understanding of a greater number of topics rather than a relatively narrow focus on a particular subfield. This may be a welcome relief if you have a variety of interest areas. When I was in graduate school, I was concerned that I was too unfocused when I found myself reading literature in psychology, health, and evaluation; in fact, this breadth of knowledge and interests has been incredibly helpful in my current career. To be clear, I am not recommending that you run out and buy a bunch of books on random topics. Rather, I suggest you pursue your interest areas, even if it is not clear at the present moment how they may relate to your future dream job.

In addition to your role as a representative of your field within the foundation, you will likely be expected to act as a representative of the foundation when traveling to conferences, grantee events, and public events. In this capacity, you will need to be able to explain the work of the foundation and of your department to many different audiences in many different settings. Therefore, in addition to being able to give a great 45-minute, subject-specific lecture to colleagues in your field, you will need to develop the skills necessary for shorter and more informal conversations with other philanthropists, practitioners, academics, journalists, and policy experts.

One way to demonstrate this skill is during the interview process. Many interviews open with statements like, "Tell me a little bit more about your experiences" or "I'm interested in hearing more about what attracted you to this position." The substance of your response is informative, but this also gives you the opportunity to demonstrate how clearly and succinctly you can communicate sophisticated research topics to individuals who may not be experts in your field. Practice different versions of these responses so that you can tailor the version you give during your interview to your audience and the available time (see Chapter 14 for more on interviewing).

Depending on the responsibilities of your specific position in the organization, you may also be called on to create a vision and possibly a strategic plan for your department. In this case, you will need to be able to outline and effectively communicate a vision that has buy in from across the foundation. In this situation, knowledge and skills in evaluation are incredibly valuable. In fact, these skills are relevant for both high-level strategy and the day-to-day grant making decisions that need to be made. If you are looking to expand your expertise, planning and evaluation are areas that will yield significant dividends to you in the future.

Finally, general business skills and knowledge are a distinct advantage in philanthropic organizations. As a program officer, you will likely interact with many different departments, including business, legal, accounting, and human resources, in service of your grant making. Familiarity with basic concepts regarding contracts, grant agreements, and budgets will be helpful, although perhaps not absolutely essential on Day 1 of your new job.

What Are the Rewards and Challenges of Working at a Foundation?

The rewards of working in philanthropy are easy to identify. In short, a program officer is able to leverage significant resources to support the most talented, innovative scholars and practitioners of our time. A program officer is afforded a window into the cutting-edge ideas that are emerging in a field and the opportunity to communicate with the leaders generating those ideas. A foundation is an intellectually stimulating environment that allows former PhD students to remain as close as possible to an academic life without actually being employed by a university.

My favorite days are when I can inform applicants that JTF will be funding their work. These are the easiest phone calls to make and e-mails to send. You know you are going to make someone happy, contribute to their work, and hopefully advance the mission and vision of the foundation.

Of course, the worst part of my job is having to explain to an applicant why we declined his or her application. As you can imagine, the funding process is extremely competitive, and we often have to say no to very talented applicants and very interesting ideas; there simply isn't enough money to fund every project. These conversations are a very difficult but necessary part of the job. The ability to have these conversations and maintain positive relationships with applicants is a critical, if not frequently discussed, feature of a program officer's job.

Fortunately, you will be surrounded by more seasoned grant makers at the foundation who will provide guidance based on their own experiences; between this guidance and your own interactions with applicants, you will find that within the first 2 years in your position, you will have acquired a new set of skills that help you build strong relationships with both applicants and grantees.

For some former PhD students, it may also be difficult to leave behind some of the benefits of academic life. Most notably, you will no longer conduct your own research, nor will you teach. Of course, in an ideal world, you may be able to continue some of these activities on a limited basis—perhaps teaching a summer course or writing a paper (e.g., journal commentary, nonempirical research chapter) every so often—but your first responsibility will be to the foundation, and you will likely find that your time to work on other endeavors is limited.

It can also be difficult to transition from an academic schedule to a business schedule. Most program officers report to the office for a standard work week—Monday through Friday, from 8:00 or 9:00 in the morning until 5:00 or 6:00 at night—and the dress is often business or business casual. So, you will need to say goodbye to the flexibility of academic hours and the casual attire. The benefit of this change in schedule and environment is that there is a degree to which work can be left at work. I can't say that I don't work occasionally at night (I do) or sometimes on weekends (guilty again), but there isn't the constant, nagging thought that I could be working on one more paper.

How Do I Find Positions at Foundations?

To search for foundation jobs, you can use several different online databases (see Additional Resources) or visit a specific foundation's website. Many nonacademic job seekers are attracted to positions located in a particular geographic region; in my case, I restricted my initial search to the Philadelphia area. To find jobs in a specific geographic region, you can either use filters in your online database search or simply do a Google search to see whether there are any foundations in your city or town and then go directly to the foundations' website. Finally, take a look at your favorite academic articles and note the funders who supported the research. This is a great way to identify foundations that support work in your areas of interest.

Advice for Future Program Officers

There are two types of advice that I would offer individuals pursuing nonacademic positions in general and foundation jobs in particular: (a) Be flexible and open to new experiences, and (b) maintain a healthy sense of humility. First, harkening back to my frustration as an undergraduate when listening to visiting scholars and other guests talk about their seemingly haphazard path to their dream job, I recommend identifying the types of positions you are interested in obtaining and building the foundation of skills that are required for those positions so that when an opportunity arises, you are prepared to seize it. Relatedly, say yes to as many opportunities as possible. If your dissertation chair suggests that you attend a particular conference or meet with specific people, do so. More importantly, once you have met new people, maintain those relationships. Program officers must navigate a large network of potential applicants, grantees, reviewers, and advisors. It will benefit you to maintain and then expand the network you first establish in graduate school.

Next, when you are on the job market and find an interesting job description but you don't quite match 100% of the listed requirements, apply anyway. If you are enthusiastic about a position and believe you have the qualifications to fulfill the responsibilities, go for it. Having been on the other side of these hiring decisions, I now see that there is rarely a perfect match between the candidate and the job description—each candidate offers a distinct profile of knowledge, interest, and experience. Do not limit yourself before you even apply.

The second type of advice I would offer, to maintain humility, is more specifically tailored to the program officer position. When I first applied to work at JTF, my future boss cautioned that I would never be smarter or funnier than when I was working on behalf of a philanthropist. It was an unexpected and humorous note, but one that should be taken incredibly seriously. As a graduate student, you may e-mail a professor at another university and pray that he or she will actually read the e-mail, let alone reply. When you are a program officer, all of your calls and e-mails are returned immediately, and almost without fail, everyone is incredibly kind and gracious. To be fair, many applicants and grantees actually are that nice! However, my point is that there is a distinct power dynamic that should not be underestimated. As Hal Harvey (2016), CEO of Energy Innovation, wrote, "Foundation leaders have a duty to . . . remember that they didn't stop having bad ideas the day they started giving away money." As a program officer, you need the humility to recognize when you are wrong and perhaps are not serving the best interest of the grantee and, by proxy, the goals of the foundation. This humble approach to philanthropy will yield the best results for you as a steward of the philanthropist's money and for the many talented grantees you fund.

Conclusion

If you are interested in maintaining a close relationship with academia, including collaborating with scholars and dedicating significant time to reading, writing, and sharing ideas about future grants, a program officer position at a foundation is an ideal career choice. With such a large number of foundations, big and small, in the United States and abroad, you have the opportunity to seek out an organization that supports research or practice in your field of interest. You may not have made your first million—or billion—yet, but you can help serve those who have, and perhaps even help change the world in the process.

Additional Resources

Bridgespan Group's nonprofit jobs board: https://www.bridgespan.org/jobs/
nonprofit-jobs/nonprofit-job-board
Council on Foundations: http://jobs.cof.org/
Idealist: https://www.idealist.org/
Philanthropy News Digest: http://philanthropynewsdigest.org/jobs
The Chronicle of Philanthropy: https://www.philanthropy.com/jobs
Versatile PhD: https://versatilephd.com/jobs/

Reference

Harvey, H. (2016, April 4). Why I regret pushing strategic philanthropy. *The Chronicle of Philanthropy*. Retrieved from https://www.philanthropy.com/article/Opinion-Why-I-Regret-Pushing/235924

Scott R. Rosas

Consulting
Applying Your Skills in New Arenas

6

I don't know that I ever set out to be a consultant. I suspect that many of my consultant colleagues would share the same sentiment. I often wonder how it is we ended up doing this for a living. Was it merely by accident that we fell into this role? Do we simply default, or is there more to the path of becoming a consultant, where the confluence of values, experiences, and skills leads us to a profession where we are able to thrive?

During graduate school, I was focused on my course work, teaching, and research while managing a full-time job in a human services agency. My graduate studies were in an applied, interdisciplinary program in human development and family studies at the University of Delaware. The program emphasized the value of practical applied research in the service of children, families, and communities. Most of the PhD students in the program intended to seek employment in academia, and their studies reflected a tightly bounded area of interest with the intent of sharpening their expertise on a particular topic. I was different.

My professional and intellectual interests were not so specific, and I seemed to be drawn more to the techniques, methods, and approaches for doing research than any one topic. I tried exploring a variety of content areas with different faculty in my program, hoping that something would pique my interest in a way that I could build a research program and hopefully an academic career. Yet at each turn, I felt like a visitor, never really finding the

http://dx.doi.org/10.1037/0000110-007
Building a Career Outside Academia: A Guide for Doctoral Students in the Behavioral and Social Sciences,
J. B. Urban and M. R. Linver (Editors)
Copyright © 2019 by the American Psychological Association. All rights reserved.

desire to remain focused on a specific topic. Although I found much of this wandering unsatisfying, each time I explored a content area, I was exposed to the way researchers examined questions and problems in those areas. I became intrigued by the research processes used by researchers, the innovative methods and tools used to conduct studies, and the variety of ways findings were represented and framed. In short, I fell in love with applied methodology.

Fortunately, with the support of my adviser, the interdisciplinary program I was in enabled me to design a course of study and propose a dissertation focused on research and evaluation methods. I was able to select qualitative and quantitative methods courses from other social science disciplines (e.g., psychology, education, public policy) and began working with a faculty member in a different department who was trained in program evaluation. Her expertise on the practice of evaluation and the use of social science research methodologies was illuminating and provided a place where my interests, competencies, and experiences were welcome.

Under her guidance, my dissertation focused on a multisite program evaluation of a nonprofit family support program using an innovative, participatory method for examining perceived benefits. In carrying out this applied research, I found myself assuming the role of a consultant when interacting and negotiating with the client agencies and the role of a researcher when focused on systematically using social science methodologies to study the principal research question. Without even thinking about it, I was preparing for a life as a behavioral and social science research consultant.

Following graduation, I spent some time in a senior management position within a state human services agency. It was here that I was exposed to how organizations plan, implement, and make decisions. I observed the role of a research consultant from the perspective of a client, and I sought out the consultants' expertise on the basis of specific organizational needs, established expectations for their work, and managed them as valuable resources. Engaging consultants from this position provided me with a unique perspective that shapes my work as a consultant even today.

Eventually, I had the opportunity to obtain a position with a small research and evaluation consulting firm, where I was able to put these skills to use. Today I continue to use my experience and expertise in research and evaluation methodologies when working with clients and colleagues in a range of contexts on issues that matter to people.

This chapter discusses consulting as a career choice for PhD students trained in the behavioral and social sciences. In particular, I highlight the similarities and differences between academia and the consulting world and discuss specific skills you will want to develop as you move from being a student to a professional. Although each path to the consulting profession may be unique, I frame what I believe to be the skills, experiences, and opportunities you as a graduate student should be mindful of if you are thinking about a career in consulting. You should be aware that consulting psychology is a distinct area of practice that provides specialized knowledge on assessment and interventions at the individual, group, and organizational levels (Lowman, 2002). Although not a focus of this chapter, consulting psychology can encompass a range of consulting services, such as coaching, mentoring, training, learning, and technology to individuals, groups, teams, or organizations. The American

Psychological Association's Society of Consulting Psychology provides more information (http://www.apa.org/about/division/div13.aspx).

What Kinds of Positions Are Available in Consulting?

Consulting can be a rewarding and productive career for behavioral and social science PhDs with an affinity for applied research. Flynn (2000) argued that social science research is dynamic and competitive, producing innovative, high-quality research that can be used by practitioners and policymakers. As expectations shift toward more pragmatic and accessible research, consulting plays a role in contributing to contemporary applied research practices, one for which PhD graduates are well positioned. Behavioral and social science research extends beyond the walls of academe, and solid research skills are often in demand. Consultants are sought after in a number of behavioral and social science disciplines, including psychology, sociology, economics, health, criminal justice, and human services. Often, they are retained less for what they know and more for what they can do.

The term *consultant* is found across a range of contexts such as business, industry, health care, and politics. In general, consultants provide expert, professional, and independent advice to clients in a variety of organizational settings to help them achieve their objectives. As external sources of expertise, consultants often provide professional experience on a temporary basis and retain no authority to implement their recommendations. As Druckman (2000) emphasized, social scientists are increasingly drawn to research consulting careers, motivated primarily by a desire to develop the practical implications of research coupled with a clientele willing to invest in applied social research. Consultants purposefully engage with clients in an active transactional relationship to provide support around a range of strategic, operational, or definitional issues. Nonprofit organizations, nongovernmental organizations, governments, and corporations hire consultants with behavioral and social science training for their ability to help make sense of a complex situation or issue, identify key components that mediate and moderate the issue, and generate ways to remedy, advance, or eliminate the issue.

Consulting can be an exciting career option because it offers the opportunity to use and expand on your knowledge in various roles while working with highly motivated colleagues. You may be called on to manage a project, serve as technical or research staff, take the lead on one or more analytical tasks, develop proposals, or produce a final product (e.g., report, presentation). Consultants work with multiple and changing clients. Most consultants are hired by consulting firms that specialize in providing research and planning services to interested clients. There are many firms in the consulting industry, and they vary in size. Some are large, with several areas of specialization and a broad array of projects in their portfolios. Consultant work in larger firms can be plentiful and often provides opportunities to travel nationally and internationally. Boutique firms are smaller and tend to focus on one particular industry or content domain. Consultant work in boutique firms is often specialized and commensurate with the size of the firm in terms of project scope, size, and available resources. Consultants can operate independently as well, and these individuals tend to work as subject matter experts in a particular area.

What Is a Typical Day Like for a Consultant?

A typical day in the consulting world usually revolves around two competing priorities. One priority is to attend to the needs of the current projects in your portfolio; the other is to seek and secure funding for the next project. You will spend considerable time preparing proposals and budgets in order to maintain the flow of work. Producing competitive proposals is key to any long and sustainable consulting career. Once you land a project, you will spend time staffing projects and preparing deliverable products. The extent to which you can maintain a balance between these two priorities determines your value to your employer.

Daily activities are framed by business rather than substantive demands. Timelines and work plans are standard tools of the trade and critical to ensuring that you and your team are able to keep the project on course to meet milestone or completion dates. Discussions during staff meetings often emphasize the status of various proposals, resourcing strategies, and internal restructuring to increase competitiveness in obtaining large contracts. In a typical day, project delivery work can be task oriented and focused on what can be billed to the client. Because you may be managing multiple projects simultaneously, each at a different stage of progress, you may find yourself working on tasks for several different projects in one day. For example, you might be working on developing a work plan for one project, conducting interviews for another, and polishing off a final report for yet another. The ability to shift across multiple tasks efficiently is critical. In the world of consulting, every day is different, and what is typical for today may not be the case tomorrow.

Despite this heavy workload, some consultants also find time for scholarly writing. Time for manuscript preparation is typically not included in project budgets, and creatively fitting scholarly work into an already busy workload can be a challenge. Occasionally, you can successfully negotiate for the production and delivery of scholarly manuscripts as one of the final project deliverables. This approach is more successful when there is alignment between your goals and objectives and those of your client. Negotiating these activities up front ensures there is time and space allotted for scholarly output.

What Are the Essential Knowledge, Skills, and Attitudes Needed to Be Successful as a Consultant?

Two types of consultants in the behavioral and social sciences are common, and their skill sets can be very different. First are consultants who possess deep expertise in a specific content area. As a domain specialist, your expertise can be distinguished by disciplinary boundaries and the culmination of a considerable record that demonstrates proficiency in your content area. Staying abreast of the current body of knowledge and trends in the discipline and communicating complex ideas are critical, as you will be sought out based on your expertise and ability to translate research findings to others. Being able to effectively judge the quality of research in your field, as well as the practical application, will be meaningful to others looking to hire you. Clients seeking consultant services from a content expert are often looking to expand their knowledge of the current state or future direction of the field. For example, an agency providing health care may retain an expert consultant to design services in anticipation of future consumer needs.

The second type of consultant is adept at working in a variety of situations and contexts providing advice on a range of issues and is often considered a generalist. Often their expertise is applicable across content areas, such as organizational dynamics, personal interactions, or strategic direction setting. These consultants tend to have a solid knowledge of methods and their application or a deep understanding of universal processes related to organizations or services, such as planning, design, and implementation. Being adept in the creative design and application of methods is important, as these consultants are often called on to develop a specific inquiry that yields usable results in unique situations, such as a specific program evaluation. The ability to be creative, adaptive, and anticipatory are key skills, as situations encountered by a consultant can be vastly different, even when working in the same content area. More than simply demonstrating proficiency with several methods, the ability to appropriately match those tools with the expectations and needs of the client is paramount.

Evaluation consultants are often viewed as generalists, even when they possess specific content expertise. It is somewhat of a misnomer to refer to these consultants as *generalists*, as their skill set is in fact specific and specialized. Although the distinctions should be noted, these two categories of consultants are not exclusive, and there is often overlap.

What Is the Difference Between Research Conducted in an Academic Setting Versus a Consulting Setting?

A major challenge in the transition from an institution of higher learning to the commercial world is the ability of new graduates to adapt to nonacademic environments. There are several important differences between the academic research for which PhDs have been specifically trained and the applied research for which behavioral and social science consultants are often sought. A primary difference is the source of the applied problem. For academics supported by government or foundation grants, for example, the problem is defined relative to current knowledge in a field and articulated in a proposal subsequently evaluated through a peer review process. In this regard, the academic's delineation of the problem is judged by his or her peers, who must decide among many proposals that are likely to offer significant contributions to the knowledge base. Performance quality of the academic is then evaluated primarily in terms of articles published in well-regarded journals.

For behavioral and social science research consultants supported by contracts that specify some product or deliverable, the problem is usually delineated by the client agency or organization. In this sense, consultants seek to address the needs of a client who must decide whether the proposal is sufficiently responsive to its needs. The consultant's performance is evaluated in terms of the value of the product to the client, timeliness of its delivery, and efficiency of the execution of the contracted expectations.

The marketplace is another important factor in the distinction between academia and consulting. In general, academic researchers tend to be less sensitive than consultants to fluctuations in the needs, budgets, and priorities of external organizations. Unlike most academics, as a consultant your survival depends on the direct support of the client, and thus vigilance and sensitivity to the client's context is paramount. To that end, your work is more likely to be influenced by market considerations and shifts in demand rather than gaps in the knowledge base.

A third difference is the orientation to and purpose of the research process. Many academic behavioral and social science researchers embrace the value of empirical investigations as framed by positivist philosophies of science. Each study is construed as part of a research program in which discoveries stimulate new inquires. Over time, new insights enable more refined explanations of human behavior or social processes.

Academics often have several responsibilities all vying for their time besides research (e.g., teaching, service) and have greater control over their schedule. In contrast, as a consultant, your research is influenced primarily by client needs, and thus you need to attend to and emphasize the development of new approaches for solving problems. Consulting projects are directed toward resolution within a particular context, with clients investing primarily in the development of tools and models rather than concepts or theories that stimulate investigation. In consulting, evaluative "how" questions take precedence over explanatory "why" questions. Timelines are imposed by the client, and the traditional project cycle tends to be more expedited in consulting than in academia. However, the rapid turnover of projects can provide more experiences, result in greater productivity and output, and expose you to a wider variety of topics in a shorter time frame.

Despite these differences, the day-to-day activities of a behavioral and social science consultant parallel those of an academic researcher, including carrying out research and data collection, conducting analysis and synthesis of information, managing projects, troubleshooting and problem solving, making recommendations, and presenting clear and concise information. As a behavioral and social science consultant, you can offer valuable technical skills likely to be in short supply within client organizations, and your formal training in research methodology is viewed as an asset.

How Can I Prepare Myself to Be a Competitive Applicant for a Consulting Position?

Behavioral and social science research consultants typically have both academic and practical experience. They frequently possess persuasive communication and instructional skills, especially valuable assets in situations in which consultants are engaged in building capacity with a client. The good news for newly minted behavioral and social science PhDs is that your graduate training has provided you with a cadre of skills valued by consulting firms. In addition, you have likely spent considerable time developing content and technical expertise important to firms needing that expertise for a particular project or line of business. Consultants are often expected to be experts in everything on which they work; successful consultants, however, are those who know how to ask questions, find and collect data, and synthesize unstructured information into insights that are practical and meaningful to their clients.

There are several transferable skills relative to a nonacademic career that many, if not all, PhD graduates possess. In graduate school, you likely had to demonstrate that you don't know all the answers but you do know how to find them. The process of searching for an answer to seemingly confounding questions relies on two skills—critical thinking and problem solving—both prized in consulting. Successful consultants have the ability to analyze and interpret data, look for patterns and trends, apply rigorous analytical processes, and draw logical conclusions. Over the course of your training, you were likely presented with obstacles that required you to learn from your struggles and missteps, such as when designing and conducting your own research. Successful problem solving and solution development are important to consulting firms and their clients. Teaching skills are also useful in consulting environments, as the practice of teaching enables you to read people; understand their thought processes, motivations, and concerns; and subsequently provide advice and feedback.

As part of your doctoral training, be sure to seek out opportunities to work both independently and as part of a collaborative team. Clients expect consultants to excel at both working effectively without constant supervision and playing well with others. If possible, look for opportunities to collaborate across disciplinary lines. The complex nature of the problems addressed in behavioral and social science consulting drive the need for interdisciplinary solutions, demanding teams with members at various levels from different disciplines.

You probably have experienced times when you needed to deal with stressful and pressure-filled environments that included competing demands and time constraints. Because life in the consulting business is never tranquil, having the ability to overcome negative events and persevere is essential. These experiences will be important; recounting such an experience and how you handled it will help convince those interviewing you for a position in their firm that you can handle the pressures of consulting. The skills you have developed to manage those challenges will come in handy when you experience similar situations as a consultant. Time management skills are essential as projects are fast paced and time sensitive and require you to prioritize activities depending on competing deliverables. Consultants who are methodologically adept in both quantitative and qualitative traditions are also of great value to their firm and clients.

By the time you attain your doctorate, you will likely have had opportunities to practice orally communicating complex ideas to scientific audiences. Meetings and conferences are settings in which graduate students can sharpen scientific communication skills. Finding opportunities to talk in front of a variety of audiences, such as giving research presentations or serving as a discussant on a research panel, are particularly valuable. As a consultant, you will need to process, synthesize, and communicate large amounts of information efficiently. Having the ability to distill large bodies of information into key takeaways within a condensed time frame will be valued in a consulting firm.

An equally important skill to develop as a consultant is the ability to effectively communicate with nonscientific audiences, which is in some ways more challenging than communicating with scientific audiences. The information demands of non-scientific audiences are critical to understand in order to ensure that your consulting work is seen as worthy of the investment. Balancing depth with clarity in communication while maintaining composure is important in consulting environments. As a student, try and find opportunities to speak about research in front of people for whom research is not the central interest. This could include presenting the results of your research at a community meeting, sharing what you have learned with study participants, or talking with high school students about the benefits of research. If possible, try and participate in planning processes in order to gain insight into how nonscientific audiences communicate about problems and potential solutions.

You have likely gained significant writing experience while in graduate school. Anticipating the types of written products you will need to produce as a consultant can help prepare you for the demanding requirements of professional written communication for client projects. One of the ways that consultants establish the legitimacy of their skills and productivity is through scholarly publications. Because a publication record is highly valued in certain consulting environments, you should find opportunities to work on developing manuscripts for publication in academic journals. Working with faculty or other graduate students on scholarly output is time well spent. Scholarly writing demands clarity and efficiency, skills that extend to all types of written products. For the nonacademic audiences you will undoubtedly encounter as a consultant, writing can be challenging, especially if you have been trained as an academic writer. You can practice translating complex research language for lay audiences by focusing on developing products more typically suited for public consumption, such as research briefs, executive summaries, or blogs about your own research. You should also identify ways to participate in report writing and other nonmanuscript writing activities while in graduate school.

Given the emphasis on the production of successful proposals in consulting, you should seek opportunities to sharpen your proposal writing skills as a graduate student.

Working with professors who are active grant writers and offering to help write sections of their proposals can help sharpen these skills. You should also explore opportunities to write your own proposals for smaller institutional or departmental grants established specifically to support student research.

Because behavioral and social science research consultants are often asked to render judgments about a particular situation, policy, program, or operation, your empirical skills must include more than those required for traditional behavioral and social science research. For example, you need to be able to synthesize relevant evaluative and factual conclusions. The ability to synthesize is the key cognitive skill needed for reconciling multiple results, which may be contradictory, so that judgments are balanced (Scriven, 1991).

Moreover, independent consultants need to model ethical business and research practices (Barrington, 2005) because they often operate without the benefit of institutional controls (e.g., review boards, advisory committees) and influences (e.g., colleagues, supervisors). Thus, if you are considering a career in consulting, while in graduate school you should acquire knowledge of ethical decision-making frameworks. This could be facilitated through a course, seminar, or colloquium in which ethical research practices are discussed in depth. Free or low-cost research ethics modules are available online as well. As a consultant, being able to ethically manage controversial values and issues is critical.

Although academic programs are not typically designed to prepare you for a career in consulting, you can anticipate the skills necessary to be competitive in the field. It should be noted, however, that there are doctoral programs for those interested in a more specialized practice related to organizational consulting psychology. Acquiring the necessary skills can be a challenge in academic programs that emphasize specialization both in content and in method. There is frequently a prescribed course of study with the goal of preparing the next generation of academics. Nevertheless, find where there is flexibility in your program of study, and take advantage of a range of experiences that will maximize your future success in the consulting sector. For example, many departments offer applied statistics, research design, or qualitative and mixed-methods courses that can expose you to a range of techniques framed within a specific disciplinary perspective, providing you with the opportunity to view research through a different lens while at the same time enhancing your skills.

What Are the Rewards and Challenges of Working in Consulting?

There are many things I enjoy about working as a consultant. Because I elected to concentrate my expertise on empirical methodologies and decision analytic approaches to problem solving, I am often involved with projects that are topically diverse. This diversity has allowed me to develop an extensive network that crosses disciplinary boundaries and has pushed my own growth and development.

As with any professional endeavor, there are drawbacks to a career in behavioral and social science consulting. I often find it difficult to maintain a balance between time spent performing research and time spent developing business. I also find that the constant transition from one project to another does not allow me as much time as I would like to be a reflective practitioner. The quality of consulting practice depends on the ability to reflect on your actions and engage in a process of continuous learning. Finally, periods of uncertainty and anxiety about work stability and the status of prospective new projects are common. I find the best way to manage this uncertainty is by taking an active approach to generating ideas combined with patience and resilience.

Advice for Future Consultants

Nonacademic work is not evidence of a substandard career, especially for behavioral and social science consultants. The reality of the job market today, as discussed in Chapter 1, is that there is a surplus of PhDs and not enough academic jobs. Most graduates will pursue employment outside of academia. If you think working as a consultant might be for you, here are several guidelines to consider.

First, as a newly minted PhD, you should be able to demonstrate you can work effectively on teams, exhibit strong communication skills, and be able to point to a record of making a difference inside and outside of your graduate program. Community service projects or organizational volunteer efforts, although not always directly related to your graduate training, provide valuable experiences in working with others toward a common goal. Nearly all consulting firms value researchers who can work with people from different fields and who understand how to problem solve across disciplines. Unfortunately, the typical graduate student experience doesn't offer enriching opportunities for teamwork and leadership. Thus, taking advantage of internships or postgraduate opportunities, especially those with consulting firms, will enable you to speak with authority about how to navigate problems that may arise in cross-disciplinary collaborations. The most beneficial experiences are those that model a consulting experience in which you work with a team to identify and solve a problem and throughout the process have opportunities to convince others that your solution is the right one.

Second, it is important to understand the value system that frames client–consultant relationships and how this drives your practice. Usually, from the client's perspective, the value added by a consultant is attributable less to knowledge of theory and more to the way knowledge is tailored or applied to problems. Value is derived from the results the consultant provides rather than from the pursuit of theoretical exposition. Thus, for graduate students interested in working in a consulting environment, attention to methodological skills should be a priority. Your ability to design and carry out applied research with proficiency and flexibility will be highly regarded in the consulting field. The more adept you are in a variety of methods and their application, the more likely it is that you will find a place in a consulting firm.

Third, although rewarding, consulting is also a demanding profession. Most consultants travel extensively and often work 60 to 80 hours a week. International work can be particularly taxing although at the same time exciting and enlightening. In order to maintain healthy work–life balance, it is important to weigh the costs and benefits of a demanding work schedule against personal commitments. Furthermore, consultants in both large and small firms are regarded by their colleagues and peers in instrumental terms or by the practical value they provide. Professional worth for consultants is measured in terms of how you contribute to the wealth and reputation of the firm. Therefore, you are typically rewarded for bringing in new work rather than for the products generated in a project or contributions to the field.

Fourth, employment listings for behavioral and social science research consultants are replete with requirements for expertise in social science research methods, both qualitative and quantitative data analysis, program evaluation, monitoring and evaluation frameworks, social impact assessment, policy analysis, strategy and program development, stakeholder engagement, and communications. Having a strong understanding of the practical applications of your own independent research will be beneficial during interviews. While in graduate school, you should take advantage of interdisciplinary course offerings, especially those with an applied focus. Experience with mixed-methods applications and newer analytical models is especially impressive on your resume.

How Do I Find Positions at Consulting Firms?

The steps you need to take to find a consulting job are not unlike those you would take for any professional position. Web-based searches and professional organization job boards frequently turn up consulting jobs from across the country. It should be noted that many consulting firms are located near urban areas, so relocation may be necessary. However, with the growth of technology and telecommuting opportunities, working from a more rural location is quite possible. In preparing for a consulting position, you should consider how to effectively use social media. For example, ResearchGate (https://www.researchgate.net/) is a platform that enables consultants and academics to share research products (e.g., publications, conference presentations, white papers) and interact with one another around specific questions or projects. Following other consultants and academics on such a platform allows you to expand your network.

Conclusion

Social science consultants are often driven by values, ideals, and a strong desire to have a positive impact on clients and their constituents. If you are able to identify necessary changes while effectively dealing with complexity, ambiguity, and challenging situations, you can be successful in the consulting sector. If you crave intellectual stimulation, seek the ability to be creative, desire a level of credibility as a subject matter expert, and work well in the company of other intellectuals, then consulting could be a good career choice. It takes up-front work, ongoing research, and good business acumen to achieve success in consulting.

Additional Resources

American Psychological Association, Society of Consulting Psychology (APA Division 13): http://www.apa.org/about/division/div13.aspx
ResearchGate: https://www.researchgate.net/

References

Barrington, G. V. (2005). Consultants, evaluation. In S. Mathison (Ed.), *Encyclopedia of evaluation* (pp. 81–82). Thousand Oaks, CA: Sage.

Druckman, D. (2000). The social scientist as consultant. *American Behavioral Scientist, 43,* 1565–1577. http://dx.doi.org/10.1177/00027640021957917

Flynn, P. (2000). The changing structure of the social science research industry and some implications for practice. *American Behavioral Scientist, 43,* 1578–1601. http://dx.doi.org/10.1177/00027640021957926

Lowman, R. L. (Ed.). (2002). *Handbook of organizational consulting psychology.* San Francisco, CA: Jossey-Bass.

Scriven, M. (1991). *Evaluation thesaurus* (4th ed.). Newbury Park, CA: Sage.

Lisa A. Gennetian

Think Tanks
Applying Your Academic Skill Set to Policy Research

7

As a first-generation college attendee, my choice to major in economics at a liberal arts college was very practical: My father, in particular, was quite convinced that this was the closest thing possible to a business degree and thus an assured path to economic security. Indeed, my objective on graduation was financial independence, which I achieved, though I was quite off course from my father's vision of a career in business. The years I spent in the formal labor market prior to attending graduate school were very influential and exposed me to nonacademic career options and helped me discover my interests. Working in a for-profit economic consulting environment provided me with exposure to senior economists and honed my technical skills. Working for a nonprofit research organization exposed me to the fiscal rhythm of grant seeking, the responsiveness of research to the political and public climate, and a different set of technical skills related to translating complex material into lay-friendly sound-bites. I eventually embarked on my PhD in economics because the discipline held a high technical standard, and I understood that my training as an economist would open doors in the nonacademic as well as academic sphere (and it certainly has delivered).

At the time that both my spouse and I were to be freshly minted economists, we conducted a very open joint job search that considered the range of

http://dx.doi.org/10.1037/0000110-008
Building a Career Outside Academia: A Guide for Doctoral Students in the Behavioral and Social Sciences,
J. B. Urban and M. R. Linver (Editors)
Copyright © 2019 by the American Psychological Association. All rights reserved.

policy, industry, and possible academic options. I feel incredibly lucky that my first post-PhD position at MDRC—a social policy evaluation nonprofit—intimately introduced me to the "business" of conducting and disseminating high-quality policy-relevant research. My tenure at MDRC also translated to acquiring research fundraising skills; engaging in interaction and exchange with the federal, state, and local policy and practitioner community; and, importantly, producing nonpartisan evidence. Organizations like MDRC are in the business of producing high-quality research that is largely responsive to the existing and near-future anticipated policy environment. Scholars juggle roles as project directors, supervisors, fundraisers, and disseminators of ideas and findings and simultaneously try to keep an active hand in the actual research.

After 8 years of experience at MDRC, it was clear that a future career path would imply more management and more vision and brand building and less actual research, particularly research to be published in peer-reviewed venues. The strong research foundation I accumulated at MDRC eased the shift to more traditional think tank environments. *Think tanks* are research institutes or organizations with groups of experts who create or use research to inform social and public policy problems and debates and guide future developments; examples are the Brookings Institution and the American Enterprise Institute. Think tanks are less reactive to demand, more proactive about interpretation and opinion about existing research and research needs, and less dependent on producing reports and briefs.

Roughly 14 years later, I was ready and eager to be a full-time academic entrepreneur (representing myself as opposed to a brand) and worked toward being fully absorbed into an academic environment. I felt very grounded in using my somewhat unconventional research path to continue to do good work with very high-quality colleagues and to produce evidence to inform policy and practice.

This chapter draws on my personal experience and the broader experience and exposure acquired working in these various sectors to describe the types of jobs available in think tanks, skills needed and valued, a typical workday, trade-offs, ways to prepare for and seek a job, and advice. Given my own experience, the term *think tank* is not referred to in its purest form; nearly every nonacademic setting I have worked in, and certainly most nonacademic research-oriented institutions, had think tank–like features and components. The descriptions that follow, therefore, also loosely translate to other nonacademic settings.

What Kinds of Positions Are Available in Think Tanks?

The entry-level position for a candidate with a PhD is usually research associate. There is typically a relatively transparent career ladder leading up to senior associate or equivalent position in increments of 3 to 5 years, with many organizations having a senior fellow distinction or chief research officer or equivalent title as an endpoint. A career track can sometimes take one of two paths: (a) primary research or methodological orientation (data collection, data collection management, chief scientific officer) or (b) operations and management (team creation, monitoring of staff, budgets and related project infrastructure).

Because think tanks hire a range of staff, it is also possible to shift gears, blending content and research expertise with task or functional expertise. This leaves open the possibility for (undiscovered) talents to develop over the course of your career without needing to transition to a different institution. In a think tank setting, a particular talent for communication and external dissemination, in addition to conducting research, can be blended in your job or open the door to a different career track of translating research for policy and feeding the communication engine of your organization.

What Are the Essential Knowledge, Skills, and Attitudes Needed to Be Successful in a Think Tank?

Reflecting on my own experience as well as the nonacademic experiences of my colleagues, there are four skill sets—outside of the substantive expertise of one's graduate degree—that nurture a productive career in the think tank sector: (a) management, (b) communication, (c) intellectual creativity and flexibility, and (d) entrepreneurship. These are described below in isolation, although in reality these skill sets closely intersect in ways I comment on later. Finally, these skill sets are discussed through the lens of career growth and progression within this sector. Unlike tenure-track academia, think tanks are not typically "up or out" environments. However, "up" will usually require some evidence of success (or exceptionalism) based in the skill sets outlined next.

The first skill set is management. In contrast to the academic sector, a PhD-level employee at any private sector organization, whether for profit or not for profit, will quickly hit barriers to internal career progression without evidence of project or people management skills. Most nonacademic work is conducted in teams. Project management entails knowing the tasks and functions to ensure a study gets off the ground with the right staff, on time, and on budget. It includes fiscal management of resources. People management means supervising staff (which is not the same as teaching students), leveraging and matching staff skills to tasks, diplomatically addressing weaknesses, having the patience to listen, and developing a people management philosophy and style that are nimble in response to individual and team dynamics.

How to be a good manager is not typically a course one takes in graduate school. It is also rare to acquire management skills over the course of completing graduate schoolwork, although this varies by discipline. For example, in applied psychology more senior graduate students may begin to take on lab management responsibilities, but even here the criteria for what is satisfactory and what is legal differ from those in the real world, where performance reviews and salaries are contingent on performance and employment regulations.

The second skill set is communication. Clear, appropriate, and professional oral and written communication is an essential function not only for professional internal and external preservation and credibility but also for being a good people manager. Work in a think tank atmosphere is almost never in isolation. It is rare that a day will go by without having to professionally correspond with at least one person in at least one format (on the phone, digitally, or in person). Some days involve a string of back-to-back professional correspondence, conference calls, and meetings. Understanding the lines between informal and formal tone in communication, use of language, and structure of feedback or inquiry matters in ways that could generate praise or reprimands. Sensitivity to perspectives—whether you agree with them or not—is important. Some aspects of communication skills are job specific, and investments are commonly made to train staff in preparation for certain kinds of communication (e.g., media interviews, speeches, presentations) because you are also representing a brand.

The third skill set is intellectual creativity and flexibility. Think tanks generate ideas that are commonly responsive to the broader political and policy climate, and demands on any one person's time will fluctuate depending on content expertise. For example, ecological or environmental research may bubble along at a manageable pace until there is an oil spill, or reauthorization of upcoming legislation may prompt redirection of time to crafting products that set the stage for informed political debate. Narrow expertise is essential to completing your dissertation, and a subsequent career path in academia commonly continues to develop and refine this narrow expertise. Think tank work, however, will often unexpectedly tap into the breadth of various experiences acquired over the course of your graduate school career, whether it is application of a methodology learned and used in a class, or an effective approach to primary data collection used by your adviser, or the application of a finding analyzed and discussed during an optional graduate seminar.

As an example, a methodological initiative was being jump-started during my second year at MDRC. A senior colleague whom I had not previously met popped into my office one afternoon and said, "I heard you have a lot of experience with instrumental variables models." I concurred and described my graduate school experience. Shortly thereafter grew an internal team for a funded project to apply these techniques in the context of experimental studies, a topic relatively far removed from my dissertation, though directly drawn from my empirical training in graduate school.

This personal example highlights another related feature of think tank environments: Efficiency and innovation that give a firm a comparative advantage over competitors or that can market the organization's brand in a niche way are highly valued. These are also valued, of course, in academic environments, but with a higher burden of proof. That exchange on methodology between myself and a colleague carved a path to an internally funded project in part because the incentives were aligned not only for colleagues (which also happens in academic environments) but also institutionally. Think tanks have a particular openness to generating better or more efficient ways to answer and inform open questions or to question existing research strategies that can be piloted or tested without first having to go through a laborious blinded peer review process.

The fourth skill set is entrepreneurship. Arguably, entrepreneurship is valued in academic as well as nonacademic settings. There are two key differences between think tank environments and typical academic settings. First, you do not necessarily have to be a self-starter in a think tank setting. The team and external demand-driven work often translate to tasks and projects being assigned versus being shaped or created from scratch. Second, generating new ideas and next directions is highly valued, but to move forward with organizational support often means that ideas and next steps have to fit, somehow, with the parameters of the institution's mission or future strategic directions.

The above four skill sets dovetail and influence each other and interact with an individual's characteristics. Superior communication and management or supervisory skills may not match well with your personal skills and characteristics. It is possible to be an introvert or socially awkward and still serve as an external ambassador presenting findings and discussing ideas with funders, but it will take more commitment and practice. It is also possible to do well in the think tank sector even if you do not excel in each or even a combination of the skills above, though you should be realistic about your career path endgame. Most individuals make it to the highest senior and executive positions as rewards for their talent in one or more of these areas.

What Is a Typical Day Like Working in a Think Tank?

At senior levels, it is uncommon to have a day at a think tank without several meetings, many of which are scheduled outside of your own control. Calendars within the institution are synced such that I or my assistant has full access to others' calendars and thus can book or release scheduled times. This has enormous efficiencies, of course, and is internally consistent with the team-building nature and accountability of institutions, but it also contributes to having back-to-back meetings (sometimes with no bathroom breaks) and an odd but effective self-discipline practice of blocking off periods of your own time (with whatever explanation) to keep others from scheduling you to be somewhere.

Although the general characteristic of having multiple daily meetings may be typical, their purpose, the needed preparation, and the coinvitees will vastly vary. Some meetings are managerial, focusing on project and staff deployment, others are internal peer reviews of analyses or findings, others are strategic preparations for a publication release or funder meeting, and yet others are substantive or skill based (e.g., meeting with an editor). The diversity of meetings very much reflects the multifaceted functions of your job.

Pragmatically, your professional time in a think tank is quantified as a typical work-week (i.e., 35 or 40 hours a week), or its official or recognized part-time equivalent, with the day generally starting around 8:30 or 9:00 a.m. and wrapping up at about 6 p.m. Its structure and predictability from a work time commitment perspective could be considered quite family friendly. One could also argue that the face time inherent in frequent meetings is actually less family friendly, because it is less accommodating to doing other things or needing to be elsewhere during those standard workweek hours. Related to this, working off site or at home and scheduling off-site writing days are not unusual. Whereas budgets and contracts are set using these hours as criteria and assumptions for invoicing purposes (as many contracts are awarded on the basis of nonnegotiable a priori assumptions about the numbers of hours to be committed to each task), as in any thinking job, it often takes more time and more work to produce the output in a high-quality manner.

Although the broader career rewards may be fewer and the path to promotion might be slower, a think tank job is not directly on the line if you do not put in extra time. In fact, staff assessments of whether the amount of work is realistically feasible under the deemed time frame and number of hours are often used as leverage to properly staff projects. There is constant recalibration of staff work responsibilities, priorities, and deadlines such that individual time may be shifted temporarily or more universally to be able to complete projects at high quality and on time. Leverage and expected off-hours work time might also depend on how much your job is contingent on raising money to cover your position (i.e., whether it is a soft-money position or a hard-money position) and how ambitious your career goals are.

In sum, a think tank job might mimic a conventionally defined typical workweek, but there is no such thing as a typical day. Outside of routine meetings and conference calls, a lot of time on the computer, and travel to locations where studies are being conducted or to Washington, DC, to debrief with policymakers or other nongovernmental organizations, the day-to-day thinking task is almost never typical. Because a job at a think tank often requires speaking to and writing for multiple types of audiences (public interest groups, advocacy organizations, public officials, academics), the challenges of research and writing are not similar to those of academic positions, for which the target audience is typically fellow academics. To have a successful career at a think tank and survive the test of time, you and the institution need to be dynamic, resilient, and responsive to a range of external factors and demands.

Not-So-Obvious Research Benefits You Should Know About

Think tanks are highly leveraged environments with available support staff at each level and expertise deemed necessary to produce output, which is usually a branded, honed, fact-checked piece of research written in multiple formats tailored to different audiences. Think tank organizations commonly rely on external funding and, as such, often have an experienced pre- and postproposal management team that assists with administrative details, budgeting, institutional review board approvals, hiring, and budget monitoring and reporting (i.e., all of the elements foundational to a good research study except the actual research). At large universities, some of this type of support is available through interdisciplinary or cross-school institutes; often, however, academic settings do not provide this support at the full range and certainly at the level of cohesiveness as it is in a think tank environment. What this implies for a think tank research staff member is that your most important job is to come up with the proposal narrative and then, once funding is in place, to plan and conduct the research without the distractions of managing the funding, staffing, budgeting, and budget reporting.

Think tanks also commonly have communications staff who are experts in translating research to technical but accessible products, ghostwriting, and interfacing with media and related platforms. Communications staff are commonly responsible for digesting your primary research and converting it into short nontechnical pieces, press releases, talking points, and prepared quotes to answer anticipated questions from the press and media. They work closely with researchers to ensure that their summaries and related highlights are technically accurate. Communications staff might also conduct practice interviews with a researcher prior to a radio, podcast, or television appearance to fine-tune the script. Often newspapers pick up or borrow quotes directly from press releases when producing a piece, never actually speaking directly to the researcher or engaging only in very light correspondence.

Think tanks, and nonacademic institutions that have think tank qualities, are rarely in the primary business of producing academic output, yet the research quality is almost always equal to or higher than typical peer-reviewed academic output. Although academic publications are not likely to be considered part of your day-to-day job definition and thus do not constitute paid work, opportunities are plentiful to produce academic offshoots and publish in peer-reviewed journals.

Finally, think tanks draw on a spectrum of disciplines, technical strengths, and experiences, and project teams are often collective efforts across this spectrum. Thus, think tanks are welcome breeding grounds for inter- and multidisciplinary work that is sometimes difficult to find or replicate in other types of research environments.

Other Practical Considerations and Trade-Offs

Early during my post-PhD career search, I was made aware of the distinction between soft and hard money, which sometimes, but not always, aligns with not-for-profit versus for-profit identities. In a nonacademic research setting, your position might be solely, partially, or not at all reliant on your ability to raise resources to cover your own salary. When I was at MDRC, my first place of employment, the organization hired hard-money positions at the senior level (i.e., the position was not technically conditioned on raising funding to cover one's own salary). Seniority at MDRC, however, almost always dictated some expectation to be engaged with and responsible for writing research proposals. Other, perhaps purer think tanks have hybrid models in which some percentage of one's salary is covered by the institution with the expectation that it is or will soon be backfilled by the employee's own fundraising. This structure can incentivize individuals to internally work on allegiances and ideas with more established and "fundable" investigators as a segue into funder networks or future coinvestigator opportunities. It can also incentivize them to externally network with potential funders and collaborators.

A second practical trade-off is compensation. Compensation and compensation progression are usually higher and faster in think tanks than in academia, but time off is more constrained. Academics are commonly appointed to 9-calendar-month terms. Nonacademics accumulate vacation time, but even if months are accumulated, it is rarely, if ever, feasible to take that time off all at once.

How Do I Find Positions at Think Tanks?

Think tanks compete for qualified candidates, at least at the PhD level, in concert with the academic market and thus follow the conventional job hiring calendar for relevant disciplines (in economics, jobs are usually posted in the autumn, with first-round interviews occurring during American Economic Association meetings in early January). Postings for think tank jobs also occur in the same outlets as postings for academic positions or relevant job exchanges for a discipline (e.g., Job Openings for Economists, the Association for Public Policy and Management, the Society for Research in Child Development; see Additional Resources).

Unlike job openings in academia, which are infrequent and require much planning to "open a line," job openings at think tanks either are opened annually, considered, and filled (putting feelers out for suitable candidates in order to keep developing a pipeline of employees) or are responsive to immediate needs of the organization (e.g., to grow a particular type of expertise for a new or anticipated project). Outside of the more formal channels, informal networking and informational interviews are valuable opportunities for bilateral introduction to think tanks and can often open the door for affiliations or one-off consultations that can also serve as a pathway to a full-time job.

How Can I Prepare Myself to Be a Competitive Applicant for a Think Tank Position?

Substantively, as a graduate student, your general path to preparation is identical whether or not you decide to pursue a think tank career. Your dissertation and technical training and any evidence of publications, presentations, or public interface of your work will be used to evaluate interest and fit. Whereas some academic positions are focused on subjects you can teach, think tank jobs are focused on verbal and written communication, depth of understanding of material (and ability to translate it to an audience that might not have the same level of topical expertise), and, in some cases, creativity or evidence of spawning independent thinking or ideas.

When I was in graduate school, I became interested in a program called Expanding Your Horizons that brought girls from the local community to Cornell University for a day to participate in various workshops. I organized an event in the economics department: a fun mock auction to demonstrate how supply and demand works. I subsequently became interested in the question of whether exposure to programs of this type actually had any impact on girls' schooling outcomes or future academic paths. The Association of American University Women happened to have a small grant competition that would allow me to conduct this independent research. I submitted the proposal, received the grant, and designed a quasi-experimental study in cooperation with the local schools. MDRC might claim that I was a fit based on my dissertation and related work, but I am betting, on the basis of my second interview, that the real tipping point for them was this experience I had basically designing a primary random assignment study.

Seeking opportunities to contribute to a research proposal or write your own, crafting a blog or one-page summary of a research idea, creating a professional website (and, correspondingly, being active on social media), and presenting at research conferences are all examples of strategies you can use to create a scholar brand complementing the foundational skills you acquired through the formal PhD process and dissertation completion. Note that these are also examples of following your passions. That I pursued conducting a small independent research study and secured funding through research assistantships (as compared with teaching assistantships) set me on a course to be well prepared for a think tank professional path.

Conclusion

A think tank career path can offer the intellectual rewards of academic settings with a more team- and brand-based structure. With self-initiation, the elements of academic settings that are not commonly associated with think tanks—teaching, publishing in peer-reviewed journals, shaping the direction of a field or discipline—are feasible to develop and pursue. Think tanks can also offer an alternative setting that is conducive to certain work styles (more structure), personal preferences, and work–personal life balance (job security not contingent on tenure).

Additional Resources

American Economic Association Job Openings for Economists: https://www.aeaweb.org/joe/listings

Association for Public Policy and Management job listings: http://www.appam.org/careers-education/job-listings/

80,000 Hours web page on think tank research: https://80000hours.org/career-reviews/ think-tank-research/#which-think-tanks-are-most-promising-to-work-at

MDRC: https://www.mdrc.org/

National Institute for Research Advancement World Directory of Think Tanks: http://www.nira.or.jp/past/ice/nwdtt/2005/index.html

Society for Research in Child Development career center job listings: http://careers. srcd.org/jobs

Worldpress.org index of international think tanks and research organizations: http://www.worldpress.org/library/ngo.cfm

Debra Mazloff

For-Profit Corporations
Finding Your Way in the World of Business

8

W hen I entered my PhD program, I knew I did not want to go into academia, but it was the most obvious path. Options outside of academia were not discussed seriously in my program. I never heard success stories about people going into business. Although some faculty consulted on the side, their primary employer was the university. All career options seemed to be academic.

I received my doctorate in communication studies. My area of focus was organizational communication. My area of research was related to wellness in the workplace. With my focus on communication and organization, going into business was not a huge leap. But as I worked on my dissertation, I dutifully launched an academic job search. At the time, tenure-track positions in communication studies programs were more abundant than other disciplines. I received an offer for a tenure-track position in a major city fairly quickly. Everyone told me I was crazy if I didn't take it, so I took the job.

Two years later, I was on track for tenure, but unhappy. Life as an academic was not a good fit for my personality. It was not an easy realization, but after many months of internal debate, I decided to make a change. Not knowing what else to do, I started with research. Alas, I am a trained academic.

I interviewed everyone and anyone, in both the public and private sector, who would speak to me about their work. I hired a professional to turn my

http://dx.doi.org/10.1037/0000110-009
Building a Career Outside Academia: A Guide for Doctoral Students in the Behavioral and Social Sciences,
J. B. Urban and M. R. Linver (Editors)
Copyright © 2019 by the American Psychological Association. All rights reserved.

10-page curriculum vita into a two-page resume. I networked and applied for jobs. Eventually, I landed a position in a large consulting firm to work with companies on human resource communication.

I have since worked for a few different large management and technology consulting firms. But after 8 years of living the "consulting lifestyle"—translate this to mean traveling and living in hotels 4 to 5 days a week, every week—I found a role in a for-profit corporation as an internal consultant, primarily working on companywide transformation projects.

I spent the next 6 years working for a property and casualty insurance carrier. Unlike large consulting firms, where you build your brand and never veer from it—much like academia—corporations allow a person the freedom to move around within the organization and experience different roles. I loved learning about the business and broadening my skill set. During my 6 years working for the insurance carrier, I worked in three different parts of the organization on projects as well as managing different support functions. Most companies regularly post open positions for employees to apply, but networking with colleagues and leadership generally leads to the best opportunities. Although the positions I found were formally posted, having relationships with the hiring managers helped me secure the jobs.

On the basis of my experience, I have found that the best place to be in any company is the front office, generating revenue. These roles are the most valued because they make rather than cost money. But in an insurance company, this means developing or selling insurance products. Because this was never a career goal, I realized that consulting was the one field I could work in using my expertise and generating revenue. So I returned to consulting.

I loved consulting because I gained entrance to the most successful companies in the world and had the opportunity to study them. But the work began to feel rote and unsatisfying because my part of the project ended before I could see the value delivered. So I recently joined a financial services asset management company in the human resources function to work on organizational change projects.

A person with a PhD can be hired to do any type of job in any type of company. The challenge is finding the right fit in terms of the company and role. I changed roles as I learned more about what I enjoyed, what was available, and where I was in my life. But there are certain skills most PhD candidates have in common that may make some roles a more natural fit than others. Roles involving research and analytic abilities, such as data scientist, product development, and organization development, are the most obvious. The most difficult roles for companies to fill are those related to data and research. Functions such as sales, human resources, marketing, and technology are all looking to fill roles requiring these skills. No role will be a perfect fit, but by exploring areas potentially related to your expertise, you can find a role that fits your needs. In my experience, my first role outside academia turned out to be the entry into business, but only a stepping-stone. All a person needs to do is find that first opportunity.

In graduate school, jobs in corporate America were not considered an acceptable career option. Not once was an alum working outside of academia brought to campus or highlighted as an example of what was possible. Because I studied organizational communication, I studied the application of theory in and on business. Yet taking a corporate job never seemed to be an option. When I finally left academia, I learned one of the many reasons why business was not promoted as a career option: A career in business is very different from a career in academia, and most faculty do not have the experience to guide graduate students toward a business career path. The schism between academia and business is vast. The work, transition, and skills required to succeed in business are not taught in graduate school. But, as I learned, many opportunities exist for doctoral candidates if they are interested.

In all of my jobs, I've helped companies solve business challenges related to organization change, human capital, and transformation. In addition, when discussing consulting, I am referring to large firms with upwards of 10,000 employees. This model is more akin to corporations and significantly differs from small firms and sole practitioners. However, the content of the consulting work is the same as what is done by sole practitioners or small firms with similar expertise, and it is the same work I currently am doing (see Chapter 6 for more details about working as a consultant).

This chapter covers what a typical day is like working in business, the biggest challenges someone with a behavioral and social sciences PhD will face, and the necessary skills to minimize these challenges. In reality, someone with a behavioral and social sciences PhD can get any type of job depending on their background and interests.

What Is a Typical Day Like in Business?

Every day in my work life is different because my role centers primarily on executing projects to help my company grow and change. At any time, I have four or five different projects in progress. So my schedule is dictated by my projects. Below are typical activities that occur throughout any given week.

ATTENDING PROJECT MEETINGS

Because my work focuses on projects, I spend a good portion of my day meeting with colleagues with whom I am collaborating. For example, we may be preparing for a working session with a leader to help redesign his or her organization, or we may be reviewing deliverables that came out of a working session. Unless I am traveling to meet the client in person, most of these meetings are conducted virtually over the phone or by video conference. Coordinating with colleagues is important for alignment on the work being done as well as for understanding the organizational challenges to getting the work done. For example, I often find leaders within my company who are not connecting with each other as they should. My role then shifts to becoming the conduit for making sure the right meetings occur. Or I am meeting with leaders to get their input or validation on the work I am doing.

DOING THE WORK

Unlike my consulting position, where I always had a team with whom I executed the work, I do most of the project work myself in business. Plus, I am one of the few people with my expertise in organizational behavior in the organization. I spend a good portion of my time collecting and analyzing data, designing solutions, and developing presentations or project plans. Between the actual work and all of the meetings, my days are very full. It is rare that I do not have meetings planned during the workweek.

NETWORKING

I am new to the company I currently work for, so I am still learning the ropes and meeting people. Relationships are critical to success regardless of the field you are in, so I spend some of my time networking with colleagues. I try to have a couple of lunch or coffee meetings each week to connect with someone new. These meetings help me learn more about what is happening in the organization and build the relationships necessary to get my work done.

COACHING AND MANAGING

In business, when I am a people manager, I spend time with my direct reports in weekly one-on-one meetings. As any manager will tell you, it takes a lot of time to manage people. The role of the manager is to enable the work to get done. This may mean helping employees understand how to do their job or helping them overcome organizational challenges. In addition, I act as a coach to colleagues who want advice on topics related to my area of expertise. For example, I may suggest how to approach a workshop or what to consider when reorganizing their team.

Regardless of where I have worked, I have always had a variety of activities to keep me interested. Plus, I have always had the flexibility to work how and where I want. If I need to take care of personal business during the day, I work it into my schedule. If I have been traveling frequently, I always prefer to take a day after the trip and work from home. It is all about prioritization. Some of my flexibility is because of my seniority, but it also depends on the organization. More companies realize the value of flexibility to employees, but not all do. It's a good idea to ask about the style of work and requirements when interviewing with companies for a position.

What Are the Biggest Challenges in Transitioning to Business?

The hardest part of breaking into corporate America is the transition from the culture of an academic institution to the culture of a corporation. Everything about business is different from academia. Although there are transferable skills, success is defined very differently in business than in academia. When you work in business, you need to modify how you do everything, from reframing your accomplishments to show how they relate to your corporate role to adjusting how you communicate with people. Business requires you to be part of the corporate team, so fitting into the corporate culture is essential to your success.

One of the biggest challenges is recognizing that traditional academic accomplishments do not count in business. Getting a PhD is a major achievement. PhD candidates are groomed for a career in academia. You are probably published and an expert in your field or at least on your topic. A doctoral degree comes with a certain amount of prestige. In response, you may have a well-developed and well-deserved ego. Individuals excel in academia because of their unique point of view and ideas. Academia celebrates eccentricities.

In business, most people are unimpressed with what you accomplished as an academic. Business insiders do not care about your academic conference papers, peer-reviewed journal articles, and awards; these are not transferable to business. Some business professionals will be impressed with your degree and where you went to school, but if you cannot do the job, they will not care about your accomplishments. In fact, business requires you to leave your academic knowledge at the door and relearn much of what you were taught. There are different expectations in business for everything, including writing, success metrics, and relationships.

What Are the Essential Knowledge, Skills, and Attitudes Needed to Be Successful in Business?

First, you will need to relearn how to write and communicate. Business and academic writing are diametrically opposed. No six-syllable words are allowed in business, and academic jargon falls on deaf ears. You should learn to write in bullet points, using sentence fragments. Messages need to be short, simple, and to the point. No one has time to read a 20-page article. A communication needs to make its point and let the reader know what's in it for them up front.

On top of tightening up what is probably a verbose writing style is the need to communicate in the style of the company or business in which you work. For example, most companies communicate primarily using PowerPoint. There is an art to developing an effective PowerPoint presentation. Executive meetings require short two- to three-slide presentations. Business executives receive hundreds of e-mails a day. Their calendars usually consist of back-to-back meetings all day with no breaks. Most do not have time to read or listen to a lengthy presentation. They need an executive summary that concisely presents options with a clear ask for what is required.

It's a good idea to practice this new communication style because your direct manager or supervisor won't want to train you in how to communicate and think differently. During interviews, candidates are evaluated on their ability to "talk the talk": Interviewers want to see that a candidate understands how the business works, has concrete transferable experience, and illustrates his or her knowledge succinctly. Managers want a new hire to hit the ground running. The inability to immediately show quick wins or accomplishments such as a successful project will lower your credibility.

In my opinion, a PhD comes with undeserved baggage in business. Many businesspeople have negative stereotypes about anyone with a PhD. The commonly held belief is that you will not be practical or get the job done. The assumption is that if you have a PhD, you will be a big thinker of esoteric ideas that are not applicable in the real world. I use my PhD strategically. Some people are impressed and want the expertise I bring to the work. But others use it as an excuse not to hire me. I keep my education at the bottom of my resume. I rarely introduce myself as having a doctorate until I know my audience. For example, some corporate cultures require credibility before finding your assertions believable. In this case, I will introduce myself as a PhD to demonstrate my expertise or credibility.

To help minimize these challenges, you should get as much business experience as possible while you are in graduate school. Consider working in an internship while finishing your degree or take business courses, in particular MBA courses. This will give you a taste of business and what is required.

The second thing you need to learn is how to be part of the team. Most work is done in a team environment; many companies have team or department goals as part of their performance assessment. There is clear recognition that success rarely rests on one person's shoulders. It is a cross-functional team that delivers a project, new product, or service. Companies are looking for more collaboration and innovation, not less. And although there are stories of one individual getting the credit or individuals who rise into leadership roles despite not being team players, these are the exception rather than the norm.

In contrast, academic success is typically up to the individual. Some scholars have coauthors or research teams, but success clearly rests on the first author's or team leader's shoulders. Universities typically do not teach PhD candidates to work as part of a team as they do with undergraduates or MBA candidates. In fact, PhDs are celebrated for their unique point of view and ideas. For many PhDs entering corporate America, this new way of working can be a challenge.

In academia, qualifications and scholarship establish credibility. On a corporate team, your title may establish your role on the team, but not much more. Team members need to build relationships with their peers, subordinates, and superiors. The expectation is that you will work as part of the team, and that includes doing things the team's way. In my first role out of academia, I felt my skills were excellent because of my academic experience and degree. I was a tenure-track professor who was on track for tenure. I thought I had so much to offer my new employer and clients. Unfortunately, my new colleagues viewed things differently. I was surprised to receive negative feedback about my previous work experience and educational background. Often I was overlooked for assignments because superiors thought it would take me too long to complete the work at the quality level needed.

The third thing you need to learn is to always be practical, not right. In addition to a team atmosphere, business has short timelines that often require less rigorous and more practical ways of getting the job done. Academia teaches the scientific method. There are clear expectations about the "right" way to conduct and publish research. Because of timelines driven by shareholders or budget, corporate leaders may be willing to take a less rigorous approach. Yet in business, academic rules are often unnecessary.

Within business, multiple stakeholders have the ability to influence the work and outcomes. Many competing demands are at play. Factors such as time, extent of change, and perception of others can all influence your work in a corporation. For example, companies may not be open to conducting a survey even though that is the best research method for data collection. Preliminary findings based on interviews may be sufficient, even though more detailed nuances of the data that could be captured only in a large-scale survey are very interesting to you. In business, the goal of research is not to further knowledge or test a hypothesis in an experimental setting. The goal is to find the information required to determine support of a proposed solution or identify recommendations. The idea of prioritizing what is most important to sufficiently complete a task is the norm. If you are someone who struggles with being flexible or sees only one way to do things, you will likely run into challenges as you move from academia to business.

Early in my business career, I struggled with how I would approach a situation in which my manager wanted me to do things in a manner other than what I thought was necessary. But I learned that my job is to provide the data and potential impacts so a client or another colleague can make an informed decision. I regularly share my point of view, including shortcomings in the research. If my client or superiors understand those shortcomings and still want to use a less than ideal approach, I work with them to get the job done.

Even with all of these challenges, probably the biggest challenge in adapting to business is the uncertainty and ambiguity. Academia tends to be a relatively predictable environment. Your career path and steps for success are clear. There are politics and personalities, but most PhDs know what is necessary for success. Business, however, is constantly in flux. Projects change, people change, and expectations change, and you must adapt quickly. In consulting, I had to get comfortable with not knowing where my next assignment would be. In sales, I have customers who make a decision and then change their mind. I have learned there are certain things I can influence but not control, and it can feel like a roller coaster at times.

How Can I Prepare Myself to Be a Competitive Applicant for a Corporate Position?

Although the transition from academia to business is challenging, there is a need in business for many of the skills PhD candidates possess. In the PricewaterhouseCoopers (2016) Global CEO Survey, 72% of CEOs surveyed were concerned about finding key skills to carry out their strategy. In addition, half of CEOs were focusing on building their future talent pipeline. The need for a "skilled, educated and adaptable workforce should be a clear priority for business," yet they struggled to find the right talent (PricewaterhouseCoopers, 2016, p. 25).

It is impossible to list all of the different talent needs in business, but currently a few key skills are in high demand. One of the most coveted skills today—data analytics—is right in many PhD candidates' sweet spot. A number of studies highlight that statistical analysis and data mining are the most in-demand skills for which companies are looking. With more and more data becoming available, companies are looking for talent who can organize, analyze, and apply data. In many cases, they are looking for PhDs who understand complex analyses (Fisher, 2016; Renzulli, Weisser, & Leonhardt, 2016), and these skills are not limited to just one business. For example, financial services, consumer products, and technical industries are looking for analytical skills.

With all of the available information in a much more complex and interconnected world, business problems have become more complex as well. Businesses are in need of critical thinking, complex problem solving, decision making, and cognitive flexibility skills (World Economic Forum, 2016). These skills are essential for companies to be able to design strategies, solutions, and products to meet market demands. However, the types of skills needed in the next 5 years will continue to change as markets continue to be disrupted. More industries and jobs will require greater levels of cognitive abilities, interpersonal skills, and creativity, while fewer jobs will require narrow technical abilities and content skills (World Economic Forum, 2016).

Finally, companies such as large consulting firms that hire classes of new hires annually are looking for smart people who can learn quickly (e.g., people who can figure out how to solve the problem or do the work, people who take initiative and are flexible). Strategy consulting firms such as McKinsey & Company (https://www.mckinsey.com/) and Boston Consulting Group (https://www.bcg.com) regularly recruit doctoral candidates, thereby allowing these individuals to use their expertise in a commercial environment.

How Do I Find Positions in Business?

There are two sides to the challenge of finding a position in business: (a) for you to find opportunities and (b) for companies to find you. Although there is a real hesitancy to hiring individuals with PhDs for the reasons described above, the bigger issue for companies is finding interested candidates. There is not a clear partnership between doctoral programs and business as there is in undergraduate or MBA programs. Most opportunities come through relationships companies have with a specific program or individual. And most PhD candidates do not know how to find a job outside the university environment. Both of these factors limit the ability to match talent to roles.

The key to finding job opportunities is twofold. First, leverage your university's career center. Countless companies come to campus to recruit candidates. Look for opportunities to network with these companies. Often, they do presentations and have networking events before they start interviewing. Attend. Do not be put off by the fact you are not getting an MBA or other degree. Get your resume into the process.

At the same time, look for roles on job boards or LinkedIn, which is a very useful resource. In addition to their job board, recruiters look at LinkedIn profiles for candidates daily. There are many ways, such as writing articles, to be noticed and build your network on LinkedIn. Plus, you can reach out to professionals at companies where you are interested in working to build a relationship. Another good resource is job listings on specialized sites related to your field of expertise. Do research to identify companies you would like to work at, and then begin finding out whom you can network with in the organization.

The best way to find a role is through networking, but at the same time, look at all of the other ways to find open positions. I have always been surprised by how I have ended up finding my positions. I actually found a job at a company's job fair that I read about in the newspaper. I had never been to a job fair before or since, but being open to something new and investing a little of my time paid off big when I landed a new job.

What Are the Rewards and Challenges of Working in Business?

Whether business is the right path for you depends on what you think is most important. The reality is that fewer faculty positions are available, as discussed in the Introduction and Chapter 1; business is becoming a more acceptable option. Most people need to move past outdated academic perceptions of business and think about what is ultimately important to them, regardless of the venue in which they work. The most commonly noted benefit to working in business is compensation. Earning power is simply greater in business than academia. Yet money may not be a motivator for you. In addition to working in a field for which you are passionate, most academics point to significant time off and flexibility. But many corporate jobs provide vacation time and leave policies that can be taken at any time of the year. In addition, many organizations are eliminating vacation policies altogether so employees can take whatever time they need (Carney, 2009). I relish the opportunity to leave work at the office when the workday is complete. I no longer worry about writing another article or grading papers. Obviously, technology makes leaving work at work more difficult, but these are behaviors fully within your control, and not limited to business.

One of the most significant benefits of working in business is the ability to make changes in your career. Good academic jobs are scarce, with a lot of talented people applying. Corporate jobs are numerous. Once you obtain your first job, the opportunities for growth and change, within and between companies, are endless. While working in business, I was able to build my knowledge and skills by working in three different functions in 5 years. These experiences made me more marketable and kept me interested in my work. Today's job market encourages professionals to change jobs regularly. The concept of lifetime loyalty is gone. I have moved back and forth from consulting to corporate and back. This flexibility allows you to craft a career path that meets your needs. You control your career. It is up to you to make the change that suits your needs. When I transitioned to a corporation, I felt the world opened up for me. If I looked, I could find interesting work that provided many of the same benefits as academia. In addition, I have been able to stay connected to academia through adjunct teaching and my network of colleagues. Although the opportunities may not be as obvious, they exist. Taking advantage of resources both inside and outside your university will help you find the right role for you. Business can open up an entirely new world of work.

Conclusion

Adapting to business can be challenging. Learning a new way of working and thinking is difficult. Finding the first position will take a lot of time and take you out of your comfort zone. Starting out at the bottom and working your way up can definitely be demoralizing after everything you have accomplished. But for individuals like myself, it was one of the best decisions I ever made.

Additional Resources

Boston Consulting Group: https://www.bcg.com
McKinsey & Company: https://www.mckinsey.com/

References

Carney, B. (2009, December 30). Yes, you should eliminate your vacation policy. *Business Insider*. Retrieved from http://www.businessinsider.com/yes-you-should-eliminate-your-vacation-policy-2009-12

Fisher, C. (2016). LinkedIn unveils top skills that can get you hired in 2017, offers free courses for a week [Blog post]. Retrieved from https://blog.linkedin.com/2016/10/20/top-skills-2016-week-of-learning-linkedin

PricewaterhouseCoopers. (2016). *Redefining business success in a changing world: CEO survey*. Retrieved from https://www.pwc.com/gx/en/ceo-survey/2016/landing-page/pwc-19th-annual-global-ceo-survey.pdf

Renzulli, K. A., Weisser, C., & Leonhardt, M. (2016, May 16). The 21 most valuable career skills now. *Money*. Retrieved from http://time.com/money/4328180/most-valuable-career-skills/

World Economic Forum. (2016). *The future of jobs: Employment, skills and workforce strategy for the forth industrial revolution*. Retrieved from http://www3.weforum.org/docs/WEF_Future_of_Jobs.pdf

Jonathan F. Zaff

Nonprofits
Bridging the Research–Practice Divide

9

have the good fortune of directing a research center for a national nonprofit, America's Promise Alliance, with a mission of ensuring that all children and youth experience the key developmental supports they need to thrive in all ways—academically, vocationally, socially, emotionally, and civically. My route to where I am today was circuitous, sprinkled with serendipity, filled with a variety of formative experiences, and facilitated by connection after connection with people who were willing to help. It all started one April while I was writing my dissertation in my 350-square-foot efficiency apartment in the Inman Park neighborhood in Atlanta. I got "the call"—this was 1999, so nontelemarketer landline phone calls were still common. I was being offered a summer policy fellowship from the National Academy of Sciences (NAS) in Washington, DC. The fellowship program, still operating today, was designed to provide graduate students with experiences in conducting policy-relevant research and in using research to influence public policy decisions.

Although I would later become a civic engagement researcher, I had not been particularly interested in politics or public policy. A job in DC was more about being in the same town as my new wife, who had moved to DC a few months prior for a too-good-to-pass-up opportunity. Soon after the call, I was packed and ready to move, subsequently spending the next few months doing my best not to trip over myself as I navigated a different environment

http://dx.doi.org/10.1037/0000110-010
Building a Career Outside Academia: A Guide for Doctoral Students in the Behavioral and Social Sciences,
J. B. Urban and M. R. Linver (Editors)
Copyright © 2019 by the American Psychological Association. All rights reserved.

and a different way of thinking about research. By the end, I had been fortunate to hang out with some fantastic fellowship recipient colleagues, meet unbelievably impressive scholars who volunteered their time to be on National Academy committees, and work with equally impressive staff who helped turn the great thinking of these scholars into tangible, actionable recommendations for policy. I was hooked. I knew I wanted to pursue a nonacademic job in which I could conduct research that would be relevant to public policymakers and actionable for practitioners.

During one of the numerous expert panels at NAS, I happened to be standing next to a senior researcher from Child Trends, a leading child and youth–focused research institute in Washington, DC (https://www.childtrends.org). By the end of this conversation, I had learned that Child Trends was looking to hire a research associate to focus on an emerging area of inquiry, positive youth development. This new way of thinking about federal and state indicators, program outcomes, and program and policy design was intriguing and aligned with my doctoral work. This conversation turned into an interview, and that interview turned into a nearly 3-year stint supporting, creating, and directing projects on youth development.

While at Child Trends, I quickly learned why adherence to rigorous scientific methods is so important. People actually listened to what we said. People who worked at federal agencies. People who worked for state governments. People who worked at foundations. People who worked in national organizations and community-based organizations. At the end of the day, as behavioral and social scientists, we need to rely on good science.

After 3 years, I had a crazy idea that I should start a nonprofit called 18to35 focused on engaging youth and young adults in politics and policy making. I left Child Trends and embarked on a nearly 2-year effort to engage youth and young adults with some strange bedfellows including professional wrestlers, staff at MTV and Rock the Vote, leaders of the Hip Hop Caucus, and a wonderful assortment of energetic nonprofit leaders who were passionate about young people as change agents. I also spent time visiting Capitol Hill and realized that e-mailing congressional staffers often resulted in meetings and discussions with them about how to better engage young voters. Once again, I learned that people actually listened to what I had to say. Although the fun and excitement of running a fledgling, bare-bones nonprofit continued, I was hit with the realization that making money would be helpful for my economic self-sufficiency (and marriage). A job search ended with a position at America's Promise Alliance.

I first learned about America's Promise Alliance during my time at Child Trends. It was founded by General Colin Powell in 1997 after the Summit for America's Future. As the director of assessment and evaluation, I supported the community mobilization efforts that defined the Alliance's work at that time. Through multiple evolutions of the organization and my own life developments, I eventually found myself in Boston (where I grew up) as the senior vice president for research and policy for the Alliance. I became affiliated with Tufts University (thanks to Dr. Richard Lerner, a professor at Tufts, whom I had been fortunate to meet while I was at Child Trends) and, over time, built the organization's internal research capacity with graduate assistants and postdoctoral associates, eventually creating the Center for Promise.

The Center for Promise is the research institute of America's Promise Alliance, now housed at the Boston University School of Education, with the mission to examine how to create the necessary conditions for all young people to have an opportunity to thrive. The findings from the Center's research are amplified by the Alliance's communications team, distributed to the more than 400 national Alliance partners and hundreds of community-based initiatives, and blasted out to nearly 15,000 people throughout our networks. The findings from our research are also integrated into the overall work of the Alliance. I have now fulfilled my aspirations developed during my NAS fellowship.

My goal with this chapter is to describe what life is like for a researcher in a non-research-focused organization. I first discuss what a nonprofit is compared with other entities. I then describe the types of research-based positions a PhD-level researcher could find at a nonprofit. I end the chapter with the skills that would be helpful for securing and sustaining a nonprofit job, the rewards and inevitable challenges that a scholar might face, and the opportunities a scholar can leverage at a nonprofit.

What Is a Nonprofit?

You just finished your doctorate, realized that a life in academia is not for you, and heard that working for a nonprofit could be a way to do applied research and conduct evaluations that could have more direct impacts on policy and practice. There are nearly 100,000 organizations that are registered with the Internal Revenue Service (IRS) as either a "youth development" or "elementary or secondary education" public charity (GuideStar, 2018). This number does not include the variety of social, human, and public health services, vocational training, and other organizational types that support children and youth in some way. In short, the United States does not have a shortage of nonprofit organizations. Nonprofits are a hugely diverse group of organizations that address a hugely diverse range of topics and function within hugely diverse geographies. *Nonprofits*, for purposes of the types described in the current chapter, are charitable organizations under the IRS designation 501(c)3 that are exempt from federal (and typically state) taxes and able to receive unlimited donations from individuals, corporations, and unions. Donations to such organizations are tax deductible. Note, though, that a nonprofit can also earn money from selling merchandise or services (think of Salvation Army stores).

A charitable organization is barred from supporting a political candidate or intervening in any way in a political election. Charitable organizations are also limited in how much they can lobby policy makers to influence legislation. Types of charitable organizations include education, public and community health, mental health and social services, and youth development organizations. In addition, social entrepreneurs and social enterprises are, by definition, mission driven, but their endeavors can be organized as either a nonprofit or for-profit entity (Martin & Osberg, 2007). A for-profit company may conduct the exact same work with the same intentions as a nonprofit organization. The difference comes down to whether the organization can distribute its profits to owners or shareholders (for-profits can) and whether profits are subject to taxes (nonprofits are not).

Some nonprofit organizations are focused on direct service, others provide support for direct service organizations (e.g., research, tools), and still others are focused on advocacy to push for public policies that support people and the programs that serve them. The organization for which I work, America's Promise Alliance, is an intermediary organization, amplifying the key issues impacting children and youth, building public will to act on those issues, creating strategic connections among organizations focused on those issues, and synthesizing and developing knowledge for organizations throughout the country to most effectively resolve those issues. MENTOR, the national mentoring partnership, provides a similar intermediary function to mentoring organizations throughout the country.

What Kinds of Positions Are Available at Nonprofits?

Research and evaluation are positioned in a variety of ways in nonprofits. Some nonprofits have research and evaluation divisions that include numerous researchers and evaluators. Other nonprofits house the research and evaluation functions within the marketing and communications department or within a strategy department that uses the knowledge generated through research and evaluation to refine the organization's strategies and programming. Still other nonprofits have bare-bones internal research capacity, with the majority of projects subcontracted to others (e.g., independent research consultants, research organizations, university-based researchers). Thus, your role as a researcher will depend on the type of organization for which you work (e.g., direct service vs. intermediary) and the way the organization positions its research and evaluation function.

With that variation a given, I lay out two general roles that are typical at a nonprofit organization: (a) evaluation-focused positions and (b) research and development–focused positions. There are other, nonresearch roles that someone with a doctorate in the behavioral and social sciences could do, such as strategy and program positions; I do not discuss these positions in detail. One important point is that the timetables for evaluation and research within nonprofits are typically much faster paced than is typical for academia. I describe two specific examples below. The first, the evaluation example, had a typical timeline, extending over 2 years. The second, the applied research example, had a condensed timeline of 1 year; within this period we conducted studies, analyzed data, wrote reports, and disseminated our findings.

EXAMPLE 1: EVALUATION

Direct-service organizations, such as YMCA, Big Brother/Big Sister, or City Year, might implement a variety of programs intended to impact different outcomes. To understand how well a given program is being implemented in different locations and its impact on participants, the organization funds program evaluations. If the organization needs an independent evaluation to preempt criticisms of not having third-party validation, the evaluation department conducts a search for an indepen-

dent evaluator or evaluation firm. This process could include developing the basic con-
tours of the evaluation (e.g., defining the scope of the project, developing the questions
to be answered), drafting the request for proposals (RFP), and selecting the individual
or firm to conduct the work. From that point, the evaluation staff at the nonprofit
organization manage the evaluation from the nonprofit's side, facilitating interactions
between the evaluator and the organization, confirming the evaluation plan is conso-
nant with the original proposal, ensuring the evaluator meets deadlines and submits
all agreed-upon reports, and facilitating the translation of the results of the evaluation
for program improvement.

In one such evaluation, America's Promise Alliance implemented an initiative
to catalyze and strengthen comprehensive community actions to resolve the high
school dropout crisis. The main intervention was engaging cities and states in holding
"dropout prevention summits" that were designed as cross-sector convenings focused
on a call to action and a forward-looking plan to support youth on their path to high
school graduation and beyond. After designing and distributing the RFP, we engaged
the Center for Child and Family Policy (CCFP) at Duke University to conduct the
evaluation. My role was to ensure alignment between the program team implement-
ing the summits and the evaluation design and implementation by the team at CCFP.

The CCFP team began working with us before the summits began, defining the
theory of action for the summits and the evaluation design. The evaluation extended to
18 months after the final summit was held so that we could understand the long-term
effects of the summits on the states' and cities' actions. CCFP found that 85% of the
summit sites still had an active cross-sector collaboration working on the dropout
issue 18 months after the summits ended. We used that and other information to
pivot our work from building public will and focusing on the dropout issue to creating
a national campaign focused on solutions around increasing the high school graduation rate; this became our GradNation Campaign.

When the evaluation purpose does not call for third-party validation, such as for
continuous improvement processes around program implementation, the evaluation staff creates internal evaluation processes to assess the quality of the organization's programming and monitor program outcomes. For this work, evaluation staff
work with program staff to codefine the program elements to be assessed and desired
outcomes, often using logic models as a tool in the process. The next step includes
developing a set of indicators and measures to assess the elements and outcomes,
developing systems for capturing the measures, and working with program staff
to deploy the evaluation systems. Finally, the evaluation team analyzes the data,
writes reports, and presents the results to executive and program staff with the inten-
tion of informing program improvements and refining the organization's strategy.

EXAMPLE 2: RESEARCH AND DEVELOPMENT

In addition to evaluation, research staff at a nonprofit may conduct applied research
studies to inform the organization's program development. The Girl Scouts Research
Institute was created by Girl Scouts of the United States of America to inform the
organization about the state of Girl Scouts, as well as the state of girls, throughout

the country (in addition to understanding the impacts of its programming). By conducting surveys with national and nationally representative samples of girls, the Girl Scouts Research Institute is able to inform the direction of Girl Scouts, including developing or sustaining programs that align with the needs identified in the research institute's studies, and to inform the broader youth development sector about the needs and strengths of girls.

For my own research center, we realized there was a group of people whom we knew very little about: those who had left high school without graduating. To most effectively support positive educational pathways for youth in the country, we needed a deeper, more authentic understanding of who these young people were, their reasons for leaving school, and ways to encourage them to stay in school. Therefore, we conducted a national, mixed-methods study of youth who left school and found that these youth often faced numerous, severe adversities without enough social support to buffer their effects. These findings have helped shape our national messages about what can be done to support all young people on a path to high school graduation and beyond. For this set of studies, my research team conducted interviews with hundreds of youth across the country and fielded two national surveys of approximately 3,000 youth per survey. We analyzed the data, wrote drafts of the report, engaged with a professional writer to ensure the report would be easily readable by multiple audiences, and worked with the Alliance communications team to develop the key messaging documents for the media, for Alliance partners, and for community-based efforts.

There is power in synthesizing existing research to capture the collective knowledge generated by the thousands of high-quality researchers conducting studies on all aspects of your field. Conducting such syntheses is one of the most important functions that a researcher at a nonprofit can perform. Because a synthesis is done to further the mission of the nonprofit, syntheses should be designed such that they bring together research in an actionable way. For the Center for Promise, we searched for a synthesis of studies on factors that promote high school graduation. We found numerous syntheses of factors that prevent dropping out of school, but we could not find such a synthesis focused on promoting graduation. Therefore, we conducted a systematic review of internal and external assets that promote high school graduation, pulling together studies that individually told a small part of a much bigger, more important story. Our resulting report provided guidance to practitioners and policy makers as part of the GradNation Campaign.

What Are the Essential Knowledge, Skills, and Attitudes Needed to Be Successful at a Nonprofit?

Making it through a doctoral program is a big achievement. A doctoral program inevitably honed your critical thinking skills, helped you establish a theoretical foundation in your area of the behavioral and social sciences, and instilled strong methodological skills. These three attributes are essential for any position you take after graduate school. Although it took a great deal of effort to gain this expertise, there are more skills and knowledge that you will need, whether you stay in academia or venture into nonacademic positions. Next, I discuss additional attributes relatively unique to the nonprofit sector. Although much of what I describe is typically not taught in graduate programs, you can find opportunities to write and conduct research with nonprofits, optimally supervised by a PhD-level researcher.

WRITING FOR A LAY AUDIENCE

In behavioral and social science graduate programs, including applied programs, you learn how to write academic papers. This makes sense, because the goal is to publish peer-reviewed journal articles, present at academic conferences, and ultimately write a dissertation. Students rarely learn how to write a research or policy brief that a non-researcher could understand or how to do a compelling, 10-minute presentation that summarizes a body of research and ends with a set of policy and practice recommendations. This type of writing and presenting for a lay audience is exactly the skill that is needed at a nonprofit because the consumers of the research are mostly program, policy, and strategy colleagues.

CRITICALLY ASSESSING RESEARCH

Whether synthesizing existing research, being asked by a nonresearch colleague for your evidence-based insights, or reviewing communications materials, as a researcher at a nonprofit you should be a constructive research critic. In my role, I am often asked to review a new evaluation report or hot-off-the-press study to see whether America's Promise Alliance should amplify the messages from the report. On the basis of my training as a developmental scientist and my continued experiences in the field, I many times find the methodologies used in the reports to be less than systematic or rigorous and the results tenuous. Gaining as much experience as possible as a graduate student learning about a variety of methodologies and finding opportunities to critically assess methodologies (e.g., as a reviewer or coreviewer of journal manuscripts) would help prepare you for this work.

WORKING WELL WITH NONRESEARCHERS

A researcher at a nonprofit inevitably works with nonresearchers, whether program, resource development, communications, or administrative staff. To implement a project successfully, coconstruct an evaluation plan, or disseminate the most powerful and valid messages, you must navigate relationships and organizational politics. As an example, for a research project, communications professionals have to get the intended audience's attention. As a researcher you have the job of making sure the findings from the project are based on systematic, valid methodologies. These two roles are not always aligned; communications professionals may oversimplify or sensationalize findings, and researchers may not go far enough in touting the findings' implications. In the end, you need to collaborate with the communications team to develop messages that are grounded firmly in research findings but provocative enough to engage a broad audience.

What Are the Rewards and Challenges of Working at a Nonprofit?

Working at a nonprofit can help facilitate the integration between research and practice that is often missing (Hamilton, 2015). This disconnect between research and practice can happen for many reasons, including because practitioners may not have time to read scholarly journals, because the questions asked by academic researchers are not consistent with the practicalities of running a nonprofit organization, because the research has not been translated into easily understandable tools that could be used by practitioners to refine their programs, or because an emphasis on research is too rare in educator and practitioner training programs (Cohen, McCabe, Michelli, & Pickeral, 2009). For a fuller discussion of this issue, Davies and Nutley's (2008) easy-to-read primer on evidence-based decision making is a good resource for understanding the ins and outs of using systematic research to inform policy and practice.

There are university-based centers that bridge the research–practice divide, such as the Ginsberg Center at the University of Michigan and the Center for Public Health Initiatives at the University of Pennsylvania, among many others. Public and community health researchers (Wallerstein & Duran, 2006), design-based implementation scientists (typically in the field of education; Fishman, Penuel, Allen, Cheng, & Sabelli, 2013), and forward-thinking developmental scientists (Zeldin, 2000) have made great strides in working hand in hand with practitioners (Granger, Tseng, & Wilcox, 2014).

Working for a nonprofit organization can provide you with an opportunity to participate in bridging the knowledge–practice gap. As Bialeschki and Conn (2011) noted, there is a bias toward knowledge published in peer-reviewed journals over knowledge issued in reports from or put into practice through nonprofits. However, numerous studies conducted by or for nonprofits could help advance your field. The research is often as rigorous and systematic as research conducted in academic settings and may even go through an external peer review process. The difference is that research and evaluations conducted by or for nonprofits are typically conducted with the specific purpose of furthering the mission of the nonprofit, and the questions for the studies are cocreated with the programmatic side of the nonprofit. Therefore, at least in theory, the findings from the studies are immediately relevant to the work of that nonprofit and to other nonprofits with similar missions or activities. Thus, working as a researcher or evaluator for a nonprofit provides a potentially fulfilling opportunity for the aspiring applied behavioral and social scientist to make a substantive impact on how organizations (and whole communities) are supporting people.

If you want to be a researcher at a nonprofit, there will inevitably be challenges, such as a lack of time to conduct research. This probably sounds strange because a research position should be about conducting research, right? If only life were that simple. Instead, there are always other nonresearch tasks competing for your time, in academia or out. For a university professor, there are classes to teach, committees to sit on, and students to advise. For a researcher at a nonprofit, the trade-offs could include helping to write nonresearch (and research) grants and being part of communications or strategic planning meetings and committees. An additional choice is between publishing high-quality research reports for your nonprofit versus papers in peer-reviewed journals. When interviewing for a job, you may want to ask about the balance between research and other responsibilities and whether there will be time to write more academically oriented manuscripts.

There are tens of thousands of nonprofits in the United States, and through their mission-driven work, these nonprofits want to effectively support their participants. However, the know-how is often lacking for how to find and use the most effective strategies and how to evaluate whether the chosen strategy works. A program developer or communications strategist is not necessarily trained to do these things. A behavioral and social scientist can provide this important expertise, and the nonprofit can provide you with a substantive way to bridge the research–practice divide.

How Do I Find Positions in Nonprofits?

Going on the job market for nonprofit jobs is different from the process for a tenure-track professor or postdoctoral fellow position. Nonprofits have changing needs based on funder demands, decisions by the organization's board of directors, the CEO's strategic redirection, or the loss of an employee (among other reasons). An organization cannot wait several months for the newly minted PhD they recruited to start. These ongoing opportunities can work to the favor of graduate students who finish at different times during a calendar year; dates that might not line up with faculty positions or postdoctoral fellowships may work perfectly for a nonprofit position. Job sites like Idealist (https://www.idealist.org) and the Bridgespan (https://www.bridgespan.org) job board are good for broad searches. Visiting the websites of organizations that you find interesting is another strategy. Like nonresearchers looking for jobs, networking can be particularly helpful in navigating available opportunities and getting your name out to people who are looking to hire.

Conclusion

Not everyone who earns a PhD wants to work in an academic position at a college or university. Jobs at nonprofits can be a rewarding alternative for those who are looking to see their training and research benefit society. By channeling the methodological and theoretical skills and knowledge you acquired in graduate school, you can be competitive for these jobs.

Additional Resources

Bridgespan: https://www.bridgespan.org
Child Trends: https://www.childtrends.org
Idealist: https://www.idealist.org

References

Bialeschki, M. D., & Conn, M. (2011). Welcome to our world: Bridging youth development research in nonprofit and academic communities. *Journal of Research on Adolescence, 21*, 300–306. http://dx.doi.org/10.1111/j.1532-7795.2010.00731.x

Cohen, J., McCabe, L., Michelli, N. M., & Pickeral, T. (2009). School climate: Research, policy, practice, and teacher education. *Teachers College Record, 111*, 180–213.

Davies, H. T. O., & Nutley, S. M. (2008, September). *Learning more about how research-based knowledge gets used: Guidance in the development of new empirical research*. New York, NY: William T. Grant Foundation.

Fishman, B. J., Penuel, W. R., Allen, A.-R., Cheng, B. H., & Sabelli, N. (2013). Design-based implementation research: An emerging model for transforming the relationship of research and practice. In B. J. Fishman & W. R. Penuel (Eds.), *Yearbook of the National Society for the Study of Education, Vol. 112: Design based implementation research* (pp. 136–156). New York, NY: Teachers College, Columbia University.

Granger, R. C., Tseng, V., & Wilcox, B. L. (2014). Connecting research and practice. In E. T. Gershoff, R. Mistry, & D. A. Crosby (Eds.), *Societal contexts of child development: Pathways of influence and implications for practice and policy* (pp. 205–219). New York, NY: Oxford University Press.

GuideStar. (2018). *Directory of charities and nonprofit organizations*. Retrieved from http://www.guidestar.org/NonprofitDirectory.aspx

Hamilton, S. F. (2015). Linking research to the practice of youth development. *Applied Developmental Science, 19*, 57–59. http://dx.doi.org/10.1080/10888691.2015.1030016

Martin, R. L., & Osberg, S. (2007). Social entrepreneurship: The case for definition. *Stanford Social Innovation Review, 5*, 28–39.

Wallerstein, N. B., & Duran, B. (2006). Using community-based participatory research to address health disparities. *Health Promotion Practice, 7*, 312–323. http://dx.doi.org/10.1177/1524839906289376

Zeldin, S. (2000). Integrating research and practice to understand and strengthen communities for adolescent development: An introduction to the special issue and current issues. *Applied Developmental Science, 4*, 2–10. http://dx.doi.org/10.1207/S1532480XADS04Suppl_1

Jane L. Powers and Lisa A. McCabe

Non-Tenure-Track Academic Jobs

The Side of Academia You Didn't Know Existed

10

During Jane's first semester of graduate school in Cornell University's Department of Human Development and Family Studies, she took an advanced seminar on theories of adolescent development that sparked her interest in adolescence. The study of adolescent development became the focus of her work—from her dissertation, in which she examined how early work experiences influenced the vocational choices and career trajectories of non–college bound teenage girls, to her current position, as director of an academic center of excellence charged with promoting the health and well-being of adolescents in New York State.

As she was finishing her dissertation, she met her husband, a member of the Cornell faculty. This restricted her job search to the Ithaca area. The first job she found was not related to her field; she worked in an office of college admissions analyzing data and generating reports to guide decision making. She knew this was not her life calling. She was fortunate to soon land a research position at the Family Life Development Center (FLDC), a multidisciplinary unit within Cornell's College of Human Ecology that housed research, training, and outreach efforts focused on the issue of child abuse and neglect. This has been her professional home ever since.

At the FLDC, she worked on a wide variety of research projects, all of which examined the impact of violence on the lives of children, youth, and families

http://dx.doi.org/10.1037/0000110-011

Building a Career Outside Academia: A Guide for Doctoral Students in the Behavioral and Social Sciences,
J. B. Urban and M. R. Linver (Editors)
Copyright © 2019 by the American Psychological Association. All rights reserved.

in different contexts and communities: among runaway and homeless youth, military families, teen mothers, and incarcerated youth. She wrote grants with her colleagues that helped build and expand the center's research and program evaluation efforts. In 2011, she served on the transition team that helped the FLDC become the Bronfenbrenner Center for Translational Research, with an expanded mission to facilitate faster connections among research, policy, and practice that enhance human development.

Her involvement with the Assets Coming Together (ACT) for Youth Center of Excellence (COE) represents a significant turning point in her professional development. Through this work, her interests shifted to more applied research activities, those that generated knowledge that would be of use to the field and benefit practitioners, educators, policymakers, and youth. In her role as project director of the ACT for Youth COE, she is at the nexus of research and practice—right where she wants to be. This work involves supporting communities and youth-serving organizations across New York State, helping them implement positive youth development strategies, and providing resources, tools, and expertise on using and evaluating evidence-based programs that promote adolescent sexual health.

Much of our work involves translating research—ensuring that findings are used to improve and strengthen practice. We work closely with our funder, the New York State Department of Health, which has incorporated the results of our evaluation efforts into developing new strategies and initiatives that best meet the needs of adolescents in New York State. It has been extremely rewarding to generate research that is of use and benefits the field.

The first job Lisa truly loved was working as a teacher in a child care center. A senior in college at the time, she found that working with preschool children allowed her to apply what she'd learned in courses about child development and social policy. She also discovered that working directly with children was fun! But despite the joy she experienced, she also knew that she did not want to make a career of working in a field in which teachers work long, inflexible hours for a minimal salary. So she began to explore opportunities to work with children, families, and child care teachers in other ways. She enrolled in graduate school to explore how research could support the child care field. Her first pieces of research (for her master's thesis and doctoral dissertation) examined a credentialing program as a means to support child care provider professional development and evaluated a classroom curriculum focused on violence prevention. From that point on, she knew that a research career would allow her to contribute to the field while still staying connected to teachers, children, and families.

As she was finishing her dissertation, her husband (a year ahead of her in graduate school) took a position as a postdoctoral associate in another city. They moved together, and she looked for part-time work that would allow her to further explore the intersection of research and practice while also finishing her dissertation. She worked in two different organizations where she helped conduct research in real-world contexts. First, she conducted phone surveys for a magazine focused on working mothers, and second, she designed questionnaires and conducted phone interviews for a child care advocacy group. These experiences reinforced her desire to continue to conduct practical research, yet also made clear that she wanted that research to be in a traditional academic setting where infrastructure is in place to support high-quality research (e.g., libraries, colleagues with expertise in research methods and analyses, easier access to funding to support research).

Her next position (still before she completed her dissertation) was as a research scientist at a small research center at a college. While in that position, she learned two important things: (a) she loved conducting applied research, and (b) she did not enjoy teaching college-level courses. She stayed in this position until she finished her dissertation and was ready to look for a longer term position at a research center.

Her first full-time position was as an extension associate in the Department of Human Development at Cornell University, the land-grant university for New York State. In that role, she served primarily as a liaison between campus research and practitioners in the field while also conducting her own applied research projects. Eventually, research became her primary focus, and she shifted to a research associate position and moved to the Bronfenbrenner Center for Translational Research at Cornell, where she connected with others with similar interests in applied research and expanded her interests to include the field of residential child care. Today, she continues to work on a variety of projects at the intersection of research and practice, including program evaluations and the development of tools and measures that serve both quality improvement and research functions.

In this chapter, we share our knowledge about non-tenure-track positions available within academic settings. In our case, we both work at Cornell University within the Bronfenbrenner Center for Translational Research. Although we work on different projects that address a variety of populations and issues, we share a common goal to link research and outreach efforts in bidirectional ways that enhance practice and strengthen research. Our perspective, based on years working in non-tenure-track positions, may differ from those in limited-term positions that serve as a stopover or stepping-stone to a tenure-track (or other) career. Similarly, our perspectives are grounded in experiences within a large research university that is part of the land-grant extension system (for more information regarding land-grant universities, see Association of Public and Land-Grant Universities, n.d.). Non-tenure-track positions within smaller academic settings may involve different benefits and challenges than those we share here.

We begin with a description of the types of non-tenure-track jobs potentially available within the academy. Next, we identify the skills needed to be competitive in this market, highlighting those that could be developed during graduate school. We describe the rewards and challenges of working in non-tenure-track academic positions, and finally, we offer advice on how to find such jobs.

What Kinds of Positions Are Available in Non-Tenure-Track Academic Settings?

Although many universities have non-tenure-track academic positions, they do not follow a one-size-fits-all model. These types of positions vary widely, as do where they are housed. Below is a brief sampling of the kinds of jobs available, along with examples of where they are typically located within the academic community.

Non-tenure-track academic positions are often found within university-affiliated centers. These centers typically focus on a specific mission or theme (e.g., child development, education, youth development) and can include researchers from multiple disciplines, such as psychology, social work, and education. Examples of such centers include

- our home, the Bronfenbrenner Center for Translational Research at Cornell University (https://www.bctr.cornell.edu/about-us/);
- Duke University's Center for Child and Family Policy (https://childandfamily policy.duke.edu);
- Field Center for Children's Policy, Practice, and Research at the University of Pennsylvania (http://impact.sp2.upenn.edu/fieldctr/);
- John W. Gardner Center for Youth and Their Communities at Stanford School of Education (https://gardnercenter.stanford.edu); and
- Child Study Center at Yale University (http://childstudycenter.yale.edu).

See the Additional Resources at the end of this chapter for a listing of other research centers that are funded by federal agencies, such as the Centers for Disease Control and Prevention and the National Institutes of Health, and located in universities across the United States.

Within these centers, non-tenure-track positions such as research scientists, research associates (at junior and senior levels), and project directors or managers are common. Data analyst and statistician positions are also frequently available. Some of these centers include work specific to program or policy development (e.g., Frank Porter Graham Child Development Institute at the University of North Carolina, http:// fpg.unc.edu) and so may also include policy analyst or implementation specialist positions. Others have a prevention focus, such as the Oregon Prevention Research Center (http://www.oregonprc.org/) and the Evidence-Based Prevention and Intervention Support Center (EPISCenter) at Penn State (http://www.episcenter.psu.edu/).

In addition, land-grant universities (e.g., University of California, Davis; University of Wisconsin–Madison) have extension systems where educators and researchers work together to deliver science-based information to stakeholders beyond the academy. Because outreach and the application of research findings are a key part of the extension system mission, you may find extension associate positions that facilitate connections between research and practice through collaborative community efforts. Researchers within extension systems are often charged with linking the academy with the field, gathering data, and translating research findings for use by practitioners and policymakers. Clinical positions are also common at university-based organizations that directly serve children and families (e.g., Mt. Hope Family Center at the University of Rochester, http://www.psych.rochester.edu/MHFC/) and may also provide students with mental health services. Some of these positions may be linked with clinical research efforts to study the impact of interventions and treatments.

If you're fresh out of graduate school, don't expect to land a research project directorship right away. You are more likely to get a junior-level position—for example, managing the data collection on someone's already funded project. Depending on your graduate school experience (or postdoctoral work), having fairly advanced statistical and methodological skills could help you obtain a data analyst position. But in our experience, junior-level positions often lead to other opportunities that offer greater responsibilities and higher level tasks. Getting your foot in the door is an essential first step. This allows you to get to know people, broaden your network, and demonstrate your skills. If and when a new project gets funded, you might be first in line to be considered.

What Are the Essential Knowledge, Skills, and Attitudes Needed to Be Successful in Non-Tenure-Track Academic Settings?

Having a broad-based set of research skills makes you competitive for non-tenure-track academic positions. A thorough understanding of research design and familiarity with a wide range of methodologies serve as a solid foundation for conducting research across disciplines and projects. Having a track record of using multiple methods—quantitative, qualitative, and mixed-methods approaches—for data collection and analyses are an asset. Strong data analysis and statistical skills are particularly valuable and generalizable to many fields of research.

In addition to these broad research skills, many non-tenure-track positions involve conducting research and/or program evaluation in real-world settings (i.e., not in laboratories) in which skills working with community members are useful. Having experience using participatory methods that include community members in the research process (i.e., in identifying questions of interest, selecting methods, gathering data, and disseminating research findings) may be of particular value to a research team or organization. Although establishing research partnerships can be difficult when community members distrust the academy, participatory research methods can be a valuable approach for addressing these challenges and bridging universities with communities.

Non-tenure-track positions often involve managing large data sets and projects. Therefore, experience with designing or working with management information systems for gathering, processing, coding, analyzing, and disseminating data is valuable for all kinds of research positions. Similarly, project management skills, such as being able to break down larger tasks into smaller components and paying attention to detail, are critical to the successful handling of projects with multiple components.

Non-tenure-track positions are commonly supported by soft money—that is, financed by grants and contracts with time-limited terms. In many cases, you are expected to raise funds to support your position to maintain employment. For this reason, having experience writing grant proposals is really important to your professional survival! How do you gain these skills? We recommend collaborating with experienced proposal writers or finding a mentor who has been successful in obtaining grants from federal or state funding streams or foundations. Take courses, which may be offered through university offices that manage grants and contracts or through funding agencies that focus on building capacity for proposal writing. In addition, take advantage of any opportunities to serve as a grant proposal reviewer. Reviewing others' work provides a unique chance to learn what successful proposals look like and how funding decisions are made.

Strong communication skills are also critical for sharing research findings with a variety of audiences. Writing research findings for peer-reviewed journals requires a more technical style. Reviewing manuscripts submitted for publication, either in the form of volunteering to review colleagues' submissions or more formally as a peer reviewer for an academic journal, can shed light on successful ways to communicate with research audiences.

But non-tenure-track positions also typically involve communicating research findings with nonacademic audiences such as policymakers or practitioners. Writing fact sheets, research reviews, tool kits, and web pages, for example, requires a succinct, summative communication style that is accessible to broad audiences. Strong public speaking skills are also an asset for non-tenure-track academic positions; audiences may include professionals from diverse backgrounds including researchers, educators, policymakers, and media representatives. Successful written and public speaking communication skills rest on your ability to translate research findings for different audiences in order to bring research to the field and advance policy and practice.

Finally, being a self-starter is a must! In our experience, one of the greatest benefits of non-tenure-track academic jobs is their flexibility. But the flip side is the need to work independently, set goals, and monitor progress to be successful.

How Can I Prepare Myself to Be a Competitive Applicant for a Non-Tenure-Track Academic Position?

Graduate school offers opportunities to develop skills and gain experience that could enhance your competitiveness on the non-tenure-track job market. Here we offer a few tips for making the most of your time as a PhD student.

LEARN ABOUT RESEARCH METHODS

In graduate school, take as many courses as you can manage on statistics and qualitative and quantitative research methodology. Gain experience working with data, for example, on faculty members' research projects. These skills are desirable and highly generalizable to multiple types of research projects.

BUILD PROFESSIONAL SKILLS AND NETWORKS

We recommend that you attend conferences to help both advance your skills and build your professional networks and connections. Submitting proposals for presentations on your work is a good start, but putting together panels of papers can enhance your chances of getting your submissions accepted and builds connections with other researchers in your field of interest. Reach out to colleagues who are doing similar work and offer to organize a panel of projects that gather similar data, tackle similar problems, or use similar methodologies. This strategy will not only build your resume but also enhance your skills at presenting and provide opportunities to learn about cutting-edge research findings and approaches.

In addition to conferences, look for opportunities to further your skills and knowledge through workshops (e.g., Cornell offers free workshops on topics such as software application and statistics) that are available to anyone in the academic community, including students and non-tenure-track faculty. Consider attending institutes that offer intensive courses in research methods (e.g., the Inter-university Consortium for Political and Social Research at the University of Michigan, https://www.icpsr. umich.edu), statistics (e.g., Stats Camp Statistical Training Institute, https://www. statscamp.org), or program evaluation (e.g., Summer Evaluation Institute offered by the American Evaluation Association, https://www.eval.org). Sometimes the organizations provide partial or full scholarships for students, but they can be worth the investment even as out-of-pocket expenses. There are also private consulting services available (for reasonable fees) to further build your knowledge and skills in areas such as statistics (e.g., The Analysis Factor, https://www.theanalysisfactor.com).

PUBLISH! BE VISIBLE!

Keep your foot in the academic door by publishing in peer-reviewed journals. Even in non-tenure-track positions, universities have a clear expectation that you will publish, although the emphasis will not be solely on peer-reviewed research journals. In addition, maintain connections to practitioners by disseminating your findings through multiple channels, such as practitioner-focused periodicals, research briefs shared with practitioners, blogs, or other social media venues. All kinds of published products will matter when it comes to your performance reviews and promotions. In addition, publications in academic journals enhance your credibility within the research community, are viewed favorably by grant reviewers, and help promote connections and collaborations with other research groups.

BE PROACTIVE IN LOOKING FOR FUNDING OPPORTUNITIES

When you have ideas for projects, explore possible federal and state funding streams. Although competition is fierce for these dollars, knowing what funding may be available, along with deadlines and procedures for submissions, will help your application be competitive. Foundations are another source of possible funding, so it is important to know areas of interest and application procedures for various local, state, and national foundations. As a researcher with a particular area of expertise and ideas, you can reach out to foundations with a letter of interest. For example, Lisa worked on a project in which a letter of interest was initially sent to a foundation (Annie E. Casey Foundation) that led to a visit from a foundation program officer and eventually to funding for 3 years to support the development, implementation, and evaluation of a new home visiting program for family child care providers.

What Are the Rewards and Challenges of Working in a Non-Tenure-Track Academic Position?

As with most things in life, there are trade-offs inherent in non-tenure-track academic jobs. Below we share what we have found wonderful about the non-tenure-track academic positions we have had, as well as some of the challenges we have faced.

First of all, we have tremendous freedom, flexibility, and autonomy. We both agree that we have a great deal of control over our time, in large part because we are not tied to a teaching schedule. Having flexible hours and being able to work at home have been especially valuable when juggling child care responsibilities and caregiving for elderly parents. As researchers, we have had a lot of flexibility in setting our schedules, and most of the time we do not have to be anywhere at any specific time. This flexibility means that we have been able to attend our children's daytime school-related events, care for them if they are sick, and offer assistance to our aging parents. Most of our job-related meetings can be shifted and rescheduled. We rarely have to be anywhere at any specific time other than during times of travel.

Another advantage is that we do not experience tenure pressure (the dreaded "publish or perish" threat). Although there is still an explicit expectation to share and disseminate our work, including in academic journals, there is less expectation to publish routinely in peer-reviewed venues. Other types of publications are valued, including those in trade publications, funder reports, self-published research briefs, and fact sheets.

We value the collaborative nature of our work with colleagues. It's common to work on joint projects as a team. We both feel that our colleagues support one another, benefit from each other, and are not competitive. We have shared goals that are mutually beneficial to all members of the team and a collective desire to advance the mission of our center.

We also like that we are based at a university, which gives us access to a wealth of resources in terms of facilities (e.g., libraries, lectures) and people (e.g., experts, consultants). The university environment also gives us enhanced credibility outside our own research center. Having the university name can open doors. But there's another, less positive side to this benefit: Nonacademic communities may not trust you because of your university affiliation. This perception can be a challenge when forming partnerships and establishing trust.

We feel appreciation from our partner practitioners, who value our contributions and are grateful for our support. Presenting findings to an audience of practitioners is fundamentally different from presenting to academic colleagues. Practitioners are extremely appreciative of your work. They thank you, value you, and let you know they will use the information you provide. In academic settings, the presentation environment often involves criticism and an atmosphere that values finding fault in your work.

Finally, we appreciate that our research is used by both our partner practitioners and policymakers. It is satisfying to see our findings advance the field and influence policy. This has been a key part of Jane's work with the New York State Department of Health, where findings from her work have been incorporated into new health initiatives and strategies to promote the health of adolescents across the state. Lisa's work has been used to improve environments for children and youth in family child care and residential child care settings. Both of us value being responsive to the needs of the field and being able to develop resources that will help practitioners do their work more effectively and improve the health and well-being of children and youth.

But there are also challenges to working in these types of positions. Perhaps the biggest challenge is the lack of long-term security. Non-tenure-track jobs typically are soft-money positions and therefore come with continuous pressure to seek and obtain funding.

Another potential downside is that you will not set your own research agenda—you will have less independence and autonomy in defining your projects and in following your own interests than in a tenure-track position. You might find yourself carrying out someone else's passion, not your own. You would have much more autonomy as a tenure-track faculty member in developing your research and in defining your goals.

Finally, non-tenure-track positions can be viewed as lower status compared with tenure-track faculty jobs. Non-tenure-track positions often do not have the same privileges that tenure-track positions have (e.g., voting on academic department issues, eligibility for submitting grant proposals). There is a sense by some within academia that non-tenure-track positions are for individuals who are not committed to long-term research in one university or who have not been granted tenure. Although it may be true that non-tenure-track positions can provide an avenue for those who have not met their tenure goals or who are looking for temporary work, it is also important to note that a non-tenure-track career can be a rewarding, intentional choice in and of itself.

How Do I Find Non-Tenure-Track Academic Positions?

There are several strategies you can pursue to find non-tenure-track positions. Listed here are some of the methods we have used, as well as what we have observed among our colleagues in our respective fields.

SCAN YOUR COMMUNITY

Become familiar with the organizations and centers that exist. What departments on campus have research programs? Are there centers (which may be located off campus) that hire researchers? Look for research talks or presentations being offered, and start attending them. Get to know the staff and organizations.

USE ALL OF YOUR NETWORKS

Contact everyone you know and let them know you are looking for employment. Use all the possible connections you might have (e.g., graduate school colleagues, former employers, faculty mentors, family friends, friends on social media sites). If there are organizations or centers that intrigue you, send letters of interest along with your resume. And be sure to follow up with additional e-mails or phone calls after sending your initial letter.

SET UP INFORMATIONAL INTERVIEWS

Contact organizations that interest you and request to speak with someone about the organization and possible opportunities. But do your homework and be as knowledgeable about the organization as possible. Review the website and publications and become familiar with the organization's goals and priority issues before your meeting.

USE SOCIAL MEDIA VENUES

Post your expertise, experience, and publications on social media sites such as LinkedIn (https://www.linkedin.com/) or ResearchGate (https://www.researchgate.net/) to connect with professionals and identify possible employment opportunities.

BE PERSISTENT!

Sometimes jobs are not immediately available, but the organization may have submitted grants that are outstanding and have yet to come through. When they do, there may be opportunities. Check in with people regularly and maintain contact with friendly reminders that you are still available and interested in possible employment.

BE OPEN AND FLEXIBLE

Sometimes available research positions are at a lower level than your qualifications merit. Recognize that there is a developmental trajectory to career paths: You might start in a lower level position that will give you a foot in the door, where you can then demonstrate your strengths and simultaneously build your skills. This approach could easily lead to more advanced professional opportunities as they become available. Likewise, a position might not be exactly in your area of interest and expertise, but there could be overlap and some crossover between disciplines, target populations, and issues. Being open to less-than-ideal opportunities might not only help you find or maintain your position but also lead to new connections.

Recognize that you might bring new knowledge to the position, along with a level of expertise that is missing and could be valuable. You can serve as a link between different areas of specialization, which could ideally have cross benefits for both areas. For example, in Jane's first position at the FLDC, she got hired on a grant that was examining the reporting of child abuse and neglect. Although the study of violence was not an area of interest or specialization initially, she began to integrate this work with her interest in adolescence. She launched a project examining maltreatment among runaway and homeless youth and later conducted studies on the impact of family violence on teen parents and then on incarcerated youth.

Conclusion

Our experiences in university-based non-tenure-track positions have been extremely positive. It's fair to say we both love our jobs and find our work to be meaningful. We feel incredibly satisfied by the range of projects on which we have worked and the opportunities we have had to build knowledge, contribute to advancing the field, support practitioners, influence policy, and make a difference in the lives of children, youth, and families. Our paths on this dynamic career track have led us in professional directions we had not intended to travel. It's a journey we highly recommend!

Additional Resources

Prevention Research Centers, supported by the Centers for Disease Control and Prevention, constitute a network of academic and community partners that conduct applied public health research. They are located in 26 universities across the United States within schools of public health. For a listing, see https://www.cdc.gov/prc/index.htm.

National Centers of Excellence in Youth Violence Prevention, funded by the Centers for Disease Control and Prevention, are located at the following universities:

- Johns Hopkins University (https://www.jhsph.edu/research/centers-and-institutes/center-for-prevention-of-youth-violence/index.html)
- University of Chicago (http://www.ssa.uchicago.edu)
- University of Colorado (https://www.colorado.edu/cspv/stepstosuccess/)
- University of Louisville (http://louisville.edu/sphis/departments/yvprc)
- University of Michigan (http://yvpc.sph.umich.edu)
- Virginia Commonwealth University (https://clarkhill.vcu.edu)

Clinical and Translational Science Institutes, funded by the National Institutes of Health (NIH), are located in more than 50 medical research institutions across the nation. For a listing, see https://ncats.nih.gov/files/ctsa-funding-information.pdf.

NIH also supports centers on topics such as autism through the Intellectual and Developmental Disabilities Branch of the National Institute of Child Health and Human Development: https://www.nichd.nih.gov/about/org/der/branches/.

The Administration for Children and Families' Early Childhood Training and Technical Assistance System includes national centers that develop and disseminate evidence-based resources and provide training and technical assistance. Centers are often housed within academic settings. For a list of national centers, see https://www.acf.hhs.gov/ecd/interagency-projects/ece-technical-assistance.

Examples of land-grant university extension systems include the following:

- Pennsylvania State University: https://extension.psu.edu/careers
- University of California, Davis: https://extension.ucdavis.edu
- University of Wisconsin–Madison: https://www.uwex.edu
- University of Minnesota: https://www.extension.umn.edu.

Reference

Association of Public and Land-Grant Universities. (n.d.). *Land-grant university FAQ*. Retrieved from http://www.aplu.org/about-us/history-of-aplu/what-is-a-land-grant-university/index.html

PREPARING YOURSELF FOR THE NONACADEMIC JOB MARKET

Patricia L. Mabry

How to Get the Most From Your Mentoring Experience

11

Finding a mentor during graduate school and early in your career can be challenging even under the best circumstances. Finding one when you are not sure you want to pursue a traditional academic career can be considerably harder. But do not be discouraged; this fact should be used to motivate you to do your due diligence and give ample attention to this important aspect of your career. I have taken a winding career path that definitely did not follow a traditional, straightforward, or even planned trajectory. And yet I feel I have had rewarding, rich experiences and have been able to make a good living. How did I do it? In this chapter, I share my reflections with you and give you my advice, but I don't recommend you try to imitate my specific moves. Rather, I offer more general recommendations for "best practices" for navigating your career.

I have divided this chapter into two parts. The first part is autobiographical, summarizing my career path to date, and is intended to demonstrate that following a strictly prescribed career path is not necessary to succeed. This professional autobiography is interspersed with lessons learned along the way. I hope these lessons will show how you can benefit from positive experiences and how you can take bad situations and make the most of them, even if

http://dx.doi.org/10.1037/0000110-012
Building a Career Outside Academia: A Guide for Doctoral Students in the Behavioral and Social Sciences,
J. B. Urban and M. R. Linver (Editors)
Copyright © 2019 by the American Psychological Association. All rights reserved.

your future doesn't look rosy at the moment. The second part of this chapter includes recommendations and advice for engaging mentors in your pursuit of a career beyond academia. My hope is that after reading this chapter, you will feel supported and encouraged to make a career choice outside of academia, if that is your desire.

It is worth considering the differences between a mentor and an adviser. I consider a *mentor* to be a person with whom you have an informal relationship that occurs during and after graduate school. An *adviser* is a formal term to indicate who is registered as your adviser with your graduate program. All graduate students must have a formal adviser who supervises and oversees their research and who makes sure they complete all of the required course work and benchmarks needed to graduate. I consider a mentor someone who can offer support, encouragement, advice, guidance, and inspiration and serve as a role model.

During graduate school, you could have both an adviser and a mentor. If you are lucky, your adviser will also be a great mentor. In this chapter, I refer to *mentor* in the generic sense, reserving *adviser* for the formal role of graduate adviser.

My Career Path: An Incredible and Improbable Journey

After earning a bachelor's degree in accounting, I worked as an accountant for a few years. I was so miserable that I sought out career counseling. Through that months-long process, I discovered that my interests and aptitudes were poorly suited to accounting and better suited to psychology. To do the type of work I was interested in would require a doctoral degree. On the advice of my counselor, I went back to school to earn a master's in psychology prior to applying to a doctoral program. The idea was to get some of the necessary prerequisites and to overcome my business background weighing against me on my application.

Looking back on my years at George Mason University, where I obtained my master's, I am grateful for the encouragement and inspiration of three people in particular. My statistics professor, Dr. Robert Pasnak, taught me critical thinking. I enjoyed how he challenged me and always made me think about the tools and methods I was learning. My clinical and health psychology professor, Dr. Jim Maddox, was an exemplary role model. He cared deeply about his students and what they were learning. He challenged me on a daily basis, and regardless of how tough his questions were, I always felt confident in his support.

Dr. Robert Smith was an incredible force in the classroom and packed so much material into each lecture. In fact, I recall audiotaping all of his lectures, not only because they were so fascinating, but also because he spoke with such fluidity that I could not always keep up. He was a professor in high demand, and if you were lucky enough to get an appointment with him, he gave you great guidance in thinking about a topic. Learning from him was like drinking from a firehose, and I regularly went directly to the library following a lecture or meeting with him in order to learn more about a topic he mentioned. I would gladly have taken any of his classes two or three times if it had been allowed. I would have loved to have had him as my formal adviser, but he did basic animal research that often involved examining the brains of deceased animals. This was intellectually interesting to me, but not something I could actually do from a squeamishness standpoint.

What all three of these professors shared was their sheer brilliance as teachers. They all challenged me to think better and more critically and yet were extremely supportive. They might not even remember me, but all had a positive impact on my early career.

Lesson 1: Look around, and see which professors are sparking your interest and motivating you to learn. If you like being in their classes, they might make great mentors. Do not be afraid of those who challenge you, as long as they are also supportive. You will learn a lot from them!

In order to demonstrate my commitment to psychology and to get real-world experience to ensure I didn't get a second degree I would regret, I volunteered for a summer in the Clinical Psychobiology Research Branch in an intramural research program at the National Institute of Mental Health. I spent three summers working for the program, the first as a volunteer and the following two as an Intramural Research Trainee Award Fellow. There, I met a terrific mentor, Dr. Ellen Leibenluft. She was trained as an MD and had a powerful intellect. She was so good because she challenged me to think, gave me difficult writing assignments, filled me with ideas, and gave me a lot of autonomy in writing. She was unafraid to critique my writing (very constructively, I should add), which both made me a much stronger writer and helped me be more receptive to criticism. Her assignments required hours in the library.

Lesson 2: Learn to make the most of criticism of your work. It will make you stronger.

Dr. Leibenluft was quite busy with her own career and mentoring several other people, which helped me learn how to get the most out of my limited time with her. Be understanding when your mentor cancels meetings on short notice. If you are fortunate enough to have a very talented mentor, he or she will be in high demand. Be self-motivated so that you do not stall in between meetings.

Lesson 3: Be efficient with your mentor's limited time. Come to all meetings prepared and with an agenda.

I entered the doctoral program in clinical psychology in the Graduate School of Arts and Sciences at the University of Virginia, which was, and still is, one of the more competitive programs in the country. That by itself was a feat. To this day, I am not sure quite how that happened. My undergraduate degree had been in accounting, so having a business background, not a science one, was unquestionably to my disadvantage.

The pressure in our graduate program was palpable; only seven of us had been admitted into the highly selective program, and of those, two were let go because of poor performance within the first year. Right off the bat, I had considerable difficulty finding a mentor or primary adviser, adding to my stress. In hindsight, I can see there were several reasons for this. On a practical level, I lived 100 miles away and commuted to school for the workweek, arriving Monday morning and leaving Friday afternoons to spend the weekends at home with my husband. This didn't leave me a lot of time to cultivate relationships among my peers and with the faculty. Another big factor was that I wasn't clear on the research area I wanted to pursue. Although my program did a very good job of matching prospective students with advisers prior to being accepted, I was one of the rare exceptions. I had a lot of interests, and I thought it was a tough enough job to narrow myself to clinical psychology (with an interest in psychobiology) from all the possible fields outside of accounting! Within the department, the person whose research coincided most closely with my interests was not a terribly good fit—he did basic research on animals, whereas I wanted to do applied work with humans. Plenty of other faculty did applied work, but few with a psychobiology angle. Ultimately, I couldn't find anyone who really shared my interests.

Lesson 4: It is a very good idea to make sure your research interests fit well with not only your program, but also at least one faculty member at your university.

Although it may seem that I made a serious error in selecting this program, I still feel that it was a reasonable choice given my circumstances at the time. I selected the program because of its reputation, emphasis on research methods and scientific rigor, ability to focus on adults versus children, and proximity to my home. Had I been willing to relocate or study a different subdiscipline in psychology, finding a mentor and adviser would have been easier.

Lesson 5: When you find a good mentor, find a way to keep him or her in your circle of influence.

During the latter half of my second year of graduate school, I finally discovered the research area I wanted to pursue—behavioral medicine. Unfortunately, it was an area of research not studied by anyone in my department. Not to be dissuaded, I discovered that my practicum professor, Dr. Daniel J. Cox, who directed the Behavioral

Medicine Center at the University of Virginia Hospital, was a great mentor. In fact, it was his passion for his work along with his deep knowledge of the field, productivity as a scholar, excellent grant writing skills, and warmth as a clinician, colleague, and mentor that ignited my own desire to pursue a career in this area. Disappointingly, he was not permitted to be my primary adviser because his academic appointment was not in my department. I overcame this by having him serve as a member of my dissertation committee and give close supervision to my research project while another faculty member in my department served as my dissertation chair.

As the clock began to tick and I was nearing completion of my degree, I began to wonder what the best career would be for me. In fact, very early on in graduate school, I got the feeling that academia might not be for me, but I didn't know what would be. During my final year, I decided I liked research, teaching, and clinical practice, but I didn't know how I could do them all. Because of personal circumstances, including a faltering marriage, as I graduated with my PhD I found myself relocating to an area where I did not have a job or any contacts. I responded to every ad in the paper and sent out countless resumes—remember, this was before the Internet was used for job searches. I cold called dozens of places. Luckily, with a bit of hard work and persistence, after about 6 weeks, I landed a job in a company for which I had worked 5 years earlier as a temporary office worker.

There were only two of us full-time PhDs, and we spent our time writing grants and running clinical trials. I learned a lot about grant writing, the National Institutes of Health (NIH), and the topic of smoking cessation from my boss and mentor, Dr. Al Jerome, who also had a doctoral degree in clinical psychology. He was very understanding and supportive as I grappled with my longer-term career decisions. Because we were working in a small business, we worked very closely together; every grant was a team effort. I believe this type of close teamwork at such a level of intensity is rare in academia. A new assistant professor, even with a good mentor, is likely to be doing more solo work, or at least to not be working elbow to elbow on all the same grant proposals as his or her mentor.

It will undoubtedly be difficult to create this type of opportunity, but if you do find it, take it. I have never in my lifetime had my critical thinking and writing skills tested with such scrutiny on a daily basis as during that time. Although we were always under tight deadlines, Al was a kind and constructive critic who took the time to explain the reasoning behind his comments and kept me going with praise when I did well.

Lesson 6: If you can find someone who will tutor you in grant writing in an apprenticeship model, do it!

I stayed less than a year at that job before my marriage completely deteriorated, so I accepted a postdoc position at the Medical University of South Carolina (MUSC), where I had completed my internship. In some ways, the position was ideal for me; it was a clinical postdoc that enabled me to get the hours of supervised practice I needed for licensure, and it was in a city where I had friends yet was some distance from my soon-to-be-ex-husband. From there, I became a tenure track assistant professor. I stayed on after the postdoc mostly because I liked my colleagues and the workplace, and I wanted to stay in Charleston, South Carolina.

I had an academic appointment, but my position was funded as a clinical one. On the upside, I could do it all: deliver clinical services, supervise clinical postdocs and interns, teach in the medical school, and pursue research. On the downside, I did not have a research mentor, and my department was not equipped for me to bring in research grant money. Moreover, trying to take on all of these responsibilities—research, clinical service and supervision, and teaching—diluted my focus on becoming an independent investigator (i.e., R01-funded NIH researcher). After a couple of years of "doing it all," I was offered a half-time position working for the National Cancer Institute (NCI) Tobacco Control Research Branch (TCRB) through the Intergovernmental Personnel Act (IPA) Mobility Program. Accepting the position meant that between grants and the IPA, I had bought out 100% of my time, so there was no time left for clinical duties. Because my job at MUSC was a clinical position, it became clear I would need to choose between keeping my current job and pursuing my research interests.

After a good bit of soul-searching, I ended up choosing research. Following the IPA, I left South Carolina for a full-time position at the TCRB. In hindsight, this was a significant decision point in my career, moving from academia to the federal government. Although it ended up being a very good decision that led to an overall positive career, it also took me off the standard academic track, with its known challenges, to some uncharted places with unidentified obstacles to overcome.

Lesson 7: Sometimes wonderful things come from the most difficult circumstances.

Because I had been an IPA, I was not permitted to be hired directly into the federal government without a cooling off period, so I came on as a contractor and served as a principal investigator for the TCRB's new Tobacco Intervention Research Clinic. The allure of this job turned out to be better than the job itself. There were numerous challenges in setting up a brand-new research entity within a large government organization, and the timing was rather poor, coming at the end of the doubling of the NIH budget. When the doubling stopped abruptly, many programs were cut, especially vulnerable new programs that had yet to demonstrate benefit (like mine), and so the Tobacco Intervention Research Clinic was closed. It was an extremely challenging time in my career. From my point of view, I had nothing but failures behind me, and I was still trying to get my career to take off. I was discouraged.

Fortunately, I had people who believed in me. Drs. Glen Morgan, Scott Leischow, and Cathy Backinger at the TCRB agreed to keep me on in my contractor role as a scientist in the TCRB. All of them deserve credit for nurturing (and sometimes just tolerating!) my ideas and giving me the autonomy and resources to pursue them. I worked hard and contributed wherever I could, but as a contractor, I was limited in how much independence I could have without doing things that were "inherently governmental" and thus prohibited for contractors. I would have applied for a position in the branch, but there was a hiring freeze. So, with an eye toward getting my foot in the door to federal service, I took a pay cut and went to work as a federal employee for the Office of Behavioral and Social Science Research (OBSSR) at NIH.

> **Lesson 8:** Don't be shortsighted. Taking a pay cut for a better opportunity can pay dividends in the long run.

My new job ended up being a perfect fit for me! Again, I had a tremendous amount of autonomy, and I immediately tried to make up for what I felt was lost time. At OBSSR, I was blessed with terrific mentors who were intellectually stimulating and supportive and allowed me to work independently. I was charged with creating a program of systems science. I learned as much as I could by reading extensively and going to meetings and conferences that were about things with which I was unfamiliar. I had the great fortune to be referred to Dr. Bobby Milstein, who was then at the Centers for Disease Control and Prevention (CDC). I cold called him, and we ended up having great conversations. Once we realized we had overlapping goals, we were able to take advantage of our unique positions at NIH and CDC to do transformative work. I was able to do gratifying work and moved up the ranks quickly, far surpassing where I would have been had I remained a contractor.

> **Lesson 9:** Mentorship can be quid pro quo—try to find ways that your work can benefit your mentor. Or, when you find someone who has similar goals, look to them as your mentor.

After 8 years at OBSSR and climbing to the rank of acting deputy director, I decided it was time for a change. I was very proud of my accomplishments at OBSSR, but I had the itch to do something different. I decided it would be prudent to stay in the federal government.

I saw a job advertised at the NIH Office of Disease Prevention (ODP) at my level, and I applied. I was excited to do something different, but the job ended up being even more different than I had expected. I had hoped to lead the team tasked with the ODP's strategic priority on "promoting the best methods for prevention research." Instead, I ended up spending the majority of my time leading the team that was tasked with developing a portfolio analysis tool for prevention research at NIH. Although it was disappointing not to do what I loved the most, it turned out to be a tremendous learning opportunity.

> **Lesson 10:** Find the positive in difficult situations. Doing something different can be a great learning opportunity!

Dr. David Murray, ODP's director, was a marvelous mentor, and I learned a lot about research design from him. He was patient and, like many previous mentors, challenged me with probing questions. He also was a great role model for how to be a good leader. He was certain about what he wanted to accomplish and gave staff very clear guidance on how to achieve the goals he had set for the office. Although he was often occupied with many other projects, he always created time to meet with us and grapple with the sticky issues we raised. I greatly appreciated his team spirit and ability to roll up his sleeves along with the rest of us.

One day, I got a call from Indiana University (IU) inviting me to apply for the executive director position at the new Network Science Institute. I was definitely flattered but unsure about leaving the federal government and its benefits. But after finding out that my (new) husband was keen on moving to Indiana (who knew!) and seeing what a good fit the opportunity was, I applied. The job at IU had the right blend of job qualifications that spoke to my scientific interests and expertise, as well as my NIH experience and the type of work I liked to do—forge collaborative, interdisciplinary research partnerships while using my skill in thinking strategically about grant applications. The two things that were missing—not being a federal job and not being located near family and friends—I felt were worth sacrificing for this once-in-a-lifetime opportunity.

Although I still miss my family and friends in the Washington, DC, area, I am enjoying the challenge of learning a new place and job. I also found new mentors at IU. Dr. Bernice Pescosolido is a well-known and highly accomplished medical sociologist, and I have learned a lot about egocentric network science as well as how to navigate the terrain of IU from Bernice. She is a formidable thinker and connector of people and projects. She challenges me to examine all aspects of my own lines of reasoning. She exudes confidence and inspires me to tackle new challenges.

Dr. Olaf Sporns is a very different type of mentor—he is not a firebrand; rather, he motivates others through his understated reflection and by example. He is the kind of guy that when he speaks, everyone sits up to listen because they know it is sure to be valuable.

Dr. Andy Saykin is located 50 miles away, but more than once in our short time knowing one another he has offered sage advice during our occasional phone calls. He is clear and compassionate and sees to the heart of the matter quickly and almost intuitively. Ten minutes of his time will get you further than 20 minutes or even an hour with most other people. It strikes me that this efficient mentorship skill may come from years of coaching his mentees and colleagues and seeing patients.

> **Lesson 11:** Look for mentors wherever you go. They won't necessarily look the same as your previous mentors, but the advantage is that you will learn new things from them.

In sum, I have not had "a mentor," but a whole host of them. I went about the mentorship experience from a completely naive and unorthodox starting point. But if I have learned anything, it has been to trust and believe in myself. I have become aware of my strengths and weaknesses. Writing this chapter has given me the chance to reflect on my career and the people who influenced it. So many people gave of themselves and helped me, which makes me think good mentors are everywhere. They are out there if you are willing to avail yourself of them. So keep your eyes peeled, and you, too, will find people to inspire and support you in your own unique journey in life.

Best Practices for Navigating Your Career Beyond Academia

Like a good scientist, gather your data. Reflect back and look forward. What has been satisfying for you in the past? What areas have you not learned about or experiences have you not had that would benefit you? What do you want out of your career—a paycheck? fame? satisfying work? chances to meet new people? Collect data on possible careers. Reflect on the ideas and concepts that interest and captivate you. Search for journal articles and other reading in these areas, taking care to look up citations that look promising. Once you find a handful or more of articles that really interest you, look up the authors and see where they are located. Read their websites to see the other topics they work on and who their collaborators are.

However you locate them, talk to people about their work and your interests, especially those whose work you admire. Did they consider any other jobs besides the one they have now? What other jobs did they hold—what was their trajectory? What current opportunities are out there? What fields of study do they say are "hot" and hiring? What articles and people influenced them? What do they recommend you read, and who can they introduce you to? Keep an open mind about your next venture, yet you need not stand idly by, waiting for it to come to you. By doing some or all of the suggested activities in this section, you will be better prepared to make career decisions as they arise. Not only that, but you will be better able to help your mentors and advisers help you.

FINDING AND SELECTING A MENTOR

You need to be proactive in reaching out to potential mentors, but not in a haphazard or premature manner. Do your due diligence in advance by observing and assessing potential mentors' fitness to be a mentor to you. This might include reading what they have written, hearing them speak, and finding out what others think of them and their work. I recommend starting with a brief e-mail introducing yourself and expressing your interest in a specific piece of work they have done and requesting a short phone or in-person meeting. In your message, offer some times you are available in the next 2 weeks. If they get back to you to set up the call—fantastic! If not, try calling, and if they don't answer, leave a message with your name, providing the reason for calling (your interest in their work), referring to the e-mail you sent and your request for a phone meeting, and leaving your call-back number. If they don't call you back at this juncture, wait another month and resend the e-mail with a brief message stating that you sent the message a while back and remain keenly interested in following up with them. If you still get nowhere, it is time to give up on them.

All is not lost, though, because if you follow my advice, you will simultaneously be pursuing more than one mentor. By the time you have reached out to two or three people you admire, you will get a call with at least one of them. Now you need to prepare for that call. In fact, you probably should prepare for the call before you even send your initial e-mail message, just in case they call you back right away. Read at least two of their recent, influential, or highly cited works, and look closely at the references and coauthors. Once you have one or more conversations that go well with someone, you can ask them about their interest in mentoring you. But you will want to be specific about how much of their time you want as well as the specific areas in which you are seeking mentorship. If you have more than one mentor, tell them about the others and the areas they cover.

I like to have more than one mentor. It is actually pretty ridiculous to expect one person to do the great big job of mentoring. Mentoring is like parenting—it takes a village. I count as mentors all kinds of people, not just those in a formal advisory role. I have learned just as much from peers, supervisees, and mentees. It comes from my core belief that I can learn something valuable from almost anyone. This philosophy has served me well.

MAINTAINING REALISTIC EXPECTATIONS

Most good mentors, as mentioned earlier, are very busy. They may or may not have funding or even time to support you to work directly with them as a volunteer. If you are invited to work with a mentor, work with them on their project in a supportive role at first. This helps you and the potential mentor get to know one another in a work setting. Most importantly, be flexible!

SPECIFIC ADVICE FOR FEMALE MENTEES

Female mentees face different obstacles than men, and it can be helpful to have a female mentor. For example, women more often than men take time out from work or school early in their careers to bear and raise children. Even if you don't take much time off, working or going to school at the same time you are parenting is often a juggling act. Many women worry that they won't be able to devote themselves to their career to the same degree they were able to prior to starting a family. Moreover, they worry they won't be a "good mom" if they are dividing their attention between work or school and family. I, too, had these concerns.

It is helpful to talk to other women, particularly those who have had some experience balancing career and family. If you have a mentor who is not exactly supportive on this issue for any reason, it does not necessarily mean you have to drop that mentor. If you are otherwise getting a lot from your mentoring relationship, you might try to stay with your mentor and get the support you are seeking in this specific area from someone else. You might find a female role model who is not in your research area whom you admire for her ability to achieve a good work–family balance. A lot of employers also have work–life balance seminars that might be a great place to go to meet other women in a similar situation.

Final Words on Mentoring

Whereas the mentor–mentee relationship is fairly formalized and strongly encouraged in academia, the path is not so clear if you work outside of academia. From my experience, most businesses don't devote a lot of resources (if any) to support formal mentoring programs within their organization. However, there are a wide range of opportunities that you could take advantage of, both informally within an organization (by approaching people inside the organization about serving as mentors) and outside the organization. Most businesses and nonprofits affiliate with one or more associations that promote the larger field in which they are situated. Therefore, you might try attending some industry-specific meetings in your field as a way to find a good source of mentors.

With respect to the federal government, I have seen mentoring programs advertised periodically. For example, Federally Employed Women (https://www.few.org) is an organization aimed at supporting and advancing careers of women in the federal workforce, including through mentoring. The Association for Women in Science (https://www.awis.org) is a transsector organization similarly devoted to promoting the careers of women in STEM fields, including behavioral and social sciences, health, and medicine.

Just remember, getting a mentor early in your career is very important, and I advise being persistent and creative in finding several mentors, formal and informal, to help guide and advise you throughout your career. And don't forget, it is almost never too soon to begin mentoring others—be supportive of your peers and more junior-level colleagues, and as you advance in your career, make time to create relationships in which you are providing mentorship. If you keep your mind and eyes open for mentoring opportunities, both as mentor and mentee, you will be surprised at how much your professional network has to offer. Good luck!

Additional Resources

American Psychological Association. (2018). *Centering on Mentoring: The task force.* Retrieved from http://www.apa.org/education/grad/mentor-task-force.aspx

American Psychological Association. (2018). *Early career psychologists.* Retrieved from http://www.apa.org/careers/early-career/index.aspx

American Psychological Association. (2018). *Get connected.* Retrieved from http://www.apa.org/careers/early-career/get-connected/index.aspx

American Psychological Association. (2018). *Introduction to mentoring: A guide for mentors and mentees.* Retrieved from http://www.apa.org/education/grad/mentoring.aspx

Association for Women in Science: https://www.awis.org

Federally Employed Women: https://www.few.org

Kram, K. E., & Isabella, L. A. (1985). Mentoring alternatives: The role of peer relationships in career development. *Academy of Management Journal, 28,* 110–132.

Kerin McQuaid Borland, Terri LaMarco, and Amy Hoag Longhi

Preparing for and Conducting Job Searches Outside Academia

12

Nonacademic job searches are not straightforward. To create a deeper understanding of what is involved, this chapter frames the process—beginning with knowing yourself and where you may best fit within an organization, highlighting ways in which to best use your job search tools, and customizing these tools to the opportunities you are pursuing—and discusses nuances inherent in job searching that are important to know to maximize success. The job search is more than submitting resumes and completing applications in the hopes of being selected for interviews. A savvy job searcher uses tools, networks, and opportunities to maximize success.

Assessing Your Skills and Interests

Preparing for a nonacademic job search is a process that seems to be driven by others—the organizations to which you are applying, the human resources representative with whom you have your first interview, or the hiring manager whose decision it will be to select the final candidate—but the reality is that the job search process starts with you. It will be the story you tell that will determine your success in translating your past into what an employer is seeking in the future. If you begin the process by only converting your

http://dx.doi.org/10.1037/0000110-013
Building a Career Outside Academia: A Guide for Doctoral Students in the Behavioral and Social Sciences,
J. B. Urban and M. R. Linver (Editors)
Copyright © 2019 by the American Psychological Association. All rights reserved.

curriculum vitae into a resume, start surfing job boards, and randomly begin submitting applications, your chances of experiencing success will likely be fairly limited. The best advice is "start at the beginning"—look at yourself from different angles, assess your past experiences, and reflect on your proud accomplishments as well as challenging times or examples when you may not have been the best fit for a task or project.

Taking time to understand who you are and what you have to offer as you begin your career journey will be a time saver as you start to identify areas in which you have interests and skills. This process of self-reflection will bring to bear the skills and attributes you wish to promote to potential employers. The process is analogous to that which you embarked on when selecting your PhD program. Broadly, you considered programs and their areas of emphasis and how they related to your educational interests. From there you narrowed your topical areas of inquiry to develop a focus on a particular question. Then, you developed a hypothesis that you needed to research, evaluate, and hone to understand what was most important.

The same is true in your job search. Consider the broad areas in which you may use your content expertise, skills, and other attributes, and then fine-tune your focus to more specific areas of interest with a keen eye on the skills needed in positions that you believe are a strong fit. You are not a PhD student or soon-to-be graduate seeking alternatives, but rather a newly defined professional seeking to make meaningful contributions. As you explore new professional opportunities and connect with professionals and mentors beyond the academy, your attitude, self-confidence, and resilience will be critical to your success. In a process that, by nature, includes rejection and subjectivity, your ability to believe in yourself and have a clear focus on the ways you can contribute is paramount.

SELF-ASSESSMENT METHODS

Knowing what you bring to an organization is vital to your job search success. There are many ways to engage in the process of self-reflection; selecting the best approach for you is a personal decision. You may decide to structure your own process, identifying key questions that have been going through your mind over the course of several months, possibly years, as you contemplated widening your career net. You may, however, prefer a more structured approach. There are several online tools that can guide you through a series of questions to help you understand your assets as well as potential liabilities.

If this approach sounds appealing, you may want to consider tools such as CareerOneStop (https://www.careeronestop.org/), hosted by the U.S. Department of Labor and Statistics (DLS). It is a comprehensive site offering insights into career exploration, skill identification, and occupational information. Another DLS resource is O*NET (https://www.onetonline.org/), which includes a free online assessment and detailed descriptions of a large number of standard occupations. A third online tool to consider is the Strong Interest Inventory (https://www.cpp.com/products/strong/index.aspx), designed to identify interests and demonstrate how they relate to various occupations and careers. Others such as CliftonStrengths (https://www.gallupstrengthscenter.com/) allow you to identify your top strengths and how those skills and attributes may be maximized in a variety of settings. These are just some examples of structured instruments designed to assist you in identifying how you have developed through your experiences, what may be important considerations as you evaluate opportunities against your personal priorities, and the tasks or responsibilities you should avoid as you consider professional opportunities.

You may also wish to engage in a more scaffolded process to uncover this important information. If you are currently in an advanced degree program, it is likely that your institution offers career support for students. Career services offices often offer a few assessment options for students as a way to develop clarity about career paths. If you are no longer a student, this type of service can be found within your community through community education classes or private career coaches. Keep in mind that the latter options will be most expensive, and so knowing what is included in a fee-based service is important. As a paying client, you should expect to have an introductory meeting to learn about the counselor and his or her approach, the administration of a validated assessment tool, and an interpretation of the assessment results that helps you establish a foundation on which to build your next career steps.

HONING IN ON SKILLS

Regardless of the way in which you come to understand your strengths and values, the goal is to identify the areas that you excel in and also that you enjoy. This package of attributes then becomes one of the filters to help you assess job descriptions and other opportunities. It is possessing the combination of a skill set and interest in applying those skills to real-life problems that will allow you to make your most valuable contributions in the workplace.

To start the process of skill identification, it may be helpful to know more about the areas of greatest interest to employers. The National Association of Colleges and Employers (n.d.) charged a task force with identifying the skill sets of most importance to employers. The resulting set of competencies is one rubric against which to evaluate yourself. The eight competencies are as follows:

1. *Critical thinking and problem solving:* Ability to exercise sound reasoning to analyze issues, make decisions, and solve problems and to obtain, interpret, and use knowledge, facts, and data in a process
2. *Oral and written communication:* Ability to articulate thoughts and ideas clearly and effectively in written and oral form, to speak in public, to express ideas to others, and to write and edit memos, letters, and complex technical reports clearly and effectively
3. *Teamwork and collaboration:* Ability to build collaborative relationships with people of diverse cultures, ages, races, genders, religions, lifestyles, and viewpoints; to work within a team structure; and to negotiate and manage conflict
4. *Information technology applications:* Ability to select and use appropriate technology to accomplish a given task and to apply computing skills to solve problems

5. *Leadership:* Ability to leverage the strengths of others to achieve common goals, to use interpersonal skills to coach and develop others, to assess and manage one's own and others' emotions, to use empathy to guide and motivate, and to organize, prioritize, and delegate work
6. *Professional work ethic:* Ability to demonstrate personal accountability, effective work habits, integrity, and ethical behavior; to act responsibly with the larger community in mind; and to learn from mistakes
7. *Career management:* Ability to identify your interests, strengths, knowledge, and experiences relative to positions and potential career goals and areas necessary for professional growth, to navigate career options, and to self-advocate for opportunities in the workplace
8. *Global and intercultural fluency:* Ability to value, respect, and learn from people of diverse cultures, races, ages, genders, sexual orientations, and religions; to demonstrate openness, inclusiveness, and sensitivity; and to interact respectfully with all people and understand individuals' differences.

As you consider positions in sectors outside of academia, compare these eight skills and attributes with your own competencies. The ways in which your experiences as a PhD student translate into the nonacademic world of work should become clear.

Chris Humphrey (2017), author of the blog Jobs on Toast (https://www.jobsontoast.com), affirmed the notion that there are many ways PhD programs prepare individuals to contribute meaningfully in the workplace. Any skill developed in one setting can be tapped and further developed in new, often unrelated arenas. Humphrey contended that doctoral programs develop skills that are desirable in a variety of employment settings and that there are four main skill areas that any well-rounded PhD has:

1. *project skills* include project management, budget management, teamwork, problem solving, and organization of meetings and events;
2. *entrepreneurship* includes thought leadership, innovation, bidding for funding, networking, and international experience;
3. *communication skills* include writing, public speaking, publicity and public relations, stakeholder management, and web, e-mail, and social media presence; and
4. *knowledge and information skills* include research, teaching and training, and information management.

You will notice that by segmenting your scholarship and related academic experiences, the work in which you have engaged can be transferred seamlessly to other work settings.

In addition, there are other areas highly valued in the nonacademic workplace that, through your experience as a PhD student, you likely possess. Take, for example, the impact multigenerational dynamics are having on the effectiveness of today's workers. Your experience working with a variety of faculty and undergraduate students may bring helpful insights to work cultures to improve teamwork and collaboration within an organization. Similarly, as recruiters become more intentional about creating diverse workplaces, any experience or training you have in this area could be an added benefit to an organization and can be part of the knowledge and skill set you bring. As you dissect your experiences and reflect on your own development, you will begin to see the strength of your candidacy beyond the academy.

To illustrate, evaluate the following job description[1] for an analytics director relative to the skills you possess from your previous scholarly work and other leadership experiences:

> The individual is capable of both designing and developing innovative analytic solutions. Qualified candidates will have a strong academic background in mathematics, statistics, or relevant field, with a passion for data science and experience in managing data-intensive projects. The candidate will have the following:
>
> - excellent professional presence, as the position will require significant interaction and communication with executives and top-tier clients;
> - excellent problem-solving skills with the ability to design algorithms, which may include data cleaning, data mining, data clustering, and subsequent data visualization and analytics;
> - high proficiency in translating complex analytic concepts into relevant business concepts and insights for a nonanalytic audience;
> - the ability to effectively communicate, synthesize, and make recommendations to business partners, executives, clients, and internal stakeholders to secure organizational engagement and effective execution; and
> - the ability to manage, develop, and mentor team members.

As a behavioral and social science PhD, you have likely engaged in research, data collection, and analysis and clearly have the background to be considered for such a position. Additionally, if you have led teams or taught courses that required you to translate information while honing your communication skills, it is likely you would be even more competitive for the opportunity. Your effectiveness at translating your past and demonstrating your competence will be the key to making a successful transition.

CONSIDERING PROFESSIONAL INTERESTS

Not all positions for which you are qualified will be of equal interest to you. Believing in the mission of the organization is part of finding the right organizational fit. Current research suggests that individuals who have a strong sense of purpose and align that purpose with organizations that have compatible missions will find the greatest fulfillment in their careers. Research by Aaron Hurst, CEO of Imperative, has indicated that "purpose driven" individuals are 64% more likely to be fulfilled at work, 54% more likely to make a meaningful impact, and 51% more likely to have strong relationships

---

[1]This is a hypothetical job description crafted from several descriptions of this type to illustrate the skills and responsibilities employers may seek.

(Hurst et al., 2016). Thus, it is key to understand the types of organizations to which you will be best suited, to know your values, and to seek opportunities that will provide the circumstances for you to flourish as a professional.

You may find that your professional interests are an outgrowth of your academic work, and for that reason you may wish to incorporate your scholarly work into your career pursuit. If you have a PhD in psychology, sociology, or statistics, you may seek opportunities to apply your content knowledge in a position in business or government. Alternatively, you may be driven by personal curiosity that represents other professional arenas to explore. For example, if you are an anthropologist who is intrigued by the way people lived centuries ago, you might apply that interest to human interaction with computers or consumer buying behaviors; if you speak a second or third language, applying your skills at a global think tank conducting work in other countries is a way to leverage your personal curiosity, combined with your skills, to launch your professional journey.

Last, you may be passionate about current issues or causes, and employers may value not only your commitment to the cause, but also the professional background you bring to advance their work. Causes such as education, sustainability, global health, and urban gentrification are examples of issues that may resonate with you and that could be platforms for engaging as a professional, deriving a sense of purpose, and continuing to understand how your skills, interests, and career journey may progress in tandem. The time spent understanding your story, your skills, your interests, and your values will pay off as you prepare to market yourself to potential employers through resumes, cover letters, job applications, and social media.

Job Search Tools

RESUME

A resume is not the same as a curriculum vitae (CV). CVs are most commonly used in academia; chances are that you have seen at least one CV of an adviser, faculty member, mentor, or friend in your department. CVs tend to be comprehensive documents showcasing extensive information on your education, experience (teaching, research, other), publications, presentations, honors and awards, research and teaching interests, professional activities, skills, and references. CVs are necessary for PhDs conducting academic job searches, but although your CV may be handy as a complete reference of your many accomplishments, it is not the document of choice for employers outside the academy. Instead, employers will request a resume—a short (1–2 page maximum), targeted summary of the skills and achievements that make you the ideal candidate for a specific job. Unlike a CV, which tends to be a static document changing only when you have new accomplishments to add, a resume needs to be modified and targeted to each industry, organization, and job to which you are applying, with the goal of quickly and concisely giving your potential employer the information needed to move you to the next step in the hiring process.

Composing a well-crafted resume begins with an understanding of the transferable skills and qualities you have to offer. Next, consider the types of positions for which you hope to apply and the specific skills and qualifications required. Matching your qualifications with the needs of the employer will help you decide what to include in (and exclude from) your resume. Finally, decide how you want to communicate your accomplishments by selecting a format for your resume that highlights the targeted story you have to tell.

The two most common resume formats are chronological and functional. A chronological format is best if you have job-related experience. This type of resume usually includes an objective or thesis statement focusing on skills related to a specific position, followed by a chronological listing (most recent first) of your educational information, employment history, related accomplishments, certifications, and special skills. A functional resume format, in contrast, is best suited for highlighting relevant skills developed through a variety of experiences. Although you still list your education and employment history, the majority of your resume is dedicated to identifying specific transferable skills that you possess and that the employer needs.

Review a variety of chronological and functional resume samples through an Internet search to find what you feel works best for you. Some experts believe that the functional resume format is ideal for PhDs translating academic experiences to non-academic settings because although you possess the necessary skills, they may not be readily apparent in a traditional chronological format. Typically, hiring managers or applicant tracking systems will spend approximately 10 seconds on your resume before they decide to reject it or take a closer look. Thus, how you organize your resume comes down to analyzing and communicating your background in relation to the employer's job description, thereby increasing your chances of progressing to the next step in the hiring process. Keep in mind these five key tips for making the most of your resume:

1. *Keep it short:* One to two pages is all that is expected.
2. *Make it scannable:* Communicate in bullet points rather than paragraphs.
3. *Focus on results:* Help the employer understand the impact of your previous roles and work.
4. *Target your resume:* Use key words that mirror job descriptions, and translate your past experiences into language familiar to the employer.
5. *Get feedback:* Share your resume with professionals in your field of interest or a career coach at your school, and listen to and incorporate their feedback.

Although your resume plays an important role in introducing your qualifications, it does not stand alone. A resume is typically accompanied by a cover letter, and most organizations also require you to submit an online application. Some employers may even turn to social media, such as Facebook or Twitter, to learn more about you before scheduling an interview.

COVER LETTER

A cover letter introduces your story and creates a first impression for employers. It specifically links your resume to the position, showcasing your knowledge of the organization and highlighting relevant skills. Start by researching the organization, then consider what intrigues you and what you have to offer. Your cover letter should include three or four paragraphs with the following information in each paragraph:

- *First paragraph:* The main purpose of the first paragraph is to introduce yourself and state why you are applying. You want to grab the employer's attention and explain why you are interested in this position and this organization. If someone has referred you to the organization (e.g., current employee, friend, family member), include his or her name in the first sentence.
- *Second and third paragraphs:* Tell your story; describe your qualifications for the position you seek using specific examples from academic, work, volunteer, cocurricular, and other professional experiences. Connect your accomplishments, skills, and knowledge directly to the position, organization, and field. Draw on all of your experiences, including research, teaching, mentoring, and data collection and analysis. The important thing here is to help the employer understand how your experiences match up with the qualities and competencies they are seeking. Avoid repeating facts outlined on your resume by focusing on key concepts.
- *Final paragraph:* Summarize or make a final statement about your interest and qualifications. Thank the employer for his or her time and consideration. Create an action step by indicating that you will follow up with a phone call or e-mail.

ONLINE APPLICATIONS AND SOCIAL MEDIA

Online applications are common today and enable hiring managers to automate, review, and store hiring documents online. A rule of thumb when submitting an online application is to complete every field, thereby providing valuable information about your qualifications and more fully demonstrating your interest in the organization and position. Believe it or not, many applicants skip questions or write "see resume," assuming that their resume will cover the required information. However, many employers (and applicant tracking systems) immediately eliminate applicants who do not complete the entire application. So do not miss this opportunity to be considered and hopefully to stand out from the competition.

Once your resume and application pass an initial screening, many employers look online for additional information about you. Keeping this in mind, you should review and edit your online presence on Facebook, Twitter, YouTube, Flickr, and so forth in order to ensure you are seen in favorable light. Here are a few recommendations about how to start:

- Google your name to see what kind of information surfaces.
- Delete questionable comments or statuses including profanity, complaints about previous employers, and discriminatory comments.
- Delete questionable photos portraying offensive or illegal activities, excessive alcohol or drug use, and partying.
- Make your profile private to prevent potential employers from accessing it.

Social media provides another opportunity to market your unique qualifications through a LinkedIn profile. LinkedIn (https://www.linkedin.com/) is a professional network designed to connect you with professionals (and potential colleagues), information, and opportunities. It is now common for hiring managers to view the LinkedIn profile of applicants, which makes it a critical tool for you to leverage. Develop an appealing, up-to-date profile highlighting your transferable skills, recommend colleagues, seek recommendations from others who can speak to your skills, and include a profile picture that creates a positive first impression. Below are a few tips to consider as you get started with LinkedIn. In addition, be sure to tap the hundreds of online articles about making the most of LinkedIn as a job search tool.

Build an Effective Profile

Although the information on your LinkedIn profile should be consistent with your resume, it does not need to be presented in the same way. Instead, LinkedIn should bring your resume to life. Use this tool to highlight more about your achievements, values, skills, and abilities and less about specific job responsibilities. Develop a compelling heading that tells your story in 120 characters. Tell readers who you are, what you do, and what makes you unique. Remember that, at least for now, your target audience is potential employers whom you want to help understand how your advanced degree could add value in their organization.

Make Connections

With a strong profile in place, begin making connections. Connections will make the other features work much better! Begin by importing contacts from your e-mail address book by clicking on "add connections" along the top navigation within "Contacts." LinkedIn automatically selects all of the imported contacts; be sure to uncheck the "select all" box. Look through the list for people with the blue "in" logo next to their name, which shows that they are already on LinkedIn. Select those with whom you want to connect, including fellow students; current and former coworkers and supervisors, advisers, and mentors; and close family friends. To find peers or colleagues for whom you do not have an e-mail address, search within LinkedIn by graduating class and company and connect directly through the system.

Join Relevant Groups

Groups are a great way to expand your network. Join alumni groups from your various academic institutions, and seek out groups related to your chosen industry. Joining relevant groups enables you to view and participate in discussions with industry leaders and professionals and allows you to get closer to connecting with other members who are already part of that group.

In summary, effectively marketing yourself requires developing a clear understanding of what you have to offer an employer; understanding the employer's specific needs, culture, and job requirements; and then communicating a fit through some fairly standard job search tools. With your tools in place, you are ready to uncover opportunities and begin searching for nonacademic positions.

Job Searching 101

For as much time as you may have invested in exploring your skills and strengths and translating your CV to a resume, the job search itself will take consistent time and energy to conclude with a successful outcome. Searching for opportunities takes persistence, commitment, creativity, confidence, and a willingness to take risks and meet people. We have worked successfully with PhD graduates at the University of Michigan and include in this section relevant quotes from real people who have been through this process.

PERSISTENCE

Your job search will be riddled with ups and downs, successes and challenges, wins and losses. If you find a fantastic position online, you need to go beyond just the "click and send" of your resume to experience a positive outcome. You may need to convince an employer that you have a set of skills they are seeking or help them see the value of the strengths you offer to a particular position. Persistence is about taking control of your job search. Be careful that persistence doesn't translate into aggression or desperation. Neither quality is attractive to employers, and both can show up in unpleasant ways, negatively impacting your job search. Persistence is about helping others understand your value through persuasive communication. A PhD graduate from the University of Michigan noted that this persistence continued to be important even after being hired:

> My biggest challenge has been helping my current company understand that my years of graduate school count as work experience. They may have the tendency to think that I've been doing the same things as undergraduates but for longer. I've had to continually remind them about my experience as a teacher and a nonprofit fellow and make the connection for them that those things count as "real" work.

COMMITMENT

Job searching takes time and dedication. You must be disciplined to manage the process (keeping track of contacts, leads, relationships, ideas, opportunities, applications) and keep your job search ever present in your mind. The job search needs to become part of your daily and weekly routine, in the same way you might train for a marathon or practice an instrument for a major performance; commitment will lead to success!

CREATIVITY

When it comes to searching for jobs, leads and opportunities are literally everywhere. As a job seeker, there is a potential lead in everything you see, read, and do. And there are potential connections in everyone you know and meet. Your next opportunity may come from the person sitting next to you on an airplane or someone being introduced to you at an event. It may be from someone on LinkedIn, a posting you find on a website, or an article you read in a journal or magazine. As you begin your search, look for leads and possibilities in everything you encounter. Ask yourself, "How can this be helpful in my search?" Maybe a posting you see online provides knowledge about vocabulary used in particular industries, or organizations that may be of interest, or possible roles and job titles. Perhaps an article you read provides knowledge about an industry, a thought leader, or an organization contributing to the causes that you find important. Find the connections, and be creative in using what you find to inform your search.

CONFIDENCE

Throughout your search, continue to repeat, "I am a talented, skilled expert in my field, and I am confident that I can translate my extensive skill set into a position outside of academia." Remind yourself of this every day. The point is, if you aren't confident enough in your abilities to speak about your strengths, employers won't be confident in hiring you. It is up to you to convince potential employers that you will be an asset in ways they have and haven't even imagined. You need to project confidence in your resume, cover letters, interviews, and networking engagements. This is why knowing your skills and strengths is so critical before venturing into the job search. Confidence is key, and if you believe in yourself, so will employers.

NETWORKING: TAKING RISKS AND PUTTING YOURSELF OUT THERE

Networking is the toughest part for many job searchers yet yields the greatest job search rewards. Networking is not about "selling yourself"; it is about building authentic and genuine relationships that allow your strengths to sell themselves. Yes, it is important to know how to pitch your skills, strengths, and interests in a concise way when speaking specifically to your intended audience, but your pitch must be grounded in who you are and what you believe about yourself. Although at times networking can feel uncomfortable or risky (e.g., reaching out to contacts, informational interviewing, asking for advice), it is what can open doors, create opportunities, and show your ability to take initiative. Generally, professionals are interested in helping others who share common interests, goals, or ideals. Finding individuals with whom you share common ground will allow networking to feel relaxed, comfortable, and genuine. As a PhD graduate from the University of Michigan advised,

> Talk, talk, talk, talk, and talk to as many people as possible. This helps you fine-tune your interests and passions and will translate to finding a job you will enjoy.

Consider the daisy chain approach. In a daisy chain, one link leads to another, and it is important to develop this framework in your job search. The idea of the daisy chain approach is that many opportunities and leads are based on smaller connections or links and that acknowledging and working through each individual connection or link to arrive at the final destination is key. To use the daisy chain approach in networking, start with someone you know, perhaps a friend, relative, acquaintance, neighbor, or mentor. Ask for advice, information, and success stories based on a position, an industry, or a geographic area of interest to you. Then, ask that person for another referral, who can be your next lead. It should be someone whom he or she thinks could be helpful to you in your search.

Remember, the key here is information gathering and relationship building. Networking is not about asking for a job. Using your network in that way will be unproductive if your contact does not have the ability to hire you or offer you a position. Successful professionals are, however, in a position to offer input, success strategies, connections, advice, and introductions—all of which can lead to future opportunities. A PhD graduate from the University of Michigan advised,

> Conduct as many informational interviews as possible; these can lead to job interviews.

The daisy chain approach can also be applied to job opportunities. It can feel like a giant leap from academia to nonacademic settings. Start by looking at links and opportunities related to things you know about yourself. As indicated earlier, your passion for a cause or product may be the starting point to identify possible organizations of interest with shared passions. Or maybe a skill you have and would like to use in the future links with a particular role or job title. Think about organizations that make products or offer services that you use daily in your academic or personal life. Could there be a link there? Look for links as a way of taking small steps toward nonacademic opportunities without feeling like you are taking a giant leap into unfamiliar territory. Now that you have a sense of how to be successful in your search, where do you look for amazing job prospects and opportunities?

Specific Job Search Strategies

Job searching requires multiple strategies, each with its own pros and cons. You want to engage in all of these strategies for optimum job search success.

ONLINE JOB POSTINGS

Search engines are by far the easiest way to find job opportunities but not the most productive, by any means. Search engines can be great tools to help identify potential job openings and to learn industry vocabulary and necessary skill sets. You can also use them to search for real job opportunities by skills, position title, geographic focus, or specialized knowledge. But when it comes to competing for a position, you and your closest 5,000 friends are likely applying for the same position through the same online portal. Although you may get lucky and be among the 1% to 3% who are called back from an online application, you are asking your resume and cover letter to do a lot of the work to allow you to stand out in a large virtual crowd. Applying to postings online alone is not likely to work.

Consider using your networking skills to connect with a current employee (even if he or she isn't in the same department as the job for which you are applying) to ask about the organization, culture, and career paths and opportunities and show interest in the position. Showing interest and gathering some insider information can help you write more persuasive cover letters and highlight necessary skills on your resume, and the employee can potentially move you forward as a referral, thereby increasing the likelihood that you will be granted an interview. If you do incorporate website search engines into your job search, focus on those that offer specific and targeted postings, such as sites offered by your institution's career services office or those that are niche or industry focused. Sites that aggregate postings, like indeed.com and simplyhired. com, can be useful in identifying options and exploring potential employers, but again, don't rely solely on applying online with the hope that your "click and send" approach will lead to success.

As you uncover opportunities, keep in mind that employers post positions with the ideal candidate in mind and, as discussed earlier, use language to help the reader understand the type of candidate they are seeking. Many times, employers are willing to be flexible on a few of the qualifications, such as degree type, level, or previous experience, particularly if you offer other skills they value. When you review postings, don't be discouraged if you don't see the desired qualifications mapping precisely to your skill sets and experiences. Look for connections between the qualifications and position description and what you have to offer, and then market your skills to clearly show the connection.

ORGANIZATIONAL WEBSITES

Slightly better than looking through job sites, visiting an employer's website for job postings and career information can lead to insights and possible opportunities. You may want to see what opportunities are posted as you begin networking to better understand typical career paths, departments, and organization-specific career progression. Again, reaching out to someone in the organization to inquire about posted jobs and opportunities not yet posted will increase the likelihood that your application will get a closer look.

ASSOCIATIONS AND DIRECTORIES

Although you may not always find actual postings with associations and directories, they can be a great help in identifying organizations on the basis of a set of criteria or themes. For example, if you want to relocate to a new city, a Chamber of Commerce in that city or region will likely have an online directory available to help identify all of the organizations, by industry, in that particular geographic area. Or if you are hoping to pursue an opportunity in a specific field, look for an association that offers access to organization membership lists, events and webinars, listservs, and possibly job opportunities. Check with your university's career services office or library system for access to other highly specific directories to help identify possible organizations of interest.

NETWORKING

As mentioned previously, networking is by far the most productive strategy, but also the most time consuming. Keep in mind that there are many ways to network. Speaker events are great places to meet others who are interested in the same topics, university-sponsored events are great for meeting other alumni who may be able to help you connect, and career services events can be helpful in meeting potential employers and other graduate students who are also seeking nonacademic positions. Again, LinkedIn can be a fantastic resource for searching for people on the basis of academic degree, interests, specific skill sets, employers, and so forth as a way to see where others have been successful. Try looking for alumni under "My Network" and then "Find Alumni" to uncover possible connections. And remember, networking can happen in places where you least expect it, including attending events not connected to your profession, volunteering with local nonprofits, and attending meet-ups, happy hours, and sporting events. There is potential to make connections literally everywhere you go (see also Chapter 13 for more advice on networking). As one of the PhD graduates from the University of Michigan said,

> You land a job by who you know, so network!

As you now can tell, there are a lot of variables at play in the job search, most of which you can directly influence. The amount of time, energy, risk, and attitude you put toward your search will be reflected in your results. Remember, the job search will take time, persistence, commitment, confidence, creativity, risk taking, and the willingness to step outside of your comfort zone to explore, engage, and connect with people you know and people you don't know. A successful search starts with knowing yourself, knowing your audience, and presenting your skills and experiences with confidence. Layer on using multiple job search strategies and truly engaging in the process, and you will find a world of amazing, attainable opportunities outside of academia, all within your reach.

Additional Resources

CareerOneStop: https://www.careeronestop.org/
CliftonStrengths: https://www.gallupstrengthscenter.com/
Jobs on Toast: https://www.jobsontoast.com
LinkedIn: https://www.linkedin.com/
O*NET: https://www.onetonline.org/
Strong Interest Inventory: https://www.cpp.com/products/strong/index.aspx

References

Humphrey, C. (2017, January 24). Discover the 20+ transferable skills that make PhDs totally employable [Blog post]. Retrieved from http://jobsontoast.com/the-20-skills-that-make-you-totally-employable/

Hurst, A., Pearce, A., Erickson, C., Parish, S., Vesty, L., Schnidman, A., . . . Pavela, A. (2016). *2016 Workforce Purpose Index: Purpose at work*. Seattle, WA: Imperative. Retrieved from https://cdn.imperative.com/media/public/Global_Purpose_Index_2016.pdf

National Association of Colleges and Employers. (n.d.). *Career readiness defined*. Retrieved from http://www.naceweb.org/career-readiness/competencies/career-readiness-defined/

Alan Pickman and Lisa Chauveron

Networking 13
How to Market Yourself and Your PhD

Alan has a PhD in counseling psychology, which, for the past 30 years, he has used to develop a special interest and expertise in working with adults and executives around career issues. He assists individuals in establishing career directions, skillfully managing their careers, and conducting effective job search campaigns. He recognized early on in his career that applying his skills in business and industry settings, rather than traditional academic or university counseling venues, was the right direction for him. He soon discovered that the field of corporate-sponsored career transition or outplacement was emerging, which focuses on helping downsized workers with career planning and job search execution. He saw corporate-sponsored outplacement as an environment in which he could pursue his passion about careers in an applied business and industry context.

He has managed internal career services units to support outplacement at Citibank, Chemical Bank, and Chase. For the past 18 years, he has been employed by Lee Hecht Harrison, the industry leader in career transition. He also runs a private career practice and has authored two books on career topics. His varied mix of professional activities over the past 30 years—career consultant and adviser, executive coach, therapist, supervisor, author, part-time university instructor—has confirmed the many ways in which a PhD psychologist can build a successful and diverse career outside academia.

http://dx.doi.org/10.1037/0000110-014
Building a Career Outside Academia: A Guide for Doctoral Students in the Behavioral and Social Sciences,
J. B. Urban and M. R. Linver (Editors)
Copyright © 2019 by the American Psychological Association. All rights reserved.

Lisa is a researcher and program evaluator with more than 16 years of experience working with urban community-based and educational organizations through engaging in program planning and implementation, developing evidence-based interventions, and supporting positive youth development and character education, largely with underserved and lesbian, gay, bisexual, transgender, and queer populations. She chose this path to marry her love of social justice, youth work, and developmental science.

After completing her BS in psychology summa cum laude, she thought she was done with academic life, so she spent a year in an antipoverty service program in New York City. Refreshed with a newfound interest in working with marginalized youth, she then pursued her master's degree in youth and family education with a concentration in prevention research. Later, she applied her knowledge at nonprofit organizations. She was excited to build internal capacity using multiple evaluation techniques and best practices from research and helped produce a program intervention currently on four national model program lists.

Eventually, she decided to work for herself on new projects with different organizations and manage a good work–life balance as the president and lead evaluator of a small consulting group, Impact Development & Assessment. Now, she helps programs and organizations scientifically determine success, empower evidence-based implementation, secure funding, and move the field forward with academic storytelling. She enjoys using rigor and credibility to support sustainable, replicable change for youth, families, and communities. She is also currently a Family Science and Human Development doctoral candidate at Montclair State University.

Need for Networking

Networking is a critical element of career management, particularly outside of the academy, and is an essential component of an effective job search. This process occurs by making personal connections to develop contacts and identify career opportunities through in-person meetings, events, or, increasingly, telecommunications such as e-mail, phone, or social media. Once you secure a job, research suggests that networking will also likely be a key aspect of your advancement throughout your career (Cruz, Schnidman, Agrawal, & De Koning, 2015). Over the past 30 years, careers have become more dynamic, making it increasingly rare for anyone to stay on a single career path. Gone are the days of retiring from decades of dedicated work with a single employer, making a strong network of contacts a professional requirement. Many new professionals mistakenly approach their career by focusing solely on the work at hand, assuming that their work product will speak for itself and ultimately lead to success. However, experts suggest that success is often a combination of positive work connections and quality work products (Pierson, 2009); therefore, networking should be viewed as a long-term aspect of successful career management.

Basically, people find jobs in three ways: through networking with personal contacts, by working with recruiters, or in response to postings. Research indicates that more than 85% of executives or midlevel managers find jobs through their personal contacts (Cruz et al., 2015), whereas just 1% to 3% (as noted in Chapter 12) secure positions from postings. Thus, we encourage you to diversify your job-hunting strategies, allocating more time and effort to networking than to the other less fruitful approaches.

Despite its importance in securing positions and advancing careers, both research and anecdotal evidence suggest that networking tends to pose difficulties for many people. In this chapter, we address those challenges while offering solutions to help you create effective networking strategies. We also discuss approaches to deal with the fact that many people outside of academia may not understand the skills that a PhD-trained scientist can bring to an organization.

Where to Begin

As a doctoral student, you developed skills and interests that are transferable to the for-profit and nonprofit sectors outside of academia (see Chapter 12). You also relied on autonomy and initiative to complete projects that required intense individual effort. Now that you have completed the self-assessment and reflection suggested in Chapter 12, you are equipped with some basic information to help you envision some ideal professional experiences. Perhaps you took one of the structured tests suggested in the previous chapter. We suggest also trying the Myers–Briggs Type Indicator (MBTI), an employment-focused personality test (Myers, McCaulley, Quenk, & Hammer, 1998).

The MBTI is a tool designed to enhance self-understanding, career exploration, or professional development along four dimensions: how people (a) focus their energy as extraverts or introverts, (b) process information through sensing or intuition, (c) make decisions by thinking or feeling, and (d) create degrees of structure in environments through judging or perceiving. These factors can influence preferences in communication style, work environment, networking approaches, and platform of introduction (electronic vs. in person). According to Daniel White (1997), an executive coach who focuses on leadership development, there are observed correlations between MBTI types and reported skills and work preferences that connect to networking. For example, White explained that Intuition–Thinking (NT) types are creative scientific people who enjoy generating new ideas. Sensing–Thinking–Judging (STJ) types are excellent at improving systems, using their focus on details to improve efficiency. Extraversion–Feeling (EF) types are good at organizing activities and usually maintain many relationships simultaneously. Extraversion–Intuition–Feeling (ENF) types enjoy brainstorming, inspiring others, and creating new approaches. We encourage you to discover your MBTI type to help you add context to your skills and interests (take the inventory at mbtionline.com).

Next, you should merge your newfound knowledge from the MBTI with your other skills and interests. To start this process, you can cross-reference your curriculum vitae with the lists of transferable skills obtained during your PhD (see Chapter 12) and begin to find people, organizations, and positions in the for-profit, nonprofit, or government sectors that interest you. Early in your networking process, you should set up meetings to learn more about organizations and the skills required to work within industries of interest. You might also want to elicit input by asking your contacts how they see your background as an asset in their field. Once relationships are established and information is gathered at these initial encounters, you should foster the relationship and follow up.

In subsequent networking meetings, as you become better informed about your target organizations and your transferable skills, you should arrange meetings with current and potential contacts. Then, be prepared to communicate how your skills as a PhD-trained scientist can support their organization's mission. Eventually you will be able to use the knowledge gained from your initial meetings to sell yourself as a good fit for an organization. You can do so by clearly illustrating the connections between your skills and interests and your contact's work. One major contribution that your PhD can offer is enhanced credibility.

Goals of Networking

Now that you have a sense of how your skills and interests match potential positions, you can use that information to inform your personal networking goals. Set some specific, measurable goals (another way to use your PhD!) to help you grow your network and showcase your strengths. Be sure to track your progress and keep yourself accountable, recounting your victories, setbacks, and new insights into your preferred career as well as opportunities for growth. Also, as you conduct networking meetings, be mindful of how increased self-knowledge of your skills and interests and your emerging understanding of potential positions can help you gain more benefit from your networking meetings.

Most of the time, when you walk into their office to network, your contacts will not have any open positions or knowledge of any open positions. Then why bother meeting? you might ask. Notably, somewhere down the road in their professional travels, your contacts may run across fellow professionals who have open positions for which you are a great fit. If you have done your due diligence by connecting to people in and around your field, your name might be offered up for such positions. Further, with one national report indicating that people change jobs an average of 12 times during their career, your contacts' position may change in the future (Bureau of Labor Statistics, 2017). Today's colleagues may become future bosses or partners, so we suggest you treat the people you meet along your professional journey with respect.

Further, because networking can help you discover strategies, contacts, and advice that can help you expand your systems of professional support and lead to future positions, it is important to develop and hone your networking skills. To do so, we recommend approaching each networking meeting with some intentional goals in mind. There are three things you should be looking to accomplish in a networking meeting:

1. *Aim to learn something about the person's organization.* This can include seeking information about what that person's organization does or asking questions about trends he or she sees in the field, or it can be more operational by learning about a typical day, such as how your connection spends his or her time, the tasks for which he or she is responsible, or how his or her career unfolded. The aim is to leave the meeting better informed about a company, field, or trend in ways that will help you sharpen your focus for your own job search.

2. *Become known or better known to people.* If the person to whom you're speaking knew you already, then your goal is to update him or her about your latest thinking or about what you've been up to since you last talked. In other words, use the opportunity to say, "Among other things, I wanted to inform you what I've been up to recently and also to orient you a little bit more toward what I'm trying to accomplish in this transition period, because I'm really looking to build on my skills in A and B as I head in Direction C." If your contact is new to you, share the same type of information so that if and when he or she hears about opportunities down the road, your contact can think of you.

3. *Aim to build enough rapport and trust through the professional manner in which you present yourself so you can be connected to your contact's network.* Doing so will allow you to continue the daisy chain process introduced in Chapter 12 to further your information gathering and expand your network. If you do receive referrals, you might ask a follow-up question to understand what about the new contact makes your connection consider him or her a good contact for you. This will facilitate your conducting a successful meeting with the next person in the daisy chain.

Role of Giving in Networking

Adam Grant (2013), an organizational psychology professor at Wharton Business School, shared findings from research on networking approaches in his book *Give and Take*. Grant found three kinds of people in the working world: takers, matchers, and givers. *Takers* view every interpersonal exchange as an opportunity to place their own needs before those of others. *Matchers* are those who are willing to give, but do it in a more measured, calibrated way; they reciprocate good deeds but maintain a quid pro quo mindset depending on how much they perceive they might receive down the road. Then there are *givers*, folks who go through life giving more freely, creating success for themselves while supporting their peers by sharing credit and adopting a pay-it-forward mindset. Overall, the givers are the most successful in the working world. However, Grant made a distinction between two kinds of givers: those who give so frequently and selflessly that often they are not very successful because they feel burnt out or taken advantage of, and those who give in what he called the "otherish" way, keeping an eye toward the other while incorporating elements that help themselves to create win–win situations. In sum, in networking, it pays both to be a giver and to connect with other givers.

Role of Temperament in Approaching Networking

Thinking back to your MBTI results, take note of the first letter in your four-letter type. For a job hunter who is more of an extravert, a person who gets energy from being in touch with other people, the process described above can feel like an invitation to potentially fun and energizing experiences. At the end of a job search process, the extraverts of the world walk away with a larger network of contacts and the feeling that they have learned a lot about the marketplace; they feel energized. On the other end of the spectrum, the introverts of the world, who get their energy from solitary activities like reading, studying, and analyzing, may find the networking process draining and scary. Yet in both cases, it is useful to use your best assets to find a networking strategy that works for you. There is no single, correct way to be a good networker. Extraverts can always improve their skills, and introverts should know that they, too, can network! For both temperament types, there will likely be a need for some movement outside of their natural comfort zone to find the most successful way to network.

For example, introverts can use their research skills to act as "high preparation people." As research suggests, introverts often mentally prepare more fully in advance and are likely to be successful if, prior to a networking meeting, they do considerable preparation. Introverts are likely to predict possible questions and prepare thorough answers as well as thoughtful questions to ask. Forethinking serves introverts well. Importantly, introverts are often people who focus a lot of attention on their relationships, specifically on the quality of the relationships they have rather than the sheer quantity of relationships. Accordingly, introverts often pick their networking meetings carefully and are very good at follow-up. They can be good at showing appreciation in the moment and promptly writing effective follow-up notes.

Extraverts, in contrast, do more on-the-spot work, often using verbal processing to share their accomplishments, determine opportunities, and generate questions in the moment. Extraverts tend to network more regularly with a larger network of people, which can mean they need extra reminders to follow up in a way that strengthens the relationship. In the moment, extraverts are often animated, excited participants who generate future possibilities and new ideas from their interactions. Although they may benefit from identifying multiple opportunities, extraverts may need to focus more on prioritizing future prospects in order to ensure they gain traction in the search process in a disciplined and focused manner.

Overcoming Barriers to Success

There are common challenges to becoming an effective networker (Pickman, 1994), including discomfort asking for help, fear of rejection, and uncertainty about marketing yourself, as well as a lack of knowledge about the process. Networkers also face the challenge of maintaining confidence in what is admittedly a difficult and time-consuming process. Below we share advice to overcome these challenges.

KNOW YOUR BRAND

Come up with a personal brand statement to help sell yourself in a clear, concise description of who you are as a professional and what you bring to the table. Your several-sentence, concise statement, often referred to as an *elevator pitch*, should communicate your professional interests, top attributes, and strengths. There are many great examples of personal brand statements online, so do some research to find models that resonate with you (e.g., Bell, 2015; Guiseppe, n.d.).

REMEMBER THAT NETWORKING IS NOT THE EQUIVALENT OF BEGGING FOR HELP

Networking is actually a chance to connect with some really interesting people (Pickman, 1994). It's also an opportunity to talk about what you love and to express interest in others through the use of thoughtful questions and active listening. So go out there and connect!

KNOW THAT INFORMATION IS POWER

Researching positions and contacts before meetings or networking events is a must. Use personal connections, Internet searches, and LinkedIn (https://www.linkedin.com/) to gather information about people and places of interest. At events, know who you want to try and meet or who you can connect to others to expand their network.

REFRAME YOUR FEAR OF REJECTION

Yes, some networking meetings will be less helpful than others in your job search. Do your part to increase the likelihood that meetings will go well by being prepared and conducting them skillfully. And remind yourself that each no is an opportunity to improve your skills, as well as a step closer to yes (Pickman, 1994).

USE THE CONTACTS YOU HAVE TO FIND CONNECTIONS AT THE RIGHT LEVEL OR INDUSTRY

Although you may not know people who make hiring decisions (Pickman, 1994), or even anyone in the organization you aim to work for in the future, you might know colleagues in a similar organization or industry. Use the daisy chain—the series of connections you have that link you to other contacts—to leverage the contacts you do have to link to those you hope to meet. You might also use the daisy chain to discover contacts that your friends, family, colleagues, and university alumni groups have in their network.

USE POSITIVE SELF-TALK TO NAVIGATE
ANY INTIMIDATION YOU FEEL

Fake it 'til you make it! Like most new activities, you'll get better at networking with practice. There may be some initial awkwardness, but keep at it. Practice in the mirror, with friends, or even at other events you attend, like weddings or social get-togethers, which offer natural opportunities for making connections.

GET COMFORTABLE TALKING ABOUT
YOUR SKILLS AND ACCOMPLISHMENTS

You are your best advocate, so sell yourself! As a PhD student, you have likely done a lot to be proud of in your career, and networking gives you the chance to share. List your skills and accomplishments within your doctoral studies and previous work experiences. Once you secure a job, you will still need to promote yourself, so networking is a great skill to develop for your career (Pickman, 1994).

OVERCOME FEAR AND LACK OF CONFIDENCE
BY RECOGNIZING THAT YOUR CONTRIBUTIONS
ALSO OCCUR OUTSIDE OF WORK

Think about your activities and achievements in an array of contexts, including family, community, and religious settings (Pickman, 1994; White, 1997). Identify the skills you used to accomplish them, and celebrate your successes. Write down three things you did well each day to remind yourself of the contributions you make to the world daily (Sandberg & Grant, 2017).

USE TOOLS FROM THE PAST

Because there will inevitably be setbacks in the networking process, draw on experiences in your own past when you demonstrated resilience by overcoming adversity or challenges. Sandberg and Grant's (2017) book illustrates the importance of resiliency and offers great advice for building it in ourselves. For instance, they encourage readers to recall a time in their lives when they successfully navigated obstacles. Remember that rough patches will pass and do not define the rest of your life.

FOLLOW THROUGH

After a meeting with contacts, be sure to send notes or e-mails thanking people for their time and advice. When referrals are offered, graciously use those connections, and thank your contact for helping make the connection. In addition, reach out again to contacts periodically to keep in touch (every 3 or 4 months), update them on your search progress, and remain in their thoughts so they can think of you for upcoming opportunities.

KNOW YOUR AUDIENCE

Networking can look different in the nonprofit, government, and for-profit sectors. Understand that although networking is necessary for making connections in each of these areas, the three have overlapping yet distinct norms. Reach out to contacts in each area to learn more about how they operate and which pitfalls to avoid.

BRING A SENSE OF HELPFULNESS WITH YOU TO YOUR NETWORKING MEETINGS

Consider which contacts and information you might offer to those in your network. Share them, and continue to look for opportunities to support others, either during a meeting or down the line. This creates mutual wins for you and your contacts.

SEEK OPPORTUNITIES TO CONNECT

Start today! Certain conferences attract academics as well as scientists who work in nonacademic jobs and practitioners who are periodically looking for academically trained professionals. Start thinking beyond papers and presentations to how you can strategically use those conference gatherings for networking and advancing your nonacademic career.

Using Social Media to Network

As indicated in Chapter 12, social media, especially LinkedIn, is popular among all networkers. LinkedIn, the social media service that executives use the most, provides an easy opportunity to discover people in a variety of organizational contexts very quickly. Your LinkedIn profile can help you find connections to people in your target organizations through first-degree, second-degree, or third-degree connections. LinkedIn can also help you learn about new potential contacts and organizations. You can approach potential contacts for information-gathering purposes and start to become known to them and their organizations. Additionally, LinkedIn offers you the chance to join networking groups. These online forums are great spaces to garner advice from people in your area of interest or attend networking events advertised online.

Conclusion

Networking will help you be better informed about aspects of the marketplace, expand your network of contacts, and sharpen your directional focus. You will be able to use your skills and style to find a networking approach that fits who you are and ultimately helps you build connections, sell yourself and your work, secure a job, and advance your career. Hopefully, through networking opportunities you will identify open positions and be able to arrange an interview with a potential employer. The next chapter explores aspects of the interview process and offers advice for successfully navigating it to secure a job.

References

Bell, J. (2015, January 22). How to create a personal brand strategy statement [Blog post]. *In the CEO Afterlife.* Retrieved from http://www.ceoafterlife.com/uncategorized/how-to-create-a-personal-brand-statement/

Bureau of Labor Statistics. (2017, August). *Number of jobs held, labor market activity, and earnings growth among the youngest baby boomers: Results from a longitudinal survey summary* [Press release]. Retrieved from https://www.bls.gov/news.release/nlsoy.nr0.htm

Cruz, E. L., Schnidman, A., Agrawal, A., & De Koning, B. (2015). *Why and how people change jobs.* San Francisco, CA: LinkedIn Corporation. Retrieved from https://business.linkedin.com/content/dam/business/talent-solutions/global/en_us/job-switchers/PDF/job-switchers-global-report-english.pdf

Grant, A. (2013). *Give and take: A revolutionary approach to success.* New York, NY: Viking.

Guiseppe, M. (n.d.). Creating your authentic personal brand statement [Blog post]. *Job-hunt.* Retrieved from https://www.job-hunt.org/personal-branding/creating-your-personal-brand.shtml

Myers, I. B., McCaulley, M. H., Quenk, N. L., & Hammer, A. L. (1998). *MBTI manual: A guide to the development and use of the Myers–Briggs Type Indicator* (Vol. 3). Palo Alto, CA: Consulting Psychologists Press.

Pickman, A. J. (1994). *The complete guide to outplacement counseling.* Hillsdale, NJ: Lawrence Erlbaum Associates.

Pierson, O. (2009). *Highly effective networking: Meet the right people and get a great job.* New York, NY: Career Press.

Sandberg, S., & Grant, A. (2017). *Option B: Facing adversity, building resilience, and finding joy.* New York, NY: Alfred A. Knopf.

White, D. (1997). Career development counseling with technologists and scientists. In A. J. Pickman (Ed.), *Special challenges in career management: Counselor perspectives* (pp. 63–76). Hillsdale, NJ: Lawrence Erlbaum Associates.

Dana M. Foney and Olivia Silber Ashley

Interviewing

What to Expect and How to Prepare

14

When Dana was in graduate school, her broad research interests were in child and adolescent development and family strengthening. She was also interested in program evaluation (e.g., developing culturally competent data collection tools). After earning her PhD, she completed a postdoc during which she put her training into practice. There, she learned that what keeps her happy is a combination of direct service and research. After working for nearly a decade as a health care and human services consultant managing projects for the federal government, state agencies, and foundations, she is now the director of data and evaluation at a nonprofit whose mission is to serve individuals living with mental illnesses and addiction disorders. She also serves as a peer reviewer for several journals in her field of expertise, including *Developmental Psychology*, *Prevention Science*, *Journal of Offender Rehabilitation*, and *Journal of Adolescent Health*.

Early in her career, Olivia worked in state government, focusing on policy, implementation, and evaluation; she thought she wanted to eventually work in federal government. Before applying to her doctoral program, she met with graduates to learn about their work, so she was familiar with nonacademic research and employers. She ended up applying for research institute, state government, federal government, and academic positions. After more than 16 years of working at a research institute, she now directs a program of

http://dx.doi.org/10.1037/0000110-015

Building a Career Outside Academia: A Guide for Doctoral Students in the Behavioral and Social Sciences,
J. B. Urban and M. R. Linver (Editors)
Copyright © 2019 by the American Psychological Association. All rights reserved.

19 researchers. Her path involved working with multidisciplinary teams, experienced project leaders, and mentors to learn about state-of-the-art research methods, project management and leadership skills, and work with funders. Seizing opportunities to lead proposal work, marketing expansion of work on existing projects, and forming a team of colleagues and midlevel staff were important to grow a body of work. And eventually learning about other staff members' career goals and trajectories was essential in helping them develop their own research.

To pursue your nonacademic career goals, it is important to understand all you can about the nonacademic interview process, which often emphasizes a different set of skills than an academic interview and therefore requires different preparation. For example, the evaluation criteria for an academic job talk and a nonacademic job talk may be different (see the "Nonacademic Job Talk" section later in this chapter). Also, a nonacademic interview tends to focus on research skills in addition to soft skills (e.g., ability to communicate effectively), and the interview structure may vary as well.

This chapter offers tips to plan for and complete a successful nonacademic interview. We offer recommendations for preparing for the interview and strategies for completing a phone interview, presenting a job talk (that is, presenting your skill set and experience to the organization), navigating the in-person visit, and following up after the interview.

Preparation

Once you decide to pursue a nonacademic career and have found a nonacademic position in which you are interested (see Chapter 12), it is important to prepare for the interview. Preparation includes researching the organization and finding out what is expected of you, preparing a writing sample, gathering your professional references, and rehearsing your job talk (if applicable) and responses to interview questions.

RESEARCH THE ORGANIZATION

Familiarizing yourself with the organization's mission, services provided, in-house experts, projects, clients served, and culture will help you ask informed questions during the interview and communicate how you have the skill set to help the organization fulfill its goals. Ask the hiring professional about the interview structure (e.g., one-on-one, panel, job talk) and about the individuals with whom you will interview (tip: read a recent article that the interviewer has published or investigate his or her recent project work).

PREPARE A WRITING SAMPLE

Many nonacademic interviews require a writing sample for which you were first author. The hiring professional may provide guidance on the subject matter and length. If no guidance is provided, select a writing sample that relates to the position for which you are applying. For example, an academic manuscript or a more applied example, such as a tip sheet (e.g., a tip sheet on opioid addiction treatment if applying to a behavioral health consulting firm), would be suitable. If you do not already have a writing sample, consider summarizing your dissertation research for a lay audience. A succinct (one- to five-page), high-quality writing sample should suffice.

GATHER PROFESSIONAL REFERENCES

The references you select may be the determining factor in whether you receive a job offer. Therefore, take time to select the best individuals to speak on your behalf, such as professors, former supervisors, graduate advisers, and colleagues. Avoid using friends or family members as references. Ask your references whether they would be willing to give you a favorable recommendation, and if so, let them know that a hiring manager may be contacting them. When you go to the interview, bring hard copies of your professional reference list in this format:

- Professional reference's name and relationship to you (e.g., graduate adviser)
- Organization name
- Organization address
- Phone number
- E-mail address

REHEARSE

Once you have researched the organization, prepared your writing sample, and gathered your professional references, spend time rehearsing your job talk (if applicable) and your responses to interview questions (for sample interview questions, see the Visit section later in this chapter). Although some questions may be unanticipated, preparing responses to common interview questions can help ease anxiety and lead to a better interview experience. Also, rehearsing with a partner or in front of a video camera can help you gauge both your verbal and nonverbal communication styles.

Phone Interview and Screening

Employers often use phone interviews to determine who will be invited for an in-person interview. Prepare for a phone interview just as you would for a regular in-person interview:

- Dress as though you are going to an in-person interview.
- Review the job description, and develop talking points about your relevant experience, qualifications, background, and skills.
- Compile a list of questions to ask the interviewer. For example, it is important to learn who funds the organization's work.

■ Ask a friend to interview you on the phone and record it to learn how you sound and help you think about how to improve your answers.

■ Have in front of you all documents you provided to the employer, because the interviewer will likely ask you about them.

During the interview, do the following:

■ When possible, look at a photo of the individual with whom you are speaking. Visualizing your audience can make you a better communicator.

■ Use a landline if possible for clear reception.

■ Smile and use your hands when talking to give your voice energy and enthusiasm.

■ Keep your answers concise, but offer to talk more about any topic as needed or provide additional information by e-mail.

■ Listen carefully to the interviewer and wait to speak until the interviewer finishes the question. If you think of something while the interviewer is talking, write it down and mention it when it is your turn to talk.

As much as possible, avoid phone interview behavior that may signal to the interviewer that you will not be a good fit for the organization (see Exhibit 14.1). Avoid speaking negatively about past employers and experiences. This may signal to the interviewer that you do not take responsibility for your own actions or learn from experiences. During the phone interview, avoid asking about time off or discussing priorities outside of the advertised position. After the organization has expressed

EXHIBIT 14.1
Interview Red Flags Signaling Lack of Fit With the Organization

---

The following red flags may signal to the interviewer (in both phone and in-person interviews) that you are not a good fit for the organization:

■ *Being long-winded:* Remember that a conversation should be a back and forth. This may be especially challenging on the phone. During an in-person interview, you can assess the interviewer's body language (positive or negative) and adjust your interaction. Whether you are participating in an in-person or telephone interview, be sure to listen carefully and wait to speak until the interviewer finishes the question. If you think of something while the interviewer is talking, write it down, and mention it when it is your turn to talk. The interviewer likely has a list of questions he or she wants to ask, so do not take 15 minutes to answer the first one. You can always ask whether you have provided adequate information or if the interviewer wants to hear more about a topic.

■ *Complaining:* If the first impression you give is that you have been unhappy in multiple positions or that others are not meeting your expectations, the interviewer may feel that you are an unhappy person who will have trouble getting your expectations met at the organization. Focus on what you have learned from challenging situations and on how your contributions can benefit the organization.

■ *Asking questions that reflect a different priority than the organization's:* The interviewer will likely ask what questions you have. Ask questions that help you learn more about the key job activities and how well you will fit into the organization. Avoid questions that convey that the job activities advertised are not your priority.

---

interest in making you an offer, you can share information about planned conference attendance, planned vacation time, or your desire for flexible scheduling. Bringing these topics up too early may signal a lack of concern about the organization's needs and priorities.

Listen for the interviewer repeating a question or probing for more information. This may signal that your response was too vague or not what the interviewer was looking for. If this happens, be sure you listen carefully to the question and make sure you understand it; after you respond, ask whether you have answered the question and offer to provide more information if needed.

Visit

NONACADEMIC JOB TALK

Your job talk is an opportunity for the organization to learn about the depth of your research skills and experience beyond what can be learned in an interview (unless your interview resembles an oral comprehensive exam). Learn from the hiring manager how much time you will have, including time for questions.

A key difference from an academic job talk is that your audience may include contract researchers instead of a mix of teaching faculty and researchers who work primarily on investigator-initiated grants. Contract researchers work under contracts issued by funders such as U.S. government agencies, state organizations, foundations, commercial clients (e.g., pharmaceutical companies), and international government organizations.

Your audience's focus will likely be on how your knowledge, skills, and contributions may serve clients with whom the organization works. A standout presentation will link your research methodology, findings, and skills to the priorities of the organization's clients and demonstrate how you will be able to help meet the organization's needs. For example, a presentation on violence research could mention how this work fits into the priorities of the Centers for Disease Control and Prevention, the Department of Justice, or the Department of Defense, depending on the organization's clients.

Unless specified, consider focusing on one study you have conducted and on which you can present detailed methodological information. Present the most complex analytic approach you are comfortable discussing (and make sure you are comfortable answering detailed questions about the approach). A brief overview of your past research, focus of the current study, and how the study fits into your career may be helpful at the beginning, particularly if you can highlight publications that have resulted from your past research. Weave in what you know about your interviewers' research and how yours is related to or may complement their research. Practice your presentation in front of people who can give you feedback to ensure you complete it on time and are concise and focused. The audience will most likely be interested in your methods so they can understand how you achieved your results. Keep the introduction and rationale for the study short enough that you have plenty of time to present methodological information. Think carefully about how you discuss findings in terms of how they fit into the current literature. Be open about limitations of your research, and be prepared to discuss (if asked) what a stronger approach would be, particularly if additional funding or time was available. Offer specific implications for practice, policy, and future research. Be prepared to discuss (if asked) what your next study would be if you had a choice.

When presenting, look at the audience's faces to gauge whether they are understanding and accepting what you are saying. People nodding and smiling are positive indicators. People frowning and looking like they are thinking hard may indicate that you need to slow down or clarify what you are talking about (see Exhibit 14.2). Offer to answer questions as you go to give the audience a chance to ask about and resolve concerns they may have. Be prepared that they may interrupt you with questions or dialogue among themselves about different ideas. It is OK to let them disagree with each other, because that is what they do at work and how good science is vetted. Keep your eye on the clock, and be prepared to speed up or shorten your presentation if needed.

When you are asked questions about your research, think about what the audience really wants to know. Are they interested in why you did not choose a different methodology? Do they want to learn about your thoughts on a current area of investigation? Do they want to more clearly understand what you did to be able to interpret your findings? Remember, this is another opportunity for dialogue, so after you answer, ask whether you answered their question. It is OK to say that you will need to look up information about your methods or findings that you do not have in front of you. Offer to follow up with the person asking the question, and be sure to do so promptly when you return home.

EXHIBIT 14.2

Job Talk Red Flags Signaling Lack of Fit With the Organization's Needs

The following red flags indicate that your job talk may not meet the organization's needs:

- Spending too much time on introduction, background, and rationale when describing your research study and not allowing enough time for methods and findings
  - *A related issue:* Not sticking to time constraints, even with repeated reminders that time is running out (e.g., if the talk is running long, not being flexible and fitting the remainder of the talk into the allotted time)
- Not providing enough information about methods for the audience to assess the validity of your results
- Presenting an overly simplistic analytic approach (e.g., no multivariate analysis)
- Presenting overly simplistic discussion and implications (e.g., more research is needed on a general topic, which could be said without seeing your presentation)
- Answering questions about methodology in a way that suggests that the study was someone else's and you just helped without a clear understanding of why methodological decisions were made
- Using language that is too casual or offensive or that includes curse words (e.g., may occur when the applicant is too young or inexperienced to realize that this language is inappropriate)

DINNER

Nonacademic employers often take candidates out for a meal, especially if the position entails interacting face-to-face with clients, to assess your etiquette and how you conduct yourself outside of an office environment (and to get to know you in a less formal setting). If invited to a meal, keep in mind that it remains part of the interview process and that in addition to assessing your hard skills, employers are simultaneously assessing your soft skills (see the Questions to Assess Soft Skills section later in this chapter). Consider the following pointers: Turn off your cell phone, dress as you would for an in-office interview, and exercise manners when interacting with wait staff. It is also a suitable practice to avoid alcohol during your meal. If the interviewer orders a bottle of wine for the table, however, use your judgment and personal preference as to whether to follow the lead of the interviewer. If you choose to consume alcohol, it is a good practice to limit your consumption to one drink. Be mindful that although alcohol may decrease anxiety, it can also have negative effects on social behavior. Your goal during dinner is to demonstrate professionalism while you and your interviewer get to know each other better.

Interview Questions

As mentioned, part of your preparation should be to rehearse your responses to interview questions. We put together a list of common interview questions to help you prepare for your interview, followed by questions to assess your strengths in research as well as your soft skills. Keep in mind that rehearsing your answers can help ease anxiety and allow you to feel more confident during the interview.

COMMON INTERVIEW QUESTIONS

Be prepared to answer questions commonly asked in interviews. Such questions may include the following:

- "Can you tell me about your research?" "Can you tell me about your trajectory and how this position fits into it?" For both of these questions, think about the story of your career—how you got started on your current path (job experience, mentor, opportunity, personal tie), how that led you to now, and what you want to do next or further into the future. Be concise. It may help to write three to five bullet points ahead of time that tell the story of your career to date.
- "I see a lot of diverse experience on your resume. What do you consider your substantive focus to be?" Be prepared to state clearly the area or areas in which you are most interested. If there is more than one area, describe how they are related.
- "What salary do you have in mind?" Be prepared to answer this question, possibly at the end of the in-person interview. Learn as much as you can in advance about what new researchers with your level of education and experience make

at the organization. Resources such as the Bureau of Labor Statistics website (https://www.bls.gov/) provide some information about compensation, but remember that these data may be outdated, so you may want to ask for a little more than they report. As important as starting salary is, it should not be your only focus. It is also important to inquire about the opportunity for growth, so ask about recent compensation increases and opportunity for merit raises and promotions.

QUESTIONS TO ASSESS RESEARCH SKILLS

Be prepared to answer questions that demonstrate your research knowledge and experience. Such questions may include the following:

- "Describe how you used [a specific research method]."
- "What are common risk and protective factors for the behavior or disease that is your substantive focus?"
- "What software did you use for a specific analysis? What procedure [or command, or code] did you use?"

QUESTIONS TO ASSESS SOFT SKILLS

Academic positions often require a clearly defined set of technical qualifications. However, when applying for nonacademic positions, soft skills can be just as important in achieving a successful interview. Soft skills are the interpersonal skills that allow you to successfully interact with others. It may take more effort to reveal these skills to the interviewer than to convey your technical qualifications. Here are several soft skills to consider:

- *Communication style:* Strong candidates are articulate, are good listeners, and demonstrate appropriate nonverbal communication (e.g., eye contact, firm handshake). You may be asked to describe a time when you were successful in overcoming resistance while securing support for ideas and initiatives. The interviewer may be assessing whether you will be able to communicate directly with funders or clients.
- *Collaboration:* You may be asked to describe a time when you removed obstacles so your team could achieve a goal.
- *Flexibility and adaptability:* Strong candidates demonstrate an ability to adapt behavior on the basis of learning something new, feedback received, and experience. This quality also demonstrates flexibility and the ability to be cooperative and a team player. You may receive a direct question about a time when you had to be flexible to cope with a changing circumstance (e.g., adapting to a changing technology, suddenly being assigned to a new role on a project). You could also weave information about your flexibility into your job talk by identifying challenges you experienced and how you engaged in midcourse corrections to address them.

- *Leadership:* You may be asked to describe an example of an instance when you had a leadership role in your professional, academic, or personal life.
- *Problem solving:* Nonacademic employers are interested in knowing how a candidate solves problems and proactively takes steps to avoid them. Be prepared for questions such as, "Can you tell me about a time when you had to handle a tough problem that may have challenged you?" or "What problems did you anticipate from a project that you worked on, and how did you plan accordingly?" Strong candidates explain what they did and what the outcomes were.
- *Innovation:* You may be asked to describe a time when you worked with others to develop new and creative ideas to solve a problem, including your role and the result.

ASKING QUESTIONS

Not asking questions could make you seem unprepared or disinterested, so take the time to have some questions of your own ready to ask. Prepare questions about your interviewers' research to help you learn how it will mesh with your goals. Remember that the interview process is about both you and the organization assessing fit, so ask questions that will help you understand how happy and fulfilled you will be if you accept an offer. Good questions to ask include the following: "What are the company's current plans for growth and development?" "What are some professional development opportunities offered to the team?" and "How does the organization evaluate success?" These questions will help you understand the priorities of the organization and what it might take to advance your career there.

Follow Up

Once you have completed an interview (phone or in-person), following up with an e-mail or handwritten note shows your continued interest in the position and provides another opportunity to showcase your skill set and potential value to the organization. If possible, collect a business card from each interviewer. After the interview, customize your message to each individual and be specific. For example, thank the individual by name for interviewing you for the specific position. Reemphasize that you would be an asset to the organization and how your skill set aligns well with the position. Let the individual know he or she is welcome to contact you with any additional questions, and close with an expression of enthusiasm about the opportunity.

Conclusion

This chapter highlighted nonacademic interview practices and strategies. Understanding the process will help you complete a successful nonacademic interview. Securing a nonacademic interview, in and of itself, is an indication that an organization thinks you might be a good fit for the position. It is your responsibility to showcase your professionalism and skill set from the moment you arrive until you follow up.

The key to a successful interview is sufficient preparation and practice. Arrive on time. Listen carefully. Make it clear you have done your research about the organization and the position. Ask thoughtful questions. Try to see yourself through the interviewers' eyes. Would you be an asset to the organization (in terms of both skill set and fit)? Strong candidates communicate clearly and thoughtfully why they are best suited for the position.

Additional Resources

Doyle, A. (2017, July 1). Best questions to ask at a job interview [Blog post]. Retrieved from https://www.thebalance.com/questions-to-ask-in-a-job-interview-2061205

Doyle, A. (2018, January 13). Get some great phone interview tips [Blog post]. Retrieved from https://www.thebalance.com/how-to-ace-a-phone-interview-2058579

Heathfield, S. M. (2017, December 28). What to consider about drinking alcohol at work events [Blog post]. Retrieved from https://www.thebalance.com/drink-at-work-events-1918788

Putzier, J., & Baker, D. (2018). Red flags and warning signs in the interview process. *Monster*. Retrieved from http://hiring.monster.com/hr/hr-best-practices/small-business/conducting-an-interview/employer-interviewing-skills.aspx#

Smith, J. (2013, January 11). How to ace the 50 most common interview questions [Blog post]. Retrieved from http://www.forbes.com/sites/jacquelynsmith/2013/01/11/how-to-ace-the-50-most-common-interview-questions/#631cca9c4873

Sobel, A. (2009, October 5). When to bring up salary in an interview [Blog post]. Retrieved from https://www.theladders.com/career-advice/when-to-bring-up-salary-interview/

U.S. Department of Labor, Bureau of Labor Statistics. (2013). *Overview of BLS statistics on pay and benefits*. Retrieved from https://www.bls.gov/bls/wages.htm

Appendix

Organizations That Hire PhDs in the Behavioral and Social Sciences

Government

Name	Location	Phone	Website
[a]Administration for Children and Families	330 C Street, SW, Washington, DC 20201	202-401-9200	https://www.acf.hhs.gov/about/jobs-contracts
Agency for Healthcare Research and Quality	5600 Fishers Lane, Rockville, MD 20857	301-427-1364	https://www.ahrq.gov/cpi/about/careers/index.html
Bureau of Economic Analysis	4600 Silver Hill Road, Washington, DC 20233	301-278-9004	https://www.bea.gov/jobs/index.htm
[a]Bureau of Educational and Cultural Affairs	SA-5, 2200 C Street, NW, Washington, DC 20522	202-632-6452	https://educationusa.state.gov/employment-and-internship-information
[a]Bureau of Labor Statistics	PSB Suite 4230, 2 Massachusetts Avenue, NE, Washington DC 20212	1-800-827-5334	https://www.bls.gov/jobs/searchjobs.htm

(continued)

Name	Location	Phone	Website
[a]Bureau of Transportation Statistics	1200 New Jersey Avenue, SE, Washington, DC 20590	800-853-1351	https://www.bts.dot.gov/learn-about-bts-and-our-work/about-bts/jobs-and-internships
[a]Census Bureau	4600 Silver Hill Road, Washington, DC 20233	800-923-8282	https://www.census.gov/about/census-careers.html
[a]Centers for Disease Control and Prevention, National Center for Health Statistics	1600 Clifton Road, Atlanta, GA 30329	800-232-4636	https://jobs.cdc.gov/
Central Intelligence Agency	Office of Public Affairs, Washington, DC 20505	703-482-0623	https://www.cia.gov/offices-of-cia/intelligence-analysis/careers-1
[a]Department of Agriculture	1400 Independence Avenue, SW, Washington, DC 20250	202-720-2791	https://www.usda.gov/our-agency/careers
[a]Department of Commerce	1401 Constitution Avenue, NW, Washington, DC 20230	202-482-2000	https://www.commerce.gov/page/career-opportunities-and-internships
[a]Department of Defense	1400 Defense Pentagon, Washington, DC 20301	703-571-3343	http://godefense.cpms.osd.mil/careers.aspx
[a]Department of Defense Education Activity	4800 Mark Center Drive, Alexandria, VA 22350	571-372-6026	http://www.dodea.edu/Offices/HR/employment/
[a]Department of Education	400 Maryland Avenue, SW, Washington, DC 20202	800-872-5327	https://www.ed.gov/jobs
[a]Department of Health and Human Services	200 Independence Avenue, SW, Washington, DC 20201	877-696-6775	https://www.hhs.gov/about/careers/apply-to-work-at-hhs/index.html
[a]Department of Housing and Urban Development	451 7th Street, SW, Washington, DC 20410	202-708-1112	https://www.hud.gov/program_offices/administration/careers

Name	Location	Phone	Website
[a]Department of Labor	200 Constitution Avenue, NW, Washington, DC 20210	866-487-2365	https://www.dol.gov/general/jobs
[a]Department of State	HR/REE, 2401 E Street, NW, Suite H-518, Washington, DC 20522	202-647-6575	https://careers.state.gov/
[a]Department of Transportation	1200 New Jersey Avenue, SE, Washington, DC 20590	202-366-1298	https://www.transportation.gov/careers/pathways-site-hiring-event-students-and-recent-graduates
[a]Department of Veterans Affairs	810 Vermont Avenue, NW, Washington, DC 20420	844-698-2311	https://www.va.gov/jobs/
Economic Research Service	355 E Street, SW, Washington, DC 20024	202-720-4623	https://www.ers.usda.gov/about-ers/careers-at-ers/
[a]Food and Drug Administration	10903 New Hampshire Avenue, Silver Spring, MD 20993	888-463-6332	https://www.fda.gov/AboutFDA/WorkingatFDA/default.htm
Institute of Education Sciences	550 12th Street, SW, Washington, DC 20024	202-245-6940	https://nces.ed.gov/whatsnew/jobs.asp
National Agricultural Statistics Service	1400 Independence Avenue, SW, Washington, DC 20250	800-727-9540	https://www.nass.usda.gov/About_NASS/Opportunities/index.php#NASSJobs
National Archives and Records Administration	8601 Adelphi Road, College Park, MD 20740	866-272-6272	https://www.archives.gov/careers
National Cancer Institute	BG 9609, MSC 9760, 9609 Medical Center Drive, Bethesda, MD 20892	800-422-6237	https://www.cancer.gov/about-nci/careers
National Center for Biotechnology Information	8600 Rockville Pike, Bethesda, MD 20894	301-496-2475	https://www.nlm.nih.gov/careers/jobopenings.html
National Endowment for the Arts	400 7th Street, SW, Washington, DC 20506	202-682-5405	https://www.arts.gov/about/employment-opportunities-nea

(*continued*)

Name	Location	Phone	Website
National Endowment for the Humanities	400 7th Street, SW, Washington, DC 20506	202-606-8400	https://www.neh.gov/about/human-resources/career-opportunities
National Institute of Child Health and Human Development	6710B Rockledge Drive, Bethesda, MD 20892	800-370-2943	https://www.nichd.nih.gov/about/jobs/Pages/index.aspx
National Institute of Food and Agriculture	800 Waterfront Centre, 9th Street, SW, Washington, DC 20024	202-720-2791	https://nifa.usda.gov/career-opportunities
National Institute of Mental Health	Science Writing, Press, and Dissemination Branch, 6001 Executive Boulevard, Room 6200, MSC 9663, Bethesda, MD 20892	866-615-6464	https://www.nimh.nih.gov/about/careers/index.shtml
National Institutes of Health	9000 Rockville Pike, Bethesda, MD 20892	301-496-4000	https://jobs.nih.gov/
National Institute on Aging	Building 31, Room 5C27, 31 Center Drive, MSC 2292, Bethesda, MD 20892	800-222-2225	https://www.nia.nih.gov/about/careers
National Institute on Alcohol Abuse and Alcoholism	9000 Rockville Pike, Bethesda, MD 20892	301-443-2857	https://www.niaaa.nih.gov/about-niaaa/jobs-training
National Science Foundation	2415 Eisenhower Avenue, Arlington, VA 22314	703-292-5111	https://www.nsf.gov/careers/openings/
[a]Navy	5722 Integrity Drive, Building 784, Millington, TN 38054	800-872-6289	https://www.navy.com/careers.html
Office of Behavioral and Social Sciences Research	31 Center Drive, Building 31, Room B1C19, Bethesda, MD 20892	301-402-1146	https://obssr.od.nih.gov/funding/funding-opportunity-announcements/

Name	Location	Phone	Website
Science and Technology Policy Institute	1899 Pennsylvania Avenue, NW, Suite 520, Washington, DC 20006	202-419-3720	https://www.ida.org/en/CareersAtIDA.aspx
State-based health and human services	Each state maintains its own database, so most job opportunities must be searched through the state database.		https://www.governmentjobs.com/
United States Institute of Peace	2301 Constitution Avenue, NW, Washington, DC 20037	202-457-1700	https://www.usip.org/about/careers/open-positions

aHas multiple office locations; address listed is headquarters.

Foundations

Name	Location	Phone	Website
Andrew W. Mellon Foundation	140 East 62nd Street, New York, NY 10065	212-838-8400	https://mellon.org/about/careers/
Autism Science Foundation	106 West 32nd Street, Suite 182, New York, NY 10001	914-810-9100	http://autismsciencefoundation.org/what-we-fund/apply-for-a-fellowship/
Bill & Melinda Gates Foundation	440 Fifth Avenue North, Seattle, WA 98109	206-709-3100	https://www.gatesfoundation.org/Careers
Bloomberg Philanthropies	25 East 78th Street, New York, NY 10075	212-205-0100	https://www.bloomberg.com/careers/
David and Lucile Packard Foundation	343 Second Street, Los Altos, CA 94022	650-948-7658	https://www.packard.org/about-the-foundation/jobs/
Ford Foundation	1440 Broadway, New York, NY 10018	212-573-5000	https://www.fordfoundation.org/careers/

(*continued*)

Name	Location	Phone	Website
Kresge Foundation	3215 West Big Beaver Road, Troy, MI 48084	248-643-9630	http://kresge.org/careers
Leona M. and Harry B. Helmsley Charitable Trust	230 Park Avenue, Suite 659, New York, NY 10169	212-679-3600	http://helmsleytrust.org/jobs-helmsley
Lilly Endowment	2801 North Meridian Street, P.O. Box 88068, Indianapolis, IN 46208	317-924-5471	https://careers.lilly.com/
[a]Pew Charitable Trusts	One Commerce Square, 2005 Market Street, Suite 2800, Philadelphia, PA 19103	215-575-9050	https://jobs-pct.icims.com/jobs/search?ss=1&searchLocation=&searchCategory=&hashed=124493942
[a]Red Cross	431 18th Street, NW, Washington, DC 20006	800-733-2767	http://www.redcross.org/about-us/careers
Rockefeller Foundation	420 5th Avenue, New York, NY 10018	212-869-8500	https://www.rockefellerfoundation.org/about-us/careers/
Russell Sage Foundation	112 East 64th Street, New York, NY 10065	212-750-6000	https://www.russellsage.org/how-to-apply
[a]Save the Children	501 Kings Highway East, Suite 400, Fairfield, CT 06825	203-221-4000	http://www.savethechildren.org/site/c.8rKLIXMGIpI4E/b.6226565/k.5717/Save_the_Children_Jobs.htm
Social Science Research Council	300 Cadman Plaza West, 15th Floor, Brooklyn, NY 11201	212-377-2700	https://www.ssrc.org/about/employment/
[a]United Way	701 North Fairfax Street, Alexandria, VA 22314	703-836-7112	https://careers.unitedway.org/jobs
W. K. Kellogg Foundation	1 Michigan Avenue East, Battle Creek, MI 49017	269-968-1611	https://www.wkkf.org/employment
Woodrow Wilson International Center for Scholars	One Woodrow Wilson Plaza, 1300 Pennsylvania Avenue, NW, Washington, DC 20004	202-691-4000	https://www.wilsoncenter.org/job-openings-the-wilson-center

[a]Has multiple office locations; address listed is headquarters.

Associations

Name	Location	Phone	Website
American Association for the Advancement of Science	1200 New York Avenue, NW, Washington, DC 20005	202-326-6400	https://www.aaas.org/careers
American Educational Research Association	1430 K Street, NW, Suite 1200, Washington, DC 20005	202-238-3200	http://careers.aera.net/jobseeker/search/results/
American Psychological Association	750 First Street, NE, Washington, DC 20002	800-374-2721	http://www.apa.org/careers/apa-jobs/index.aspx
American Sociological Association	1430 K Street, NW, Suite 600, Washington, DC 20005	202-383-9005	http://www.asanet.org/about-asa/jobs-asa
Association for Behavioral Analysis International	550 West Centre Avenue, Suite 1, Portage, MI 49024	269-762-5317	http://jobs.abainternational.org/jobseeker/search/results/
Association for Psychological Science	1800 Massachusetts Avenue, NW, Suite 402, Washington, DC 20036	202-293-9300	http://jobs.psychologicalscience.org http://www.psychologicalscience.org/career-resources
Consortium of Social Science Associations	1430 K Street, NW, Suite 550, Washington, DC 20005	202-842-3525	http://www.cossa.org/
Gerontological Society of America	1220 L Street NW, Suite 901, Washington, DC 20005	202-842-1275	https://www.geron.org/career-center
Good Samaritan Community Services	1600 Saltillo Street, San Antonio, TX 78207	210-434-5531	http://www.goodsamaritancommunityservices.org/about-us/job-openings
National Association of Science Writers	P.O. Box 7905, Berkeley, CA 94707	510-647-9500	https://www.nasw.org/services-employers-and-writers

(*continued*)

Name	Location	Phone	Website
National Bureau of Economic Research	1050 Massachusetts Avenue, Cambridge, MA 02138	617-868-3900	http://www.nber.org/jobs/
National Organization of Research Development Professionals	20 North Wacker Drive, Suite 2250, Chicago, IL 60606	855-737-3381	http://www.nordp.org/jobs
National Academies of Sciences, Engineering, and Medicine	500 Fifth Street, NW, Washington, DC 20001	202-334-2000	https://chk.tbe.taleo.net/chk06/ats/careers/jobSearch.jsp?org=NAS&cws=1
Population Association of America	8630 Fenton Street, Suite 722, Silver Spring, MD 20910	301-565-6710	http://www.populationassociation.org/careers/
Rural Sociological Society	Stipes 521, 1 University Circle, Macomb, IL 61455	309-298-3518	http://www.ruralsociology.org/employment-opportunities
Society for Applied Anthropology	P.O. Box 2436, Oklahoma City, OK 73101	405-843-5113	https://www.sfaa.net/resources/career/
Society for Research in Child Development	1825 K Street, NW, Suite 325, Washington, DC 20006	202-800-0677	http://careers.srcd.org/

Institutes for Research

Name	Location	Phone	Website
[a]Amnesty International	5 Pennsylvania Plaza, 16th Floor, New York, NY 10001	212-807-8400	https://careers.amnesty.org/
Howard Hughes Medical Institute	4000 Jones Bridge Road, Chevy Chase, MD 20815	301-215-8500	https://hhmicareers.silkroad.com/
[a]Human Rights Watch	350 Fifth Avenue, 34th Floor, New York, NY 10118	212-290-4700	https://careers.hrw.org/
[a]United Nations	405 East 42nd Street, New York, NY 10017	212-963-4475	https://careers.un.org/lbw/home.aspx
[a]World Health Organization	525 23rd Street, NW, Washington, DC 20037	202-974-3000	http://www.who.int/careers/en/

[a]Has multiple office locations; address listed is headquarters.

Think Tanks

Name	Location	Phone	Website
American Enterprise Institute	1789 Massachusetts Avenue, NW, Washington, DC 20036	202-862-5800	http://www.aei.org/jobs/
ªAmerican Institutes for Research	1000 Thomas Jefferson Street, NW, Washington, DC 20007	202-403-5000	http://www.air.org/page/careers
Brookings Institution	1775 Massachusetts Avenue, NW, Washington, DC 20036	202-797-6210	https://www.brookings.edu/careers/
Carnegie Council for Ethics in International Affairs	170 East 64th Street, New York, NY 10065	212-838-4120	https://www.carnegiecouncil.org/about/jobs
Cato Institute	1000 Massachusetts Avenue, NW, Washington, DC 20001	202-842-0200	https://www.cato.org/about/jobs
Center for American Progress	1333 H Street, NW, 10th Floor, Washington, DC 20005	202-682-1611	https://www.americanprogress.org/job-listings/
ªCenter for Global Development	2055 L Street, NW, Fifth Floor, Washington DC 20036	202-416-4000	https://www.cgdev.org/page/job-opportunities-0
Center for Naval Analyses	3003 Washington Boulevard, Arlington, VA 22201	703-824-2000	https://www.cna.org/careers/
ªCenter for Strategic and International Studies	1616 Rhode Island Avenue, NW, Washington, DC 20036	202-887-0200	https://www.csis.org/about-us/careers
Child Trends	7315 Wisconsin Avenue, Suite 1200W, Bethesda, MD 20814	240-223-9200	https://www.childtrends.org/about-us/careers/
ªCouncil on Foreign Relations	58 East 68th Street, New York, NY 10065	212-434-9400	https://www.cfr.org/career-opportunities

Name	Location	Phone	Website
Heritage Foundation	214 Massachusetts Avenue, NE, Washington DC 20002	202-546-4400	http://www.heritage.org/about-heritage/careers
Mathematica Policy Research	600 Alexander Park, Suite 100, Princeton, NJ 08543	609-799-3535	https://www.mathematica-mpr.com/career-opportunities
[a]MDRC	16 East 34 Street, 19th Floor, New York, NY 10016	212-532-3200	https://chm.tbe.taleo.net/chm01/ats/careers/searchResults.jsp?org=MDRC&cws=1
[a]RAND Corporation	1776 Main Street, Santa Monica, CA 90401	310-393-0411	https://www.rand.org/jobs.html
[a]Rotary International	One Rotary Center, 1560 Sherman Avenue, Evanston, IL 60201	847-866-3000	https://www.rotary.org/en/about-rotary/careers
RTI Health Solutions	3040 Cornwallis Road, Research Triangle Park, NC 27709	919-541-6000	https://www.rtihs.org/careers
RTI International	East Cornwallis Road, Post Office Box 12194, Research Triangle Park, NC 27709	919-541-6000	https://www.rti.org/careers
Urban Institute	2100 M Street, NW, Washington, DC 20037	202-833-7200	http://www.urban.org/about/careers

[a]Has multiple office locations; address listed is headquarters.

Index

A

AAAS (American Association for the Advancement of Science), 46–48

Academic jobs. *See* Non-tenure-track academic jobs; Tenure-track academic positions

ACT (Assets Coming Together), 110

Adaptability, 168

Administration for Children and Families, 120

Administration work
  in private foundation jobs, 60
  in think tanks, 85
  time spent on, 15

Advice, 40

Advisers, 124. *See also* Mentee experiences

Ages, 138

Alcohol, 167

Alumni groups, 157

American Association for the Advancement of Science (AAAS), 46–48

American Economic Association, 86

American Enterprise Institute, 80

American Psychological Association (APA), 39, 69

America's Promise Alliance, 99–105

Anthropology
  percentage of social science degrees received in, 17
  trends of post-PhD career plans in, 19

APA (American Psychological Association), 39, 69

Applied research, 16–17

APS (Association for Psychological Science), 39

Assessments, 135–140

Assets Coming Together (ACT), 110

Association for Psychological Science (APS), 39

Associations
  business affiliations with, 133
  contact information of major, 177–178
  and extramural community, 53
  job postings and directories from, 148

Autonomy, 116, 153

B

Backinger, Cathy, 128

Behavioral science degrees, 17

Bialeschki, M. D., 106

Boston Consulting Group, 96

Boutique firms, 69–70

Bronfenbrenner Center for Translational Research, 111, 112

Brookings Institution, 80

Budgeting, 85

Businesses. *See* For-profit corporations

C

Career decision making, 11–20
  and applied research, 16–17
  compensation as factor in, 12

Career decision making, *continued*
and day-to-day tasks, 14–15
geography as factor in, 12–13
and getting your career off the ground, 12
and intellectual freedom, 14
job market landscape for, 17–18
job security as factor in, 13–14
and mentorship opportunities, 15–16
and postdoctoral positions, 37–38
and teaching opportunities, 16
and time management, 15
travel as factor in, 13
and trends in postgraduation career paths, 18–19
Career management, 138
CareerOneStop, 136
CCFP (Center for Child and Family Policy), 103, 112
CDC (Centers for Disease Control and Prevention), 119, 129
Center for Child and Family Policy (CCFP), 103, 112
Center for Public Health Initiatives, 106
Centers for Disease Control and Prevention (CDC), 119, 129
Child psychology, 17
Children
and gender disparities, 17–18
and returning to academia later in life, 23–24
Child Study Center, 112
Child Trends (research institute), 100
The Chronicle of Higher Education, 39
Chronological résumés, 141
CliftonStrengths, 137
Clinical and Translational Science Institutes, 119
Clinical psychology, 17
Coaching, 68, 92
Cognitive psychology, 17
Collaboration
as competency, 137
in government jobs, 55
interview questions about, 168
Commitment, 144
Communications, 50, 85
Communication skills
as competency, 137
for consulting, 76
and for-profit corporations, 93
in government jobs, 52
and interviews, 168
in non-tenure-track academic jobs, 114
as skill area, 138
and think tanks, 81, 82, 87
Compensation
as factor in career decision making, 12
in for-profit corporations, 97
in think tanks, 86

The Compleat Academic (Darley, Zanna, & Roediger), 4
Complex problem solving, 96
Conferences
and postdoctoral positions, 40
for private foundation jobs, 60
Confidence, 144, 145, 158
Conn, M., 106
Consulting, 67–78
advice for working in, 76–77
finding positions in, 77
in government jobs, 53
opportunities for publishing in, 26
overview, 67–69
preparation for, 73–75
in research vs. academic settings, 71–72
rewards and challenges in, 75–76
skills needed for, 70–71
types of positions in, 69–70
typical day in, 70
Consulting psychology, 68–69
Consumer products, 96
Contracts
for consulting, 72
in think tanks, 84
Counseling psychology, 17
Coursework, 39
Cover letters, 141–142
Cox, Daniel J, 126–127
Creativity
and job search process, 144, 145
as skill for working at think tank, 81, 82
Criminology, 17
Critical thinking, 96, 104, 137
Curriculum vitae (CV)
and converting to résumés, 136
and postdoctoral positions, 34, 39
résumé vs., 140

D
Daisy chain approach (networking), 146, 157
Data analytics, 96, 112
Data mining, 96
Davies, H. T. O., 106
Debt, 12, 17
Decision making
career. *See* Career decision making
and for-profit corporations, 96
through thinking vs. feeling, 153
Developmental psychology
percentage of social science degrees received in, 17
postdoctoral positions in, 40
Developmental Psychology (journal), 161
Dinner interviews, 167
Directories, 148
Diversity, 18, 138

DLS (U.S. Department of Labor and Statistics), 136, 168
Druckman, D., 69

E
Economics
    in percentage of social science degrees received in, 17
    trends of post-PhD career plans in, 19
Education, 140
18to35 nonprofit organization, 100
Elementary and secondary school employment, 19
E-mails, 132
Enthusiasm, 40
Entrepreneurship
    as skill area, 138
    and think tanks, 81, 83
Ethics, 75
Ethnic diversity, 18
Eunice Kennedy Shriver National Institute of Child Health and Human Development, 41, 46
Evaluation-focused positions, 102–103
Evidence-based decision making, 106
Expanding Your Horizons program, 87
Expectations, 132
Experimental psychology, 17
Expertise, 70–71
    in clinical interventions, 20
    in consulting, 69–71, 73, 77, 82
    content, 82, 136
    expansion of, 62, 67
    in government jobs, 49, 51–52
    in nonprofits, 105, 107
    and non-tenure-track academic jobs, 118, 119
    and post-doctoral positions, 37
    research, 20, 81, 110, 111
Extramural community, 53–54
Extraversion, 153, 156

F
Facebook, 142
Family, 13. *See also* Children
Family Life Development Center (FLDC), 109–110, 119
FBI (Federal Bureau of Investigation), 36, 42, 43
Fear, 158
Feeling style (decision making), 153
Fellowships, 39–40, 42. *See also* Postdoctoral positions
Field Center for Children's Policy, Practice, and Research, 112
Financial services, 96
First-authored publications, 38–39, 61
FLDC (Family Life Development Center), 109–110

Flexibility
    and for-profit corporations, 96
    and interview questions, 168
    and non-tenure-track academic jobs, 116, 118–119
    as skill for working at think tank, 81, 82
Flickr, 142
Flynn, P., 69
FOAs (funding opportunity announcements), 54
For-profit corporations, 89–98
    challenges in transitioning to work for, 92–93
    consulting for, 69
    finding jobs in, 96–97
    networking with, 159
    preparation for, 95–96
    rewards and challenges of working in, 97–98
    skills needed for, 93–95
    typical day in, 91–92
Foundation jobs. *See* Private foundation jobs
Freedom, 116
F32 awards, 41
Functional résumés, 141
Funding opportunity announcements (FOAs), 54

G
Gender
    and intercultural fluency, 138
    and mentee experiences, 132–133
    and post-PhD career plans, 19
    and returning to academia later in life, 23–25
    types of disparities based on, 17–18
Gender studies, 17
Generalists (consulting), 71
Gentrification, 140
Geography
    as factor in career decision making, 12–13
    and retiring to academia later in life, 25
    and trends of PhD graduates, 18, 19
Ginsberg Center, 106
Ginther, D. K., 18
Girl Scouts Research Institute, 103–104
Give and Take (Grant), 155
Giving (networking), 155
Global fluency, 138
Global health, 140
Government degrees
    percentage of social science degrees received in, 17
    trends of post-PhD careers in, 19
Government jobs, 45–56
    as alternative to academia, 3
    and consulting, 69
    job security with, 14
    looking for, 47–48
    and mentee experiences, 133
    networking with, 159
    opportunities for publishing in, 26

Government jobs, *continued*
    organizations hiring for, 171–175
    preparation for, 50–51
    rewards and challenges of, 55–56
    skills required for, 51–52
    trends in, 19
    types of, 48–50
    typical day in, 52–55
Grant, Adam, 155, 158
Grants
    and consulting, 71
    for funding of postdoctoral positions,
        40, 41
    and government jobs, 47–49, 52–53, 55
    and nonprofit organizations, 107
    and non-tenure-track academic jobs,
        113–114
    in private foundation jobs, 60
    time spent in pursuit of, 15

H
Hard money, 85
Harvey, Hal, 64
Health care sector, 69
Health Education & Behavior (journal), 27
Health scientist administrators (HSAs), 51
Helpfulness, 159
Hiring, 85
Hospitals, 42
"How" questions (consulting), 72
HSAs (health scientist administrators), 51
Human development and family studies, 17
Humility, 64
Humphrey, Chris, 138
Hurst, Aaron, 139

I
ICs. *See* Institutes and Centers
Impact Development & Assessment
        (consulting group), 152
Implementation specialists, 112
Independent postdoctoral positions, 35
Indiana University (IU), 130
Industrial and organizational psychology, 17
Industry employment
    consulting in, 69
    opportunities for publishing in, 26
    trends in, 18
Informational interviews, 118
Information processing, 153
Information skills, 138
Information technology, 137
Innovation, 169
Institutes and Centers (ICs), 48, 49, 53, 54
Institutional review boards, 85
Intellectual freedom, 14
Intercultural fluency, 138

Interests assessment, 135–140
Intergovernmental Personnel Act (IPA)
        Mobility Program, 128
Internal Revenue Service, 100
International work, 77
Internet searches, 157
Internships, 57, 76, 94
Interviews, 161–170
    dinner, 167
    following up after, 169
    information, 118
    job talks as, 165–166
    phone, 163–165
    preparation for, 162–163
    types of questions asked in, 167–169
Intramural researchers, 50
Introversion, 153, 156
Intuition, 153
IPA (Intergovernmental Personnel Act)
        Mobility Program, 128
IU (Indiana University), 130

J
Job boards, 97, 136
Job market landscape, 17–18
Job search process, 135–148
    personal attributes for success in, 144–146
    skills and interests assessment in, 135–140
    strategies for, 146–148
    tools for, 140–144
Job search websites, 39
Job security, 13–14
Jobs on Toast, 138
Job talks, 165–166
John Templeton Foundation (JTF), 58–60, 62
John W. Gardner Center for Youth and Their
        Communities, 112
Journal of Adolescent Health (journal), 161
Journal of Offender Rehabilitation (journal), 161
JTF (John Templeton Foundation), 58–60, 62
Judgment, 153

K
K-awards, 41
Knowledge skills, 138

L
Land-grant universities, 16, 112, 120
Law enforcement, 43
Lay audiences, 105
Leadership, 138, 169
Learning department evaluations, 59
Learning opportunities, 68
Lee Hecht Harrison, 151
Legislation, 49–50
Leibenluft, Ellen, 125
Leischow, Scott, 128

LinkedIn
    gathering information from, 157
    and job search process, 143, 145, 148
    uses of, 97, 159
Local opportunities, 28

M
Maddox, Jim, 124
Management skills
    in for-profit corporations, 92
    in think tanks, 81–82
Matchers (networking), 155
MBTI (Myers–Briggs Type Indicator), 153, 156
McKinsey & Company, 96
Medical University of South Carolina (MUSC),
    127–128
Meetings, 83, 84, 91
Mentee experiences, 123–134
    and best practices for navigating your career,
        131–133
    case example, 124–131
    outside of academia, 133
MENTOR organization, 102
Mentorship opportunities
    and career decision making, 15–16
    and consulting, 68
    in government jobs, 54
    time spent on, 15
Methodological skills
    and consulting, 74, 76
    and nonprofit organizations, 104
    for non-tenure-track academic jobs, 113, 114
    and post-doctoral positions, 37
    and think tanks, 81
Milstein, Bobby, 129
Morgan, Glen, 128
Murray, David, 130
MUSC (Medical University of South Carolina),
    127–128
Myers–Briggs Type Indicator (MBTI), 153, 156

N
National Academy of Sciences (NAS), 99, 100
National Association of Colleges and
    Employers, 137
National Cancer Institute (NCI), 128
National Centers of Excellence in Youth Violence
    Prevention, 119
National Institute of Child Health and Human
    Development (NICHD)
    Child and Family Research Section of, 50
    Division of Intramural Population Health
        Research of, 50
    Intellectual and Developmental Disabilities
        Branch of, 120
    positions at, 46, 47
    post-doctoral positions with, 36
National Institute of Mental Health (NIMH), 41

National Institutes of Health (NIH)
    applying to positions in, 50–51
    Clinical Center of, 50
    collaboration opportunities at, 55
    and extramural community, 53–54
    funding from, 41
    and mentee experiences, 127
    and non-tenure-track academic jobs,
        119–120
    Office of Disease Prevention, 129–130
    opportunities at, 48–50
    and Plain Writing Act, 52
National Science Foundation (NSF), 41
NCI (National Cancer Institute), 128
Networking, 151–160
    and for-profit corporations, 92, 97
    getting started with, 153–154
    goals of, 154–155
    in job search process, 145–146, 148
    need for, 152–153
    for non-tenure-track academic jobs, 115, 118
    overcoming challenges with, 156–159
    role of giving in, 155
    role of temperament in, 156
    with social media, 159
Neuropsychology, 17
NGOs (nongovernmental organizations), 69
NICHD. *See* National Institute of Child Health
    and Human Development
NIH. *See* National Institutes of Health
NIMH (National Institute of Mental Health), 41
Nonacademic career paths. *See also specific headings*
    compensation in, 12
    geographical considerations with, 13
    intellectual freedom in, 14
    and job security, 14
    mentoring opportunities in, 15–16
    pros and cons of, 11
    travel time with, 13
Nongovernmental organizations (NGOs), 69
Nonprofit organizations, 99–107
    consulting in, 69
    contact information of major, 178
    defined, 101–102
    finding positions in, 107
    networking with, 159
    opportunities for publishing in, 26
    rewards and challenges of working at,
        106–107
    skills needed for, 104–106
    trends in, 19
    types of positions in, 102–104
Non-tenure-track academic jobs, 109–120
    looking for, 117–119
    preparation for, 114–116
    rewards and challenges in, 116–117
    skills needed for, 113–114
    types of, 111–113

NSF (National Science Foundation), 41
Nutley, S. M., 106

O

Oak Ridge Institute for Science and Education, 39
Obama, Barack, 52
Office of Legislation and Public Policy (OLPP), 49
OLPP (Office of Legislation and Public Policy), 49
O*NET, 136
Online applications, 142–144
Online job postings, 147
Operations (think tanks), 81
Oregon Prevention Research Center, 112
Organizational websites, 147

P

Participatory research methods, 113
PAs (program announcements), 54
Pasnak, Robert, 124
Peer review
    components of, 27
    evaluation through, 71
    and nonprofit organizations, 106
    and program officers, 59
    in publishing process, 48
    and think tanks, 83, 85
Perception, 153
Persistence, 118, 144
Personal brand, 157
Pescosolido, Bernice, 130
Philanthropy, 59
Phone interviews, 163–165
Plain Writing Act, 52
Policy analysts, 112
Policy department positions, 59
Political consulting, 69
Political science
    percentage of social science degrees
        received in, 17
    trends of post-PhD careers in, 19
Portfolio analysis, 54
Positive self-talk, 158
Postdoctoral positions, 33–43
    acceptance of, 12
    activities in, 35–36
    decision making for, 37–38
    discovery of, 39–42
    graduate school skills used in, 36–37
    overview, 35
    preparation for, 38–39
    qualifications gained from, 42–43
    trends in, 18–19
Powell, Colin, 100
PowerPoint presentations, 93
Presidential Management Internship, 48
Prevention Research Centers, 119
Prevention Science (journal), 161
PricewaterhouseCoopers, 95

Primary research, 81
Private foundation jobs, 57–65
    advice for, 63–64
    foundations hiring for, 175–176
    looking for, 63
    opportunities for publishing in, 26
    responsibilities in, 59–60
    rewards and challenges of, 62–63
    skills needed for, 61–62
    types of, 59
Problem solving skills, 137, 169
Professional development courses, 3–4
Professionalism, 40
Professional organizations
    and consulting jobs, 77
    involvement in, 25, 27, 28
    and job search process, 148
    opportunities in, 40
Professional references, 163
Program announcements (PAs), 54
Program development, 54
Program evaluation, 113
Program officers, 59–60
Program officials, 48–51
Project directors, 112
Project meetings, 91
Project skills, 138
Project-specific postdoctoral positions, 35
Proposal writing skills, 74–75
Psychiatric clinics, 42
Psycholinguistics, 17
Psychology doctorate degrees, 3, 17. *See also
        specific specializations,* e.g.: Developmental
        psychology
Public interest, 52
Public policy, 49–50
Publishing
    and consulting, 74
    in consulting, 70
    and government jobs, 51
    and intellectual freedom, 14
    and nonprofit organizations, 106
    and non-tenure-track academic jobs, 115, 116
    and postdoctoral positions, 38–39
    and returning to academia later in life, 25–27

R

Racial diversity, 18, 138
Recruiters, 152
References, professional, 163
Referrals, 158
Rejection, 157
Religion, 138
Research. *See also specific headings*
    applied, 16–17
    and consulting, 71–72
    participatory methods in, 113
    primary, 81

Research and development, 102–104
Research associates, 80–81, 112
Research institutes, 178
Research labs, 15
Research scientists, 112
Resilience, 158
Résumés, 136, 140–141
Retirement, 25
Returning to academia, 21–28
    feasibility of, 25
    and gender, 23–25
    requirements for, 25–28
    and retirement, 25
Rice, S., 24
Risk taking, 144

S
Sandberg, S., 158
Saykin, Andy, 130
School psychology, 17
Science policy, 49–50
Scientific review officers (SROs), 49–51
Self-assessment, 136–137
Self-reflection, 136
Sensing (information processing), 153
Sexual orientation, 138
Skills assessment, 135–140
Smith, Robert, 124–125
Social media
    in job search process, 142–144
    networking with, 159
    and non-tenure-track academic jobs, 118
Social psychology, 17
Social science doctorate degrees, 3, 17. *See also
    specific headings*
Society for Research in Child Development,
    40, 46, 48
Sociology
    percentage of social science degrees
        received in, 17
    trends of post-PhD careers in, 19
Soft money, 47, 85, 113, 117
Soft skills, 168–169
Sporns, Olaf, 130
SROs (scientific review officers), 49–51
Statistical analysis, 96, 112
Strong Interest Inventory, 136
Supervision, 54
Survey of Doctorate Recipients, 17
Sustainability, 140
Synthesizing (cognitive skill), 75

T
Takers (networking), 155
Teaching opportunities
    and career decision making, 16
    and consulting, 73

and returning to academia later in life,
    25, 27
    time spent on, 14
Teamwork
    as competency, 137
    and consulting, 76
    and for-profit corporations, 94
    in think tanks, 81
Technical assistance, 52–53
Technical industries, 96
Technology
    and consulting, 68
    information, 137
    and leaving work at work, 97
Temperament, 156
Tenure-track academic positions
    compensation in, 12
    decline in, 3
    gender disparities in, 17
    geographical considerations with, 13
    job security with, 13–14
    pros and cons of, 11
    teaching in, 14, 16
Theoretical foundations, 104
Thinking style (decision making), 153
Think tanks, 79–87
    considerations with, 85–86
    contact information of major, 179–180
    defined, 80
    finding positions in, 86
    opportunities for publishing in, 26
    positions available in, 80–81
    preparation for careers within, 86–87
    research benefits of, 84–85
    skills needed for working in, 81–83
    typical day working in, 83–84
Timelines, 70
Time management
    and consulting, 74
    flexibility in, 15
Trainings, 68
Travel
    and consulting, 77
    as factor in career decision making, 13
Twitter, 142
Two-body problem, 13
Twombly, S., 24
Typical day at work, 14–15

U
University-affiliated centers, 112
University policies, 24
U.S. Congress, 49
U.S. Department of Health and Human Services,
    49, 53
U.S. Department of Labor and Statistics (DLS),
    136, 168

V

Versatile PhD website, 58

W

White, Daniel, 153
"Why" questions (consulting), 72
Wolf-Wendel, L., 24
Work ethic, 138

Work-life balance, 47
Work plans, 70
Writing, 15. *See also* Publishing
Writing samples, 162–163

Y

Youth Center of Excellence, 110
YouTube, 142

About the Editors

Jennifer Brown Urban, PhD, is a professor in the Department of Family Science and Human Development at Montclair State University, where she also codirects the Institute for Research on Youth Thriving and Evaluation. Dr. Urban is trained as a developmental scientist with specific expertise in youth character development and program evaluation. Her scholarship is encapsulated under the umbrella of systems science, including both theoretical approaches and methodologies, and consists of three strands: (a) systems evaluation, the development, testing, and implementation of a systems science approach to program evaluation and planning to enhance internal evaluation capacity, particularly for youth program practitioners and evaluators; (b) innovative approaches to advancing developmental science by developing and promoting a social justice perspective, the use of innovative methods, and professional development resources; and (c) building the evidence base in developmental science, specifically to determine the key features of character development programs that promote positive youth development and advance the application of character science in multiple contexts to enhance human flourishing across the lifespan. Dr. Urban is currently principal investigator (PI) on several grant-funded projects, and her most recent research focuses on character development and innovative approaches to program evaluation and planning. She uses mixed-methods approaches in her own research and has mentored many undergraduate and graduate students in designing and executing applied research projects. She developed and has taught a doctoral professional development course for several years and is passionate about mentoring students.

Miriam R. Linver, PhD, is a professor in the Department of Family Science and Human Development at Montclair State University and codirects the Institute for Research on Youth Thriving and Evaluation (RYTE Institute). Previously, Dr. Linver was a postdoctoral fellow and research scientist at the National Center for Children and Families, Teachers College, Columbia University. Her research reflects Bronfenbrenner's ecological paradigm, focusing on the contexts of child and adolescent development. She has expertise in the importance of the home environment for infants, children, and adolescents; the ways school and out-of-school experiences matter for children and youth; and flourishing and character development as key outcomes. She has served as guest editor of several journal special issues, including *Parenting: Science and Practice* ("Parenting at HOME"), *Infant Mental Health Journal* ("New Directions in Young Children's Socio-emotional Measures"), and *Research in Human Development* ("'My Life Purpose Is . . .': Assessment of Youth Purpose in Context"). Dr. Linver is co-principle investigator on several funded projects in the RYTE Institute focused on program evaluation and character development outcomes in youth. She enjoys the challenges and rewards of mentoring and collaborating with undergraduate and graduate students, postdoctoral fellows, and colleagues.